Life Like Dolls

Life Like Dolls

The Collector Doll
Phenomenon and the
Lives of the Women
Who Love Them

A. F. Robertson

Routledge
New York and London

Published in 2004 by
Routledge
29 West 35th Street
New York, NY 10001
www.routledge-ny.com

Published in Great Britain by
Routledge
11 New Fetter Lane
London EC4P 4EE
www.routledge.co.uk

Routledge is an imprint of the Taylor & Francis Group.
Printed in the United States of America on acid-free paper.

10 9 8 7 6 5 4 3 2 1

Library of Congress Cataloging-in-Publication Data

Robertson, A. F.
    Life like dolls : the collector doll phenomenon and the lives of the
    women who love them / A.F. Robertson.
        p. cm.
    Includes bibliographical references.
    ISBN 0-415-94450-3 (hardback : alk. paper) — ISBN 0-415-94451-1 (pbk. : alk.
    paper)
    1. Dolls—Collectors and collecting—Psychological aspects. 2. Women—United
States—Psychology. I. Title.
    NK4893.R62 2003
    688.7'221'075—dc21   2003009895

*For my sister
Elizabeth Stanger,
who collects grandchildren.*

Contents

List of Pictures ix

List of Figures xi

Preface xiii

Chapter One

Introduction 1

Chapter Two

The Commodity 21

Chapter Three

The Collection Just Grows and Grows 61

Chapter Four

The Doll That Needs You 95

Chapter Five

Dollification 117

Chapter Six

More Than Real 151

Chapter Seven

Forever Young 189

Chapter Eight

Innocence and Fear 221

Appendices 231

Notes 253

Bibliography 267

Index 277

List of Pictures

Picture 1   Elderly woman nursing a doll, 3

Picture 2   Advertisement for *Caroline* (Georgetown Collection), 30

Picture 3   Marketplace doll stall. Richelieu, France, November 1995, 51

Picture 4   Certificates of authenticity for two collector dolls, 56

Picture 5   At Debbie's house—dolls everywhere you look . . . , 73

Picture 6   Eva's dolls—at home, 74

Picture 7   Waiting for you to take her home, 96

Picture 8   Two American Girl play dolls and the collector doll *Gwendolyn*, 154

Picture 9   *Rose Vanilla*, without her bonnet, 177

Picture 10   Rosie, age 3, grooming Barbie, 178

Picture 11   Rosie nursing doll, 195

Picture 12   The Lenox Christening Doll, 203

Picture 13   Sarah with her MyTwinn, and MyTwinn's own look-alike doll, 210

Picture 14   *Noelle,* the Christmas Angel, 214

Picture 15   Unwrapping and wrapping *Noelle,* the Christmas Angel, 216

Picture 16   *Mary Jane,* 230

List of Figures

Figure 2-a   Number of doll manufacturers and total sales in the United States, 1967–97, 41

Figure 2-b   Total sales of U.S. doll firms, and wages of production workers, 1967–97, 41

Figure 2-c   Total employees and total production workers in U.S. doll firms, 1967–97, 42

Figure 2-d   Number of production workers in U.S. doll firms and average wage, 1967–97, 42

Figure 2-e   Annual average price of dolls in advertisement sample, 1991–99, 48

Figure 2-f   Price ranges of dolls by main doll firms in advertisement sample, 1991–99, 52

Figure 3-a   Age of U.S. doll collectors (1994), 88

Figure 6-a   Development of the facial mask, 161

Figure 6-b   Facial development, 163

Figure 6-c   Infantilizing facial features, 164

Figure 6-d   Comparison of doll face forms, 170

Figure 6-e   Mouth forms. Antique doll, play doll, real child, and
              two PCDs, 174

Figure 7-a   Infantilization, 197

Figure 7-b   "Infantilized" and "normal" boys, 198

Figure 7-c   Adultified dolls, 202

Figure 7-d   Mean and variation in the height of the nasal septum
              in sample of 118 girl dolls, 204

Preface

In North America and in Europe producing dolls for adult women is a large and lucrative industry. Commercially linked to the collection of "real" antique porcelain dolls, the new commodity differs quite radically in form, function, aesthetics, and many other ways from dolls intended for children. In marketing terms the dolls are targeted at women in the "empty nest" stage of their lives: they have finished rearing their own children (or perhaps never had any) and can expect to live much longer than in the past. Most of them can afford the price tag of around $100 for a doll, and many believe that their purchase is a sound investment. The sales pitch is backed up by certificates of authenticity, limited edition numbers, artists' signatures, and the exhortation to *collect*.

The design of these dolls has obviously been researched with care. A major selling point is elaborate realism that rarely applies in the design of dolls for children. Much attention is paid to such details as the curl of eyelashes and the molding of nostrils and fingernails. The dolls all have names and personal identities that are fleshed out in the advertising copy and the packaging.

This quest for realism often seems overdone. Exaggeratedly large infant eyes are combined with voluptuous post-adolescent mouths, big hair, and elaborate clothes. This is the child who, ambiguously, has and has not grown up, who is alive but inert; lifelike, but preserved in the fragile chill of porcelain from the change and loss that life itself implies.

While the women who collect these dolls gaze at them in rapture, the rest of us may only glimpse them from the corner of our eyes: an advertisement in *Parade* magazine, a window display in a high street store, a late-night program on one of the TV shopping channels. This billion-dollar industry has catered for a very private sort of desire. The collectors, many of whom have turned whole sections of their homes into "nurseries" for their dolls, are distant from (and are often shunned by) the clubs to which serious, up-market, antique doll aficionadas belong. But gradually these new doll enthusiasts are "coming out," contacting one another at fairs, on TV sales marathons, in Internet chat rooms, and even in one another's homes.

Authentically unreal, a bizarre concoction of childlike and adult traits, novelties that profess to be antiques, precious trash: these dolls are the joint product of human passions and big business. Certainly, they are in some sense magical, deceptive: words like "enchanting," "charming," "irresistible," and "captivating" are part of the sales talk. But however mendacious and however inert these dolls may appear to others, for the women who buy them their beauty rests in the fact that they are "so natural," so very much alive.

It would be easy to dismiss this realism as merely metaphoric: "of course they don't *really think* these dolls are alive." But as soon as we started talking to these women we discovered that that is how they *really feel.* If we are to engage more sympathetically with the collectors' feelings we have to ask some deeper questions about what aspects of "real life" are embodied in the dolls and how they are put there. Part of the answer can be found in the clever details of manufacture, but it is of course mainly the women themselves who imbue the dolls with life. How and why do they do it?

For all its apparent childish triviality, the porcelain collector doll (PCD) obliges us to think again about the distinctions we habitually make between people and things, feelings and meanings, passion and reason. In exploring the PCD phenomenon we have had to take a very broad view, pursuing the meaning of these dolls from the intimate details of physiology, sexuality, and family growth, through to the demographic, political, economic, and historical processes of the nineteenth and twentieth centuries. The collectors are identifiable by their age and family circumstances, they are comfortable economically, they have a nostalgic interest in dolls both as antiques and as relics of their own childhood. Over the last thirty years an industry has developed to cater to their desires. But there's more to it than that. At the heart of the matter there is an ambiguity that I have sought to capture in the title of this book. To the collectors, the dolls are lifelike, but in the collector's dreams life is also doll-like: stable, immortal, perfected.

There is an exquisite, sensuous tension between the bodies of the women and the bodies of the dolls that defies simple explanation. Feelings are so fundamental to our human experience and yet, as psychologists, doctors, and others are painfully aware, they are notoriously difficult to capture "scientifically." One reason for this difficulty is that when we start analyzing bodies they become *less* lifelike: anatomical specimens, cultural artifacts, neurological systems.

As a remedy, I have suggested that we refocus our attention on how people *grow*, recognizing that for human beings this growth is simultaneously physical and social.[1] We don't reproduce ourselves, other people do that for us, making our bodies, and passing on to us the ideas and tactics we need to "do" life. But the other side of the coin is no less important: how we grow animates society—that large-scale, long-lasting aggregation of human beings held together by the symbolic apparatus we call "culture." Human growth, in other words, is the active link between the biological and the historical aspects of our being, which implies that it should be of as much interest to historians and students of culture as to biologists and physiologists.

I have been drawn to these dolls and their collectors because they seem a very apt illustration of how the meanings people attach to things change as they grow, and how the way we grow in some sense differentiates everything out there in the world around us that we lump together as "culture." Car, mother, and delicious, are all ideas that change quite radically as we proceed through our lives. The

PCDs are dolls, but they are not the dolls we familiarly associate with children. What makes them seem natural or freaky depends not just on who you are, nor even how old you are, but how you grew up, how you have lived, and how you view your own past and future. In this strange phenomenon of the collector doll, some aspects of the way women have grown during the course of the twentieth century have been fixed in porcelain. If we can read the features of these dolls with sufficiently open minds, they may tell us something interesting about our collective history, and perhaps also something significant about our constitution as human beings.

This project was an offshoot of my undergraduate and graduate classes on the family at the University of California, Santa Barbara. Around 1990, we noticed the increasing number of advertisements for porcelain collector dolls (PCDs) in the Sunday newspapers and mailbox fillers. It was immediately obvious that they were intended for adult women rather than children, and that they could tell us something interesting about family life in contemporary America. The 440 advertisements we clipped and discussed became the core of the project, as it developed.

Many people may think it odd that a man should have started and carried through this particular project. In our radically gendered society, a male with a large stack of pictures and texts dealing with effigies of little children will inevitably attract some suspicion. I offer no apologies. Apart from the captivating strangeness of the phenomenon, I came to the dolls from a lifelong interest in the ways in which human reproduction is socially organized. American and European women who seemed to be accumulating substitute children were obvious grist to my mill. The collectors I got to know seemed relaxed about or even indifferent to my sex. There are men everywhere in the doll business, sculpting and trading, driving to fairs and minding stalls, helping their spouses at home with care and maintenance. A few look sheepish, but most are breezy and self-confident. One of my early mentors and sources of inspiration, the anthropologist Meyer Fortes, used to declare bluntly that you couldn't be a proper anthropologist if you had never raised a family of your own. I argued back vehemently that someone like myself, married but without children, may actually be *more* observant about family life than someone afflicted with diapers, teenage delinquency, and school bills. I certainly see no reason to believe that a good family man—or even a good family woman—would necessarily have made better anthropological sense of the doll collectors.

The project developed as a means of giving students at Santa Barbara some practical experience of doing anthropology. My own fieldwork has been mainly in Africa, and the logistical problems of taking students there are legion. Instead, we tend to encourage students to take a practical interest in "the exotic in our midst"—to explore the unfamiliar worlds that crowd around our own. Typically, we have directed students to ethnic enclaves, strange occupations, communities of the very poor or the very rich. On the principle that our own families are full of aliens, I have had students write about their parents and siblings, domestic rituals, or financial crises—often with startlingly illuminating results that I have ploughed back into teaching. Introducing the doll phenomenon to a large undergraduate class always brought several students with some direct interest (usually a close relative with a collection) to my office afterward.

I introduced the dolls to a small undergraduate seminar on research and writing. I could see no reason why the students, mostly in their late teens and early twenties, should know anything, or care about the PCDs. My hope was that their detachment from the phenomenon would raise interesting objective questions, and I was often rewarded. Some plainly felt they had been hijacked, but played along patiently, digging out facts and figures, studying dolls in different times and places, and talking to collectors. The writing is nearly all my own, so they are absolved from blame, although I use the "we" pronoun to signal their involvement. Those who were smitten continued to work with me as relays of research assistants, processing the advertisements, monitoring the TV shows, collecting statistics. Our treatment of the topic benefited not only from the great variety of their backgrounds, but also from the breadth of their disciplinary interests—biology, sociology, psychology, history, and economics. Their greatest assets were their direct contacts with the collectors themselves—grandmothers, aunts, family friends—with whom they struck up conversations that often were mutually gratifying. This personal transgenerational network proved to be an unusual and productive way of collecting information. The project extended throughout the 1990s, including a year when I was teaching at Manchester University in England. This long time frame, coinciding with the boom in PCDs, allowed us to track changes in the commodity, marketing styles, and clientele.

The students were well aware, from their anthropological class-work, that there can be something unpleasantly smug about making a study of the exotic and learning other people's secrets. Though many students' first reaction to the topic was "yuck!", the vast major-ity ended up with sympathetic feelings for the collectors and for the older women in their families more generally. It reminded me of the anthropologist's tendency to fall in love with one's "tribe" and to use its customs to measure off all that's wrong with our own society (overindulgent parenting, rudeness in public, etc.).

For my own part, I feel puzzled about the obsessive aspects of col-lecting, but I have much sympathy for the passion with which the col-lectors relate to their dolls. My fundamental concern is that social sci-entists, for all their fancy theories, can now make very little sense of these intense feelings. I have written quite a lot about this in recent years, and I live in hope that we may find better ways of bringing feel-ing and meaning back together, thus improving our understanding of what life is about. The porcelain collector dolls have always seemed as good a starting point as any.

Only one student researcher, a surfing dude who became the dar-ling of his local doll club and made a sterling contribution to our project, said he did not want to be named. I'll call him Frank. The rest are listed below, in alphabetical order. The contribution of some of them went far beyond the call of duty. I thank them all most sincerely for their patience, diligence, good humor, and apparently genuine interest in the goals of the project.

I also acknowledge very gratefully the help of many colleagues, friends, and relatives, especially Francesca Bray, the Gerngross family (thank you, Anna and Emily), Ramon Guardans, Keith Hart, Ilene

Kalish, Eva Kuhn, David and Sarah Lawson, Debbie Madrigal, Juliet Mitchell, Harvey Molotch, Elizabeth Stanger, Don Symons, and Phil Walker. My thanks to Dona Porter of the Bradford Group, and to doll artists Dianna Effner, Linda Mason, and Pamela Phillips for permissions and technical advice.

The student researchers: Claire Ardis, Kathleen Berglund, Beth McWaters Bjorkman, Timea Bradley, Corinna Bridges, Angel Browning, Celise Chilcote, Emily Christian, Jennifer Cullen, Roya Daizadeh, Cindy De Witt, Rebecca Denman, Marilyn Gomez, Carolyn Gregorio, Cristina Maria Gueco, Robyn Hagle, Laura Izuel, Brandon Johnson, Susie Kim, Jaime Lomonaco, Stacey Pedersen, Jamie Porter, Jennifer Ramirez, Virginia Ray, Jenade Scott, Tracy Sellman, Lorraine Tennyson, and Amanda Wade.

Chapter One

Introduction

"This is not a toy."

Most people looking at porcelain collector dolls (PCDs) for the first time find them odd. They don't look at all like the sort of thing you would give to a child: they are too fragile, too elaborate. Unlike so many children's dolls they are startlingly realistic, and yet their realism looks overdone, distorted. The fact that they are made to imitate real live children, and that their owners treat them as such, is somehow disturbing. Odder still, they are often collected in large numbers. The industry works on the assumption that buyers will not be content with just one but will accumulate dozens or even hundreds.

On the one hand we see a commodity manufactured in very large quantities by successful business corporations. *Stevie*,[1] also known as "Catch Me If You Can!" is advertised as a "Collectible Doll with Investment Potential":

The doll you buy today may be a wise investment for the future. Once an edition is sold out, those who want a doll from the edition must pay whatever the market will bear, if and when one becomes available from dealers or at auction. That's why fine collectible

1

dolls often sell for more then their original prices within only a few years of being issued. Of course, not all dolls increase in value; values can go down . . .

On the other hand, we see an object that arouses very passionate feelings and which is treated by the collector as a real little person: "I'm transported when I see a doll," says Anne R. "I go into another world." Anne has an "extraordinary spiritual feeling" for her dolls. They are "magical," she insists: "Dolls appear alive to me. . . . [I]t's almost as if you can breathe life into them. . . . [T]hey can collect their life force, a warmth from you. You can almost see through their little eyes."[2]

Why are some people so deeply enthralled by these dolls, and others so appalled? This was the basic question pursued by our student researchers, most of whom were women between 18 and 24 years of age and who were not in the market for these dolls. Their initial reactions ranged from a shrug of indifference to outright disgust:

"It's obsessional. These women have a mental problem."
"Dolls are creepy—they bother little girls."
"They don't look like dolls. They look older . . . like women."
"Very weird . . . Freaky . . . Distorted . . . "
"It's like taxidermy."
"Makes me think of JonBenet Ramsey."
"They're promising something that's already gone."
"They're, like, untouchable."
"They try to capture life, but they are deathly."

These responses were mild compared with what many women in their thirties and forties had to say. Academics especially were "shocked" or "nauseated," and a few were critical of our motives in studying them. Of course, the censure and the disgust only increased our curiosity— the topic was plainly hot.

The collectors themselves are usually well aware of the oddity of their obsession: "Many blushed and others started laughing when asked about their compulsion to collect dolls."[3] They know it's considered shameful for fully grown adults to be so interested in dolls. It hovers on the brink of madness—it is well known that clinically senile

Picture 1: Elderly woman nursing a doll.
The woman's son died of pneumonia when he was a baby. She was taking
stuffed animals from other residents in the clinic, so the staff got her the plastic
child's doll. She addresses it as "son." Photo by Elizabeth Stanger.

women often nurse dolls (Picture 1). To be interested in such elaborate dolls—lots of them—provokes a good deal of guilt. But there is
strength in numbers: to see collectors emerging from domestic seclu-
sion into the daylight of clubs, fairs, TV phone-ins, and Web chat rooms
is very evocative of gay people "coming out" in the 1960s and 1970s.

Adults routinely disparage dolls. This is very evident in the dictionary definitions, which were almost certainly concocted by adult
males. The word maybe originated in the Old Dutch *dol*, a whipping
top, or in the Old English *doil* or *dold*, meaning stupid.[4] We are told
that "doll" is a diminutive of "Dorothy," a name commonly given to
dolls and puppets, and that it is also the "smallest pig in a litter." The
Oxford English Dictionary defines it as "an image of a human being
(commonly of a child or lady) used as a plaything; a girl's toy-baby."
By transference it is also "a pretty, but unintelligent or empty person,
esp. when dressed-up; a pretty, but silly or frivolous woman." "A doll's
face" is one that is "conventionally pretty, but without life or expression." Around the nineteenth century it was used to refer to "a common woman, a prostitute."

Scholars have been particularly stand-offish about dolls. People
who make a serious study of such apparently trivial things seem to fear
the stigma of indulging in "Mickey Mouse academics."[5] Even more
bizarre is the tendency for books about dolls to *look* like toys: Audrey
Vincente Dean's useful book *Dolls*, published in 1997, measures three
and a half by five inches. Anything that looks like a toy seems to get
this treatment—even when it is actually a human being: what can have
possessed the publishers of Gaby Wood's remarkable study of the
dwarf Caroline Crachami to produce the book itself as a miniature?[6]
We are reminded that "mannequin" or "manikin," the word we use
for the people or dummies (or in the nineteenth century, the "dolls")
that model clothes, is a contemptuous allusion to a dwarf.

In this project we kept encountering the complaint that even
developmental psychologists don't pay much attention to dolls
(indeed, to toys in general) although they are so much at the center
of our early lives. Eva-Maria Simms points to a sexist undercurrent:
"The doll, although featuring prominently in many female children's
lives, has found little attention from the academic community." While

"the doll barely exists in psychological theory," the little attention that has been paid to the topic is decidedly androcentric, loosely concerned with oedipal struggles, little girls who (mis)treat their dolls "phallically," and boys with an "unhealthy" fixation on girlish things.[7] On the other hand, our worries about dolls are treated very extensively in modern art. Dolls have been used copiously by artists like Hans Bellmer and Cindy Sherman, and especially surrealists like May Wilson, to make statements of every conceivable sort, most of them erotically or morbidly disturbing. Jason Hunsiger's picture *Boy in the Bush* "is a self portrait of the artist at age six playing with a doll in his secret hideout under the hedge. The doll, held by the boy, is dressed like the boy, in shirt, shorts, and sneakers, but appears as a menacing adult." And in *The Woman Without Children,* a 1992 watercolor that is very evocative of the passion for PCDs, Ellen Phelan portrays a lone figure gazing longingly at a trio of dolls.[8] The photographer Richard Avedon has made particularly bizarre use of battered, naked dolls in his sequence of fashion plates titled *In Memory of the Late Mr. and Mrs. Comfort.*[9]

If we belittle girls and their dolls, we have also belittled the second childhood of old age. We have disparaged older women especially, a problem that the founding generation of feminist scholars have themselves become aware of as they, too, age.[10] The increasing demographic weight of this segment of our population is forcing their special concerns on our attention. Women die later and more slowly of chronic ailments than men. Most of them live alone, at home; in the 65–69 age bracket, 34 percent of women are widowed, 7 percent of men.[11] One reason why they are less likely to live with their children than in the past is simply that they have fewer children.[12] Loneliness is the dominant affliction of later life, from which many women are seeking relief in the company of dolls. Far from trivial, doll play is a key to understanding the damaging processes of isolation and neglect that have developed relentlessly along with the poisoned chalice of increasing longevity.

Not all societies take such a dim view of adult relationships with dolls. They seem to have happier connotations in the romance languages: the French *poupée* (see our "puppet") probably derived from the Latin *pupa*, a little girl, which in turn probably came from the Sanskrit root *push*, meaning to nourish. In other languages, what we call a "doll" would be translated simply as a "made-child."[13] In Japan there is a long tradition of dolls, which are integrated into the ceremonial life of women and their families. In the past, a girl got two *hina* when she was born, she took them with her when she was married, and they were passed down by women through the generations. On the third day of the third month there was a "feast of dolls" (*hina matsuri*) focused on girls, in which the dolls and their often very elaborate accessories were displayed. A motif of this feast was that the "living" dolls (the ones belonging to live girls) entertained the "dead" ones.[14]

How you see the porcelain collector dolls, and the values you attach to them, depends very much on who you are—crudely, your gender and your age. Interestingly, young children don't like them, and prefer something that looks and feels quite different. Not many adult men are enthused by the PCDs, or are in any way sensitive to the purposes they serve, although there are reports of "serious" male Barbie collectors.[15] There have been some very famous male doll designers down the years, including Johnny Greulle, the creator of *Raggedy Ann*, and Pierre François Jumeau, who in the nineteenth century made the porcelain dolls that are now prized as antiques. But we shall return often to the central role that women have played in the design, if not the manufacture, of almost every doll. This is as true of the large-scale production of PCDs today as it was in past centuries. Male designers have played their part in finding durable materials for play dolls, and ways of producing them in large numbers. But they also seem unable to resist the temptation to turn them into mechanical marvels. Casimir Bru, father of the famous *Bébé Bru*, experimented tirelessly with dolls that slept, ate, blew kisses, and chattered.[16] Women and children get bored with such claptrap, preferring dolls they can animate with their own imaginations. More generally, male interest in dolls is assumed to be warped, signaling pedophilia or some unhealthy fetishism.

The different life-bound meanings of dolls are highly charged emotionally. Men's problems with dolls hark back to their childhood, when at a certain stage they were made to feel guilty about showing any interest in them. "That boys are naturally fond of and should play with dolls as well as girls, there is abundant indication" declared Hall and Ellis in their classic study of dolls at the end of the nineteenth century. "The danger, too, of making boy milliners is of course obvious, but we are convinced that on the whole, more play with girl dolls by boys would tend to make them more sympathetic with girls as children if not more tender with their wives and with women later."[17] Kenneth Loyal Smith, curator of the Toy Collection at the New York City Museum, speaks for doll enthusiasts today: "Dressing them, talking to them, having a friend a child can really trust serves a great function in preparing us for adulthood, regardless of gender."[18] In spite of such liberal views, boys habitually react with venom against dolls. Our study is packed with tales of girls who suffered mightily from the destructive urges of their brothers, and who have sought restitution later in life by filling their homes with PCDs. The penance for these boy doll-destroyers is often a guilty terror of dolls later in life. Repeatedly, we found it was boys and men who most disliked and feared dolls, and who were intimidated by their glassy gaze or could not bear their frilly prettiness. These are themes that weave their way through countless folk tales, novels, and horror movies. A sense of guilt and shame may also dog the girl who is told at puberty that she must put away her dolls and grow up. Reckoning with this loss is part of the agony of adolescence, and in due course the ecstasy of collecting dolls later in life.

Our modern Western idea that it is sick or abnormal for grown-ups to have a passion for dolls has been carried over to criticism of other cultures and societies. Until quite recently, "primitive" (in a perverse sense, "childlike") peoples were reckoned to have a weakness for dolls, or doll-like objects, to the extent that they actually worshiped them. This was "fetishism," a naive tendency to imagine that objects are alive and behave like real people. Holding such objects in reverence was "idolatry," and although there is no semantic relationship between "idol" and "doll," it was felt that "some psychic connection cannot be doubted."[19] This made it easy to believe that children's interest in dolls was a measure of their uncivilized, savage condition; and that the savages' interest in dolls was in turn a measure of their childishness. An adult in civilized society who took an interest in dolls

was truly anomalous: women who played with dolls were either mad
or witches.

In our societies we have not scrupled about referring to the icons
of other cultures—the *kachina* of the Hopi or the *akuaba* of West
Africa—as "dolls." If we shrink from the notion of referring to the crucifix as a doll, it is presumably because we cannot tolerate the suggestion that it is merely a plaything. The Christian church has always had
a very equivocal view of dolls, sometimes banning them as idolatrous,
otherwise incorporating them in images of the Christ child, or cheru-
bim. Is the same sort of ambivalence at work in the aficionadas' insistence that the PCDs are "serious" and should not be mistaken for toys?
Jennifer, one of our researchers, remembered that her grandmother's
dolls were as untouchable as that other figure that dominated her
house—a massive, eight-foot-tall crucifix. And yet religious icons come
close to being toys in such forms as the Nativity scenes set up in households throughout the Christian world. In Catalonia, Spain, each of
these must have its *caganer*, or "shitter," the fun being to place this
squatting figure, unmistakable in his red beret, somewhere obvious yet
unexpected among the little plaster cattle, kings, and holy family. If we
are prepared to admit sacred objects to the category of "dolls" we
could surely trace the lineage of our PCDs in one direction to the
putti, those exquisitely molded cherubs rising in clusters amid the
baroque decor of churches throughout the Roman Catholic world.

Standard Western children's dolls pop up in all sorts of strange
and highly ritualized contexts around the world. Pink plastic dolls
dangle from the headdresses of young male initiates of the Kabre people of northern Togo, West Africa.[20] In the children's section of
Japanese cemeteries, dolls have appeared in remarkable profusion, in
the form of *Mizuko-jizò* memorializing miscarried, aborted, or stillborn fetuses. William LaFleur describes the "Purple Cloud Temple"
near Tokyo, given over exclusively to *jizò*. They apparently represent
diminutive monks, but wear bibs and little sweaters, and often have
toys. "Jizò is quite remarkable in that it is a stand-in for *both* the dead
infant and the savior figure who supposedly takes care of it in its oth-
erworld journey. The double-take effect—one moment a child and
the next a Buddhist savior in monkish robes—is intentional."

Children are welcome at these cemeteries—there is even a playground. "The sense of kitsch arises because two things are conflated here that we in the West usually want to separate as much as possible—that is, the cemetery and the nursery."[21]

There are some interesting parallels with the phenomenally successful Precious Moments dolls, manufactured by Enesco, that are to be seen from time to time among the motley objects that appear in American cemeteries. This is a highly standardized, hand-sized, androgynous doll reminiscent of the earlier Kewpie. The signature feature is the eyes, which are tear-shaped (set vertically in "drop" mode), evocative of dewy-eyed newborn innocence. The originator of the Precious Moments dolls, Samuel Butcher, hoped that "these figurines, fashioned after my artwork, would be little messengers delivering the inspirational thoughts and teachings of the Lord."[22] One Precious Moments collection of about 22 dolls is "Sugar Town," whose styles and accompanying texts closely reflect an essentially white, Christian-right market. A worldwide complex of collector clubs has sprung up around these dolls, focused by Butcher on a chapel to which Precious Moments enthusiasts can make pilgrimage. It has a ceiling in the Sistine style, but decorated with the familiar Precious Moments figures. With the motto "Loving, Sharing, and Caring," the Precious Moments movement raises charitable funds, notably for the Easter Seal Society. We traced 477,000 Web sites related to Precious Moments.

FEELING, MEANING, AND GROWTH

Our attitudes to dolls are loaded with very passionate and contradictory feelings of love and hate, security and fear, pride and shame, innocence and guilt. These are not fleeting emotions; they are embedded within us, accumulating from our earliest experiences. We may grow up, but we never really get dolls out of our systems. The life of the doll and the child are intertwined, laying down complex layers of sensation and significance, from the erotic and maternal to the guilty and aggressive. By the time a collector is in her fifties and has more than a couple of hundred porcelain dolls, the meanings and feelings will have piled up to almost impenetrable density.

In our pursuit of a sympathetic understanding of this small but telling fragment of contemporary culture, we have had to dig down through these layers of feeling and meaning, looking back at the childhood experiences of the collectors earlier in the twentieth century, and at the history of the dolls themselves. Approaching the topic from the perspective of a self-consciously "holistic" anthropology, our focus is on how people grow, both physically and socially, in the cultural contexts that are distinctively human. Pursuing the meaning of dolls along this growth axis inevitably takes us through different fields of study, tracing connections between the biology of the human body on the one hand and social history on the other.

I should clarify at the outset several aspects of this developmental or biohistorical perspective on culture that I have found helpful in resolving the perplexing ambiguities presented by the PCDs.[23] Growth is a process that goes on *between* people. I grow as an individual, but also as a person in the context of developing social relationships. Human lives are finite, but the modern fixation on *individual* human lives as a span of years extending from conception to death is a very special and painfully narrow sort of cultural construction. In cultures other than ours, our bodies and all their psychic components are more usually seen as shared rather than as personal private property. This is surely a more generous view of who and what we are.

We do not reproduce ourselves or raise ourselves. Other people do most of that for us, in the context of families and communities. Being phenomenally slow developers among the mammals, we can't survive after birth without protracted care from other people, most immediately our mothers. Over periods longer than our personal lives, human growth links one generation to the next in the process we dully call "reproduction." It involves relays of people, their individual lives extending through many decades within the historical fabric of community and society. Growth is thus both a personal experience and, extending through history, a social and demographic process. This is the life-sustaining nexus into which dolls are inserted, acting as surrogates for or supplements to "real" people.

A corollary of this intergenerational view of growth is that aging and death are as much facts of life as birth and maturation. Biologists are mainly to blame for the notion that growth ends with adulthood, when we have acquired the sexual and social capacities to produce and rear offspring. From a Darwinian point of view, older women such as our doll collectors are not very interesting because their reproductive days and thus their role in evolution are over. But if our genes appear to have little interest in our survival past middle age, we as human individuals assuredly do. The perpetuation of culture (as distinct from the human species) likewise depends on there being senior generations to consolidate and pass on knowledge and understanding.

Moreover, these days aging has become a very conspicuous *historical* fact: dramatically increased longevity means that there are proportionately very many more older people—women especially—than ever before. We have only recently started coming to terms with the economic, political, and social implications of this. The PCDs are witness to the impact that the demographics of aging are having on culture. We are just beginning to assess the implications of a social environment that is peopled, as never before in human experience, with grandparents and, increasingly, great-grandparents. In these new circumstances, meanings and functions of familiar objects like dolls mutate and multiply.

This broader, historical understanding of human growth helps to bridge the gaps between physiology, psychology, and culture. One of the casualties of the intellectual estrangement of biology and culture is our inability to explain the vital connections between how things *feel* and what they *mean*. As we grow, feeling and meaning are not discrete aspects of our experience, they emerge together. We put our feelings into words and gestures, and the symbolic languages of art or ritual stir our deepest feelings. We build up our understanding of things gradually by experience and association, not like dictionary definitions. Nor is meaning something that adults draw ready-made from the cultural repository and dump into the minds of children. The anthropologist Christina Toren reminds us that "humans are biologically structured to be at once products and producers of their own, collective and personal, histories."[24] An infant and its mother commune by intense feelings but *know* very different things. You can look up the word "mother" in a dictionary and get a very basic definition, stripped of the feelings that give the meanings of the word their real force. For like everything else in life, being or having a "mother" is not a state but a process, an unfolding sequence of events, experiences, obligations, sensations. In other words, to know what "mother" really means, you have to understand how humans grow. Likewise, if children have an idea of what a "house" is before they can say the word, it is because they have crawled around it, tasted it, fallen off it, been lost in it, felt happy in it. Our understanding of semantics would be enriched if we could trace how these sensuous meanings are assembled, through time, in the human experiences of growth.

From this it follows that individuals take and make meanings differentially, according to their current relationships in the intergenerational cycle of growth. There is no such thing as "a doll" in some absolute, generally agreed, standardized sense. One way of drawing the many sorts of "doll" back into a general cultural framework of understanding is to discover how they thread their way through our *whole* lives, changing their meaning—and changing us—in the process. The "doll" that we see in dictionary definition is stripped of most of the meanings that really matter: the passion that a child or an older woman invests in the doll, the shame and ridicule it brings to the grown-up man. Rather than one meaning, we have a portfolio of basic life-bound definitions.[25] To suggest that this is actually not very interesting or important in the long term (history) and on the grand scale (society, culture) is to underrate the power of the underlying feelings, as well as the centrality of objects like dolls in millions of individual lives.

If we disparage dolls it is because we have grown out of them. It's not they that have changed, it's our perception of them *and* of ourselves. If the collectors' own children, raised in the 1960s and 1970s, have a distaste for the PCDs, it is partly because they have grown up in different historical circumstances. But the generation gap is not a permanent expression of political, economic, or cultural difference, it is the difference between one episode and another in the human regenerative cycle. In time, the collectors' children may themselves turn to doll collecting or find some other ways of filling the gaps in their lives.

It is intriguing to imagine "culture"—something we usually think of as very uniform and static—as composed of all these different, emergent, serial understandings. What makes growth processes distinctively human is their dependence on the "webs of meaning"—cultures—built up over time in social groups. But the corollary is often overlooked: culture does not "reproduce" itself; it depends on the physical regeneration of people—their growth. Culture depends on human growth as much as human growth depends on culture.

The mistake earlier generations of anthropologists made was to assume that culture could be reduced to one basic, homogeneous view of the world. This "tradition" was tacitly assumed to be the understanding of a typical older male—the "tribal elder" to whom anthropologists went for the authoritative story. A few decades ago, women objected to this bias, and feminist scholars showed us that the world could look very different through women's eyes. More recently, there has been a similar shift in attention to children's understandings of the world.[26] With this new focus of interest has come a tendency to insist that children have their own culture, distinct from that of the adult world. By focusing on growth I find it more illuminating to see the differences as a progression, with childhood as the experience from which adulthood emerges, and childish understandings being endemic to culture generally, rather than alien to it. After all, every adult was once a child, and although growing up means putting away childish things, our earliest experiences weigh heavily upon us throughout our lives, shaping the culture that we in turn try to impose on our children. In our adult world, we tend to lose track of the connections between "playful" and "serious" things: the links between roller skates and cars, model-making and engineering, dolls and parenting. Without these subtle transitions we simply would not have that grand collective accomplishment we call "culture." "What is important," says Roger Cox, "is not the memory, which in any case is almost certainly illusory, but the possibility of finding in childish things, and with luck in children themselves, a renewed humanity."[27]

The meanings we attach to everything in our lives change, to some degree, as we get older. This is partly because our bodies change over time, and partly because history moves on and one generation

experiences youth differently from the next. But we still make believe
that the things that matter to us most (say, family, apple pie, honesty)
have basic, stable meanings of their own. These are the things we call
"culture." We tacitly assume that there is some sort of system of values
"out there" beyond ourselves, calling the shots in our lives, while in
fact culture depends entirely on each generation keeping the faith,
passing the consolidated values on to their children. Meaning is fluid,
continually being made, lost, and remade in the relentless cycle of
human growth. This is the medium within which culture happens, the
matrix in which human societies adapt and change, the regenerative
process on which our progress as a species has depended. The trouble is we are not very good at perceiving how it happens. After all, the
growth process in its transgenerational sense stretches far beyond the
compass of our small individual lives.

The passion for porcelain collector dolls is a very particular but
illuminating example of how bodies and symbols, feelings and meanings, and material and emotional values converge in that aggregate
we call "culture." Dolls have a powerful and pervasive significance in
our culture generally, and children have had a central role in making
dolls mean what they do. Dolls affect all of us because all of us were,
once upon a time, children. However, not all of us have been collectors of porcelain dolls, although it seems fair to claim that they are
now as much a part of our culture as most other things. (In the fullness of time they may even be among the more durable relics of our
civilization.) It is older adult women who give the PCDs meaning, and
who (abetted by the manufacturers) implant them and maintain
them in our culture. To understand how and why this happens we
have to know how these women have grown and the broader social
and historical contexts within which this growth has taken place.

It's sad that our current interpretations of culture can take so little account of all those powerful feelings that are incorporated in the
emergent meanings of "mother" or "house" or "doll." Cultures,
nations, and all the other ways we imagine our collective being can't
feel. To feel, you need a body, and to know how feelings permeate the
meanings of things (dolls, cake, horror) we need a sympathetic
understanding of how bodies work. Biologists know at least as much

about this as cultural theorists; but alas, these days, the very syllable "bio-" has become a red flag to those who prefer to explain things in "strictly cultural" terms. In focusing on these dolls, one of my intentions is to show that reducing our bodies analytically to symbolic abstractions (a schematic assemblage of surfaces, members, orifices) doesn't tell us enough, and that flesh-and-blood understandings are a vital part of cultural explanation. If this is part of the mounting rebellion against disciplinary dogmatism in anthropology, I am happy to be part of it.

"Biology" and "culture" are not discrete facts of life, although they are treated as such in our intellectual culture. As we live and grow we don't keep crossing thresholds between biology and history, or between science and culture. These are distinctions that scholars make for their own convenience. It is our explanations that have come asunder—witness the biocultural wars that rage on in the academy—not the life process itself. The dogmatic assertion that biology has no relevance to the study of culture is based on an argument that if all humans have the same physical constitution, and cultures are so diverse, then biology can have nothing interesting to say about the constitution of culture.[28] But human beings are not all the same, physically or socially, for at least one obvious reason: we *grow*. The biological differences between child and adult, and between women and men, are hugely influential in the shaping of the collective representations we call culture. The rejection of everything tainted by biology has fostered the absurd notion that children—or women—are of little relevance to culture: in the patriarchal world they consume culture and are dominated by it, but they don't produce it. This is exactly the trap from which I want to escape in our consideration of children, women, and dolls.

In a recent book, the biologist Linda Birke makes a lucid appeal, on feminist grounds, for closing the biocultural gap. The challenge to biological determinism was necessary, she argues, but has led feminists to lose track of their own physical constitution, their own insides. Science is undoubtedly a politically loaded, historical product; the dominant image of "the biological body as a set of constraints" explicitly or tacitly "supports political practices which fail women."[29] At the same time, she objects to the feminist fixation on the exterior of the body, and its reduction to symbols and metaphors: "While recent sociological and feminist theory has made enormously important claims about the processes of cultural inscription *on* the body, and about the cultural representation of the body, the body that appears in this new theory seems to be disembodied—or at the very least disemboweled. Theory, it seems, is only skin deep."[30] On the other hand, biology tends to reduce the insides of the body to its component parts, widening the gap between the *whole* body and the practical understanding of its place in society and history which feminists have sought. "There is no well-developed theory of the organism in biology," says Birke.[31] Nor, I would add, are there clear, academically respectable ways of tracing the *growth* of this organism from its microbiological beginnings, organs and all, to its social construction in historic time spans.

Understanding of the body, says Birke, is a victim of "the long-standing separation of the disciplines of academic inquiry." But it is also a victim of the old and futile tendency to separate "nurture" and "nature": "Ignoring or playing down the biological, material body helps to perpetuate dualisms of mind versus body, with all their gendered connotations."[32] The modern academic disciplines have set themselves up around this schism, with biologists, historians, geologists, and psychologists going about their own separate business. But discussion of heredity and environment is now shifting its axis, cutting across these disciplines and breaking them up into warring factions: the biosocial versus the cultural anthropologists, the evolutionary and the humanist psychologists, the fugitives from, and to, "science."

In the twenty-first century many of us are finding it necessary to return to the quest for a more comprehensive understanding of human nature and of its history in our individual and collective lives. Increasing concern about the disjunction between global political-economic processes and long-term human welfare has focused critical attention on the relationships between individual greed and social welfare, environmental, and cultural systems. Part of this is a concern about what we grow and *how* we grow: not just a selfish progression from birth to death but, as one recent book has it, transgenerationally from "cradle to cradle."[33]

Closing the gap between our knowledge of the physical processes in which we are born, mature, reproduce, and die, and the historical processes by which we make our way collectively from one epoch to the next remains one of our biggest intellectual challenges. Anthropology used to pride itself on this inclusive view of humanity, tracing the connections between very intimate and very large-scale phenomena. There are many things we need to know about youth and age in the contemporary world that no longer seem to fit the professional way we have been parceling out knowledge. To understand childhood and old age better we must come to terms not simply with academic biases, but with the biases of mature adulthood itself. Viewing the dolls from within the lives of the women who collect them may help us to see that the connections between our physical being and the moral systems in which we live are more intimate than we generally imagine.

THE BOOK AND THE PROJECT

With these ideas about growth in mind, we begin by putting the objects themselves into historical context, tracing the development of the PCD as a successful manufactured commodity in North America and Europe since the early 1980s. Their "ancestry" can be traced to two phases in the broader history of dolls, the most recent of which is the immense surge in the manufacture of play dolls for children during the twentieth century. But even more influential was an earlier boom in fine porcelain dolls that were treasured by children and women during the second half of the nineteenth century. These have been translated by time into *antiques*, and their high value, styles, and the nostalgia that surrounds them is a basic inspiration for the design, production, and manufacture of the PCDs today.

In chapters 3 and 4 we consider why some women should want to buy these dolls in the large numbers suggested by "collecting." If this has the driving force of a *need*, we can see it developing as their lives have unfolded in historical time: growing up in the Depression, raising families in years of postwar recovery, and experiencing the "empty nest" phase in times of relative affluence. In the fifth chapter we explore how the dolls enter the lives of the women, taking their place in the fabric of family relationships, serving as surrogates for "real" children, and helping to create new sorts of community and identity for the collectors.

In chapter 6 we take a close look at the dolls as physical artifacts, focusing on how "realism" is built into their bodies. To be truly alive the dolls should change physically, but their main attraction is that they have transcended the ultimate tragedy of human growth: they are immortal—or, as the advertisements so often put it, *timeless*. All dolls that imitate life must also deny growth, an ambiguity that makes them fascinating, powerful, dreadful. In the seventh chapter we explore how the PCDs do not simply capture essences of childhood, but physically incorporate aspects of the lives of the women themselves. A peculiar attraction of these exquisite effigies is that many of them also fix in porcelain memories of the women's once-fertile bodies.

I have introduced our student researchers, the backbone of the project, in the preface. We gathered detailed case studies of some 25 collectors, mostly from the western states of the United States. The students also searched bibliographies, museum catalogs, the Web, and the copious literature on antiques and doll history. The most laborious work was on the advertisements we clipped from magazines. Between 1991 and 2000 we collected 440 of these, and by sifting out repetitions, incomplete advertisements, those whose provenance was unclear, and outliers of various sorts (plastic dolls, religious images, etc.) we reduced these to a core list of 267. This included 28 dolls marketed in Britain. It was the striking uniformity of these advertisements, each for a single doll, that convinced us that we were looking at a distinctive product. The set became our main point of reference for identifying and talking about the PCD phenomenon, and we will refer frequently to this sample in the chapters that follow. We felt that no statement—with the possible exception of what the collectors themselves told us—was more heavily loaded with information than the pictures and the texts of these advertisements. They are also very costly to produce and place, and there is no doubt that they were based on intense market research and the most purposeful writing and editing. We subjected each advertisement to various forms of content analysis, ranging from the dolls' facial proportions, clothes, and accessories to the vocabulary of the text (see appendices A and B). We looked for the words most frequently used, and compared them with every other aspect of the doll (price, size, age, sex, race) we could think of.

The advertisements soon drew our attention to the six principal firms competing in this multimillion-dollar market during the 1990s. We discuss these, and the commodity they have produced, in the next chapter. We tried persistently but unsuccessfully to get information directly from these companies. One problem has been the speed with which one firm has consumed another in the brief and dynamic history of this commodity. More generally, business corporations are skeptical about journalistic and scholarly research, and disinclined to cooperate.[34] In the case of dolls, the problem probably lies in innumerable critical studies of Barbie and her phenomenally successful manufacturer, Mattel.[35] Possibly a firm that produces can openers or toasters would be more forthcoming. But within the limits of our shoestring project we found out quite a lot about the commodity and the people who produce and sell it, by other means.

Today, doll collectors are not hard to find. Since the phenomenon got under way some 25 years ago, they have been "coming out" in increasing numbers. If you are curious, log onto the Internet, or drop by your local doll store and chat with the proprietor and the shoppers who linger there. It's a passion to share, and of course you might also succumb to the charms of *Madeleine* or *Dana* or little *Christopher:* as the advertisement says, "Who could say 'no' to such a cute little boy? With that mischievous grin, those deep blue eyes and incredible dimples, Christopher can get away with just about anything—including stealing your heart!" And just think, you can "bring the joy of this adorable little boy into your home for only $76!"

Chapter Two

The Commodity

"Julia is attractively priced at $89."

The porcelain collector doll "epidemic" of the 1980s and '90s is not, as we might suppose, an entirely new development. If we were to think of the PCDs as freakish distortions of children's dolls, then the opposite has also been true: over several centuries dolls very specifically intended for women were models for children's dolls. Here, we shall track the descent of the contemporary PCD from its two most direct ancestors: the elaborate "fashion dolls" of the nineteenth century, which have since become valuable antiques; and the children's play dolls that proliferated during the twentieth century. These are European and North American traditions, which helps to explain why, although production of the PCDs is now a global enterprise, the principal markets are in the United States, Britain, France, and Germany.

ANTIQUE DOLLS

Dolls, however we may define them, have been around for a very long time. A 2,000-year-old doll from a child's grave in Peru is "a fine example of the cross-culturally ubiquitous style of doll: its soft responsive body, warm colours and appealingly stylized face offered the tactile pleasure and reassurance that children have always sought from dolls."[1] Similar objects have been found in the ancient Egyptian, Greek, and Roman graves of adults as well as children. Such dolls were evidently made at home, and it is interesting that the doll industry today still draws much of its creative energy from very small scale "kitchen table" design and production, mostly by women.

The first clear evidence of large-scale manufacturing of dolls comes from Germany in the fifteenth century. From the workshops in cities like Augsburg and Nürnberg we have early indications of "mass production," such as the "ring" method, by which a profile was cut horizontally through a piece of timber then sliced vertically and carved into dozens of figures.[2] The dolls produced in these workshops were mostly female adult figures, made in simple materials (wood, clay, wax) and costumed in local styles. The baby doll of the modern period was not yet born. These earlier dolls were evidently intended for women as well as children, and the more elaborate ones were exchanged as gifts among the expanding European middle class and aristocracy. These were the forerunners of the "character," "fashion," and "ladies'" dolls of the nineteenth century, important strands in the ancestry of today's collector dolls.

The elaborate dolls of the eighteenth and nineteenth centuries were developed not for lucky children, but to model women's clothes. This is probably the origin of the expression "all dolled up." Scaled down to less than half life-size, these were despatched by European couturiers to clients around the world, and became treasured items in their own right. They were exchanged as gifts at Easter (the start of the new fashion season) and to commemorate weddings, originating the enduringly popular tradition of the bridal doll. As the craze caught on, celebrities like the young Queen Victoria (herself a doll collector), the Empress Eugénie of France, and the Swedish singer Jenny Lind were used as models. Subsidiary industries developed to provide clothes and accessories: seamstresses, milliners, shoemakers, jewelers specializing in the trade. These dolls were much desired by (rich) little girls, to whom they were entrusted as icons of femininity, models of etiquette, and exercises in needlework, not as playthings in the "rag doll" mode. In these mannequin figures there is at least a hint of Barbie, the pre-cocious mini-adult with a passion for fashion.[3]

Germany and south-central Europe remained the historic centers of doll production through to the nineteenth century, when specific artists and firms were defining the basic materials, designs, and crafts-manship that made them valued antiques for the twentieth century. In 1810, Johann Daniel Kestner of Waltershausen, Germany, started producing up-market dolls in fine porcelain, elaborately dressed and hand-painted, and sold throughout Europe and North America. Realism was the key to their fame: "We feel that the only difference between a WPM [Walterhausen Puppenmanufaktur] doll and a human being is a heartbeat!" As Paris emerged as the women's fash-ion capital of the world, competition with Germany in the production of dolls intensified. This was partly resolved by partnerships in pro-duction, with the heads and bodies being manufactured in Germany and the final product assembled and clothed in France.[4]

The favored material for molding the faces of these "fashion" and "character" dolls was porcelain, whose texture and luster lent itself so well to the modeling of a child's or a young woman's complexion. Porcelain is made from kaolin, a pure white clay derived naturally from granite, and named after the hill in Jiangxi province that was the source of the original "china." It can be molded very finely and, when fired at high temperatures (1,200–1,440°C), is very strong and translucent. Left unglazed, it acquires a rich luster and matte surface. Modern bisque porcelain was developed in the early eighteenth cen-tury in Europe for the production of vases, tableware, and other lux-ury items, and it was these firms that fired the early dolls' heads and limbs. The technical processes are very demanding, and it took a long time and much experimentation for porcelain production to diffuse to other parts of Europe and eventually, early in the twentieth cen-tury, to North America. It is interesting that the revival of porcelain dolls at the end of the twentieth century depended, like their eigh-teenth- and nineteenth-century predecessors, on firms that produced domestic crockery, where resources and expertise in the manufacture of this delicate material were always concentrated.

The increasing enthusiasm for fashion dolls brought a demand for greater realism, and thus the development of materials and techniques. The "Poupées de Luxe" or "Parisians" of the French producer Pierre François Jumeau set the standards: bisque dolls with human hair, glass eyes with real lashes, detachable swiveling heads mounted on shoulder plates, and an abundance of furs, jewelry, and other valuable accessories. Jumeau was responsible for two major innovations: the industrial, factory-based manufacture of dolls (hitherto large-scale production was subcontracted to a network of workshops); and from 1855 the production of *bébé* dolls. These were not "babies" as we would recognize them today, but were modeled on children about four to eight years old. "*Bébés* resembled idealized young children with big eyes, chubby cheeks, and small rosebud mouths," and were often modeled on members of the manufacturer's own family.[5] When Jumeau and his son Emile moved the enterprise in 1873 to a new state-of-the-art factory, these child dolls were the mainstay of production.[6] They "clearly appealed to both children and adults" and their success was phenomenal: Jumeau claimed that in 1889 they sold 300,000.[7] Their great rival was Casimir Bru Jeune, who was producing his famous *Bébé Bru* dolls in his own factory in 1868. And early in the twentieth century a new giant dominated production: the Société Française de Fabrication des Bébés et Jouets (SFBJ).

True to the age of mass production the dolls were now displayed in retail stores and advertised in new magazines, which drew attention to the quality, realism, construction, and clothing of the dolls, and instructed owners on selection, care, and maintenance. The doll craze of the late nineteenth century gave rise to a new word, *dollatry*— "the worship of dolls," a borrowing from the etymologically unrelated "idolatry." The extravagance drew an official complaint from the Russian Toy Congress about "large, elegant French dolls which teach love of dress and suggest luxury."[8] The assumption that children were being corrupted was probably misplaced: the bébé-doll boom at the turn of the century was still very much an adult affair.

CHILDREN'S DOLLS

The twentieth century is the epoch of the child's doll. From the seventeenth century onward, play dolls in robust materials (wood, cloth, leather) intended for "real" children were produced in increasing quantities, but not in the factories of Pierre Jumeau or Casimir Bru. The classic bébés and mannequins of the nineteenth century became antiques in the twentieth: old-fashioned, highly valued, and definitively in the display rather than the play category. There was a brief revival of the adult character and fashion dolls in the 1920s in the craze for "boudoir dolls." These languorous, stagey, decorative dolls with cigarettes and spit curls were much influenced by the cinema and such personalities as Clara Bow, Rudolph Valentino, and Jean Harlow. But the Great Depression "marked a sudden end to this creative fantasy."[9]

In the twentieth century dolls were adjusting to a new historical phenomenon, recently dubbed "the invention of childhood":

> The period between 1850 and 1950 represents the high-watermark of childhood. In America . . . successful attempts were made during these years to get all children into school and out of factories, into their own clothing, their own furniture, their own literature, their own games, their own social world. In a hundred laws children were classified as qualitatively different from adults; in a hundred customs, assigned a preferred status and offered protection from the vagaries of adult life.[10]

The display dolls of the late nineteenth century impressed themselves on the design of dolls in the twentieth century. The adult and bébé forms, elaborate dress, and a concern for realistic detail were noted by Hall and Ellis in the survey of children's dolls at the turn of the century.[11] But if dolls had hitherto been "adultified," they would now be "childified," and increasingly this would be done not in the European heartland of doll production, but in the United States. At the turn of the century American stores like Macy's stocked imported European dolls, many of them very expensive by contemporary standards. "A revolution in European doll production enabled jobbers, manufacturers' agents, importers, and distributors to channel European toys to American retail stores where mothers and fathers purchased great quantities of dolls made out of china or bisque." The doll collectors were now little girls, and the wealthier their families, the larger the collection.[12]

Increasing resentment about European cultural dominance, directed especially against the Germans at the time of the World War I, did much to stimulate American doll production. The Kewpie doll made its appearance in 1913, Raggedy Ann five years later. For "fine" dolls, the main inhibition had been the satisfactory production of bisque porcelain, but with the shift to the production of children's play dolls that quickly lost its significance. For appearance, especially for faces, porcelain has never been bettered, but for play it is clunky and potentially harmful when it breaks. The quest for durable, impact-resistant, realistic materials had taxed the inventiveness of nineteenth-century producers. Although used for centuries, wax (beeswax, paraffin, or spermaceti) could be as fragile as china, scratched and blemished easily, was difficult to paint, and tended to discolor. Papier-mâché was difficult to mold in detail, and paste surfaces tended to flake and peel. Gutta-percha and gum tragacanth (hardened, rubber-like substances) were more resilient and better textured but, like rubber, tended to perish and decompose. Celluloid, used in production as early as 1869, was durable and lightweight, the forerunner of hard plastics. Through to the twentieth century the great mass of dolls were made out of "composition," a catch-all term for almost any materials (wood, paper, cloth, plaster, eggshells, glycerin, glue) mixed according to secret recipes into a pulp and pressed into molds. Depending on the ingredients, composition had a tendency to go sticky or peel, craze, and crack open. All these substances looked good for a while, but porcelain—if left untouched—could last forever.

Plastics, developed for other industrial purposes during the twentieth century, could be poured into elaborate and detailed molds, hardened into strong rigid forms, resist moisture and changes in temperature, and withstand the rigors of child's play. But they also produced unrealistically shiny surfaces, and could not be colored and painted with much subtlety. Many of these disadvantages were overcome with vinyl (polyvinylchloride), the substance from which most children's dolls are now made. The surface texture is softer and more skinlike, will hold hair and eyelashes more firmly, allows more convincing matte coloring and smoothly functioning joints, and is virtually unbreakable.

Although dolls like Kewpie in the "character" tradition were cartoon distortions, some of the biggest-selling dolls were modeled fairly closely on real people. The child movie star Shirley Temple has had a truly astonishing career as a doll. In the 1930s the Ideal Novelty and Toy Company of New York sold six million 24–inch Shirley Temple dolls, made of "unbreakable" composition and featuring mischievous "roving" eyes. Even in the Depression, one woman recalled, "everybody had a Shirley Temple," not least because of her modest price.[13] She appeared in plastics of various sorts, and in 1982, Ideal reissued a vinyl version with a profusion of nylon curls.[14] She is a long-established genre in her own right, merging all three categories of antique, child's play doll, and adult collector item. She combines perky images of childhood with the precociousness of the miniature adult.[15] She has made numerous appearances, in porcelain, in the collector doll range.

The 1920s launched the era of truly large-scale mass production of dolls for children. The development of techniques and materials, and the intensification of market research and merchandising techniques, produced the Cabbage Patch Kids and the Sasha series, which, have sold in their millions and imprinted their personae deeply in the subconsciousness of countless children. The proliferation of forms and functions is almost infinite, from the miniaturization of Action Man to giant Bart Simpsons to grace your sofa, from mutants and TransFormers to life-size Barbies that wear the same clothes as your child and can walk hand-in-hand with her. For all their variety, these are unmistakably playthings. Of course, any of them that survive that prime function may graduate to the status of antique, and any of them can be set aside, like virtually any other manufactured object, as a "collectible." But that was not why they were made.

THE PORCELAIN COLLECTOR DOLLS (PCDS)

From the point of view of the adult collector, "dolls were dead" in the mid-1970s.[16] Adult women looking for dolls quickly exhausted the antiques market—prices soon outstripped what the ordinary collector could pay. They turned first to the major American producer of high-quality children's dolls. Beatrice Alexander Behrman, alias Madame Alexander, is the historic doyenne of the U.S. doll industry. The daughter of a Russian porcelain repairer and doll doctor, her opportunity came with the end of German doll imports to the United States in the First World War. She opened the Alexander Doll Company in 1923 and developed the plastic standard-mold "Madame Alexander" doll range over the next twenty years. Her classic dolls remain collectors' favorites, but Madame Alexander was resolute that her dolls were for children, hence their relatively simple, highly standardized designs and materials. The new adult collectors were looking for something more. In the 1970s two companies catering to collectors moved in: first Effanbee Dolls, which produced limited-edition "prospective antiques" exploring "intuitively" quite new designs and sales techniques. With their button eyes and tiny mouths, the dolls have a distinctly late-nineteenth-century appearance. They were followed by another New York firm, Royal House of Dolls, which produced a "Curio Cabinet Collection" of bisque porcelain dolls in 1975. At the 1983 Toy Fair, Royal, Effanbee, and Alexander were surrounded by more than 30 rivals. Thereafter, Madame Alexander went into eclipse. Since her death in 1990, sporadic efforts have been made to revive the fortunes of her company: an investment group set up a batch manufacturing system which took sales up from $23.8 million in 1995 to an estimated $32 million for 1998.[17] However, these "retro-antiques" remained definitively children's dolls, and could not compete seriously with the PCDs for the cardinal reason that they lacked the desired realism and individualism.

At this stage, a different sort of firm moved in: companies that had never dealt with dolls, but had experience with the medium (porcelain) and, more significantly, direct sales through magazines, TV, and mailings of crockery, memorabilia, and jewelry. In the early 1980s the trade of these companies began to coalesce around a new sort of commodity, the collectible. Its growth was spectacular, rising from estimated sales of $30 million in the United States in 1983 to $7.6 billion in 1994.

The new species of fine porcelain doll, manufactured specially for adult collectors, is noted in the specialist catalogs and price guides from the early 1980s onward. Technically, they bore the influence of the twentieth-century developments in play dolls, in the material of eyes and hair, the beanbag bodies with their "natural" heft, the jointing of heads and limbs, and much else. But as imitation or "neo" antiques, the basic concept of the dolls and much of the styling reverted to the classic *bébés* of the late nineteenth century (see picture 2). They are often represented as "a turn-of-the-century treasure," or having "the special beauty of old-fashioned girls." And yet, as we shall see, the design and detailing of most of the PCDs differ markedly from these earlier models. Both aimed to be "lifelike" but achieved this in quite different ways.

In one key respect, the PCDs have remained true to the antique originals. Virtually all of them are porcelain: 91 percent of the advertisements in our sample make this explicit, the exceptions being 20 of the 53 Georgetown collection dolls, which we know to be porcelain. A couple of vinyl dolls may have sneaked into our sample under the "material unspecified" heading. The touted virtue of vinyl is that it will allow a collector doll to double as a play doll, a great convenience for grandmothers who feel obliged to share their collections with little visitors. We kept *Patsy* ("Crafted in hard collectible vinyl") on our list mainly on these grounds. She was offered as a "perfect 'first collectible' for a child, and yet is a lovely addition to any home and collection."

The advertisements press home the point that making porcelain is an old and very demanding art. Without great care and expertise in production, loss and wastage are high. Today, the doll's head and body parts are modeled by the artist in synthetic (polymer) clay, and a production mold is made from this sculpt. In the factory, the kaolin compound is pressed into the mold, the shell released and retouched, washed with a complexion-colored slip of creamy clay, and fired (sometimes two or three times) at temperatures in excess of 1, 200°C. This produces a hard, impervious matte texture that can be painted by hand. The result, as *Nicole* will testify, is "Old world craftsmanship in a collector's treasure for today."

Picture 2: Advertisement for *Caroline*.
(Georgetown Collection) © Pamela Phillips.
Photo by Dave Tuemmler, Stretch Studio.

INVENTING THE COMMODITY

Dolls were a distinct commodity in Europe as early as the seventeeth century, and a separate niche for collectible fashion dolls for adults was clearly established by the late nineteenth century. These were important precedents for the collector doll, which by 1990 had emerged as a new version of the old commodity, with distinctive forms, functions and clientele. The PCD may not have been as widely known as other manufactured commodities, like automobiles or hamburgers, but the people who wanted to buy it knew what it was and where to look for it, and the people who wanted to sell it knew how to make it, how and where to present it to their customers, and roughly how much to charge.

Things don't become commodities simply by sitting in a shop window or a closet at home. In its simplest terms, a commodity is something that is bought and sold—in Shakespearean English, "an article of traffic." It is made in the active relationship between producer and consumer: they recognize it and give it value, mainly in the repeated act of selling and buying, as an object distinct from other kinds of object. If enough people like the special spoon I invented to deal with ice cream, we have a new commodity: the ice cream scoop. Pretty much anything, from concrete objects like houses and oranges to abstract things like work (farm or factory labor) and information (legal advice) can become a commodity. Precious few things, such as the air we breathe, are not for sale, and thus don't qualify as commodities. But this doesn't stop people from trying to capture them and make a buck out of them (for a start, you can buy "fresh" Scottish air in cans).

One of the key devices for turning objects into commodities is *money*—which is itself built on social relationships and loaded with special social meanings. To use cash to buy and sell the ice cream scoop or the legal advice we need to agree what the coins and notes are, and what they can do. The government of whatever country we are in usually validates the coins for us, leaving us to sort out between us how many of them should mark out this or that particular deal. But even though sellers and buyers make their deals in cash without knowing each other personally, the meaning of the commodity depends on some sort of shared interest that brings them together. The buyers and sellers of PCDs may never have understood one another perfectly, but I shall return repeatedly to the point that the dolls—right down to details of their lips and names—are the product of an intricate collaboration between them. In the terms suggested by anthropologist Arjun Appadurai, the gap between "production knowledge that is read into a commodity" and "consumption knowledge that is read from the commodity" is, in this case, quite narrow.[18] But to understand the product we have to know a lot more about this relationship than the economic laws of supply and demand alone could tell us.

One of the most significant things we can say about a commodity is that it expresses relationships among people: not simply between the seller and the buyer, but among the relays of people involved from the earliest stages of the production process (the quarrying of clay for the porcelain, the spinning of yarn for the dolls' dresses) to the packaging and mailing of the finished product to your home— and even to the people who come to admire your dolls there. Marx pointed out that although we may not always be conscious of the fact, every commodity has social meaning built into it, whether it's a block of steel or a Porsche, a brick or a porcelain collector doll. In Marxian terms, "the social character of people's relationships with each other is disguised as an objective relationship between them and things."[19] Although the purchaser may not be fully aware of it, the doll embodies a relationship she has with persons as remote as the women in Thailand or Mexico who assembled it and stitched its clothes.

If all commodities carry lots of social baggage, the doll does this in a startlingly and exceptionally explicit way. This commodity is not a thousand tons of cocoa or a block of steel, it is an object masquerading as a real little person in its own right. But the fact that this particular commodity has a face and a body is actually a distraction from the "social identity" of the object which Marx and the political economists imagined. Gazing at the finished product, we can be duped into thinking that it is a lot sweeter and nicer than the real relationships among the people who produced it would imply. To the worker in Thailand who paints the lips and eyelashes for $3 a day, or for the man in Illinois shifting boxes with a forklift truck, the commodity might as well be a block of steel. It seems unlikely that either has any interest in the "use values" of the doll as they are intended by the manufacturer or perceived by the collector.

Recently, anthropologists have been looking more closely at the ways in which objects absorb identities as they move around between people—bought and sold, exchanged, given as gifts. In one sense, each specific item (grandpa's gold watch) has a biography. "Though the biographical aspect of some things (such as heirlooms, postage stamps, and antiques) may be more noticeable than that of some others (such as steel bars, salt, or sugar), this component is never completely irrelevant."[20] As a particular *category* of objects, a commodity also has a social history (the gentleman's pocket watch) recountable in varying degrees of cultural detail (the gold watch as a typical retirement gift).

Reflecting on this "social life of things," we may note two further peculiarities of the PCD as a commodity. First, compared with bread or cars, this product is *enclaved*: it is made and traded in a restricted sphere, outside of which much of its meaning is lost. You have to be quite specifically involved in the production and consumption of this commodity to know what's going on, and to give any sort of value to it. Second, much of its value depends on moving it as quickly as possible out of the status of mere merchandise and into the status of socially meaningful object (*Kimberly*, *"Angel hugs"*): the "commodity phase" of the PCD is ideally brief. As we shall see, building a very particular social identity into the commodity (names, birth certificates, etc.) is an important part of the manufacturing process itself.[21]

One of the ways we know a commodity exists is because people talk about it—they give it a name. This makes it easier to buy and to sell the object. We have all had the experience of going into a shop (so often it's a hardware store) and being unable to name the object we want to buy. Without a name, even an object with a very distinct form and function (a bradawl) may be hard to distinguish from the objects on the shelves around it (hand tools). We may not even agree on the use to which a commodity will be put—you're selling me a brick, I'm buying a doorstop, but if I can't ask for a brick, I may not get my doorstop.

Giving it a name is usually essential to establishing the object's identity as a separate commodity. *Differentiating* a product in this way means you can sell more of it more easily. But to do this you have to communicate with your customers, and in modern times we have depended on advertising to do much of this job. Patents and trade-marks are the means by which a new product can be claimed and pre-sented to the market. Occasionally such a proprietary name may iden-tify the commodity more generally (Scotch Tape and Post-its are favorite examples). By the time sales peaked around 1995, the phrase "porcelain collector doll" was generally established as the key indica-tor of the new product we are concerned with here. It appeared in advertisements, packaging, trade journals, and other places (shops, TV programs, toy fairs) where the goods were transacted. Augmented by a few other words (heirloom, classic, premier), it picked the PCD out from the broader categories of "toy" and "doll" by specifying the material (porcelain) and the adult purpose (collecting) it served.

While the sellers and buyers were evidently communicating about the product quite effectively, people compiling trade statistics or com-menting on the industry have been more uncertain about the identity of the commodity and the environment to which it belongs: are the PCDs "toys" or "ornaments and souvenirs" or "giftware"? By the early 1990s the U.S. Department of Commerce had identified them as a growing and anomalous category, but was referring to them by the antique label "fashion doll" and lumping them into statistics along with children's dolls and stuffed animals. The fact that the producers and consumers regard the new commodity as neither a fashion doll, nor a play doll, nor a stuffed animal has still not penetrated official understandings.

On the grounds that knowing what a product *is* depends to a large extent on distinguishing it from those it *is not*, we identified some product counter-indicators for the dolls. Apart from junk shops and garage sales, you would be very unlikely to find the PCDs for sale in the same place as menswear, sports utility vehicles, or teen products like pop music. One diligent researcher sifting through stacks of mag-azines noticed that ads for PCDs never appeared anywhere near a scratch-'n'-sniff perfume advertisement. The aversion is mutual: the advertising director of *Country Home* says other advertisers, fearing the grandma image of doll advertisements, ask to be positioned at least six pages away.[22] You won't find any doll advertisements in *Vogue* magazine, nor will you see them in any of the mass of parenting magazines on the racks today. Although the dolls imitate babies and children, they are traded in a separate world.

The more clearly defined a commodity, the more perceptible the identity of the purchasers, and the more directly the producer can communicate with them. Who you are as a consumer plays a powerful role in the definition of the product, which is why it may be invisible outside of the group or social segment (region, ethnic group, social class, profession) for which it was made. The people who buy PCDs are predominantly white and lower middle class, but gender and age are even more basic to the definition of this commodity. This reminds us that the structure of our lives, our growth as human beings, is a basic property of the things we make, buy, and sell. Manufacturers of sports utility vehicles do not waste much time trying to sell them to little children or elderly women. But the same sort of discrimination is latent in virtually any commodity—foodstuffs, entertainment, clothing, houses. For all of these, and for better or worse, your gender and the stage you have got to in your life connect you with some commodities or versions of them and not with others. If you don't connect with them, chances are you won't even notice them.

It is impossible to understand the PCDs without paying close attention to the life circumstances of the women who buy them. To dismiss the PCD craze as "childish" would miss the distinctively adult meanings the collectors, *as older women*, attach to the dolls. And yet, children are the models for the dolls, and it is to childhood passions that the women's desire for these particular dolls harks back. Making sense of this, putting together a convincing objective explanation, turned out to be less easy than we supposed when we began looking at PCDs in 1991. But there is no doubt that the doll manufacturers were already very smart at reading, and catering for, those very special demands.

THE FIRMS

The trade in collectibles, through which the main firms came to doll production, generated an estimated $7.6 billion in sales in 1994.[23] They were the companies best placed to manufacture and distribute the new commodity when demand for it arose, and it was from this motley product environment—not "dolls and stuffed animals"—that the PCD emerged.

We latched onto the PCD phenomenon through the advertising campaigns, and soon identified the leading firms. All of them were, or soon became, parts of larger conglomerates dealing in collectibles, and all specialized in direct sales to customers through intensive advertising:

Ashton-Drake Galleries, Niles, Illinois
The Georgetown Collection, Portland, Maine
The Hamilton Collection, Jacksonville, Florida
The Danbury Mint, Norwalk, Connecticut
Franklin Heirloom Dolls, Philadelphia, Pennsylvania
Lenox Collections, Langhorne, Pennsylvania[24]

Teasing out information about these firms and the PCDs from the limited, publicly available information about their parent companies was a tough task. The industry in the mid-1990s was "brutally competitive."[25] According to business journalist Phyllis Berman, Danbury, a subsidiary of MBI Inc. with revenues of about $300 million in 1991, was formed by one of the colorful characters in the trade, Ralph Glendinning, "to produce knockoffs of Franklin's expensive collectibles."[26] In these circumstances trade information is not bandied about openly.

One thing was certain: the business was big. Between them, Bradford (owners of Ashton-Drake), Stanhome (Hamilton), MBI (Danbury), Roll International (Franklin), and Brown Forman (Lenox) grossed $1.5 billion in 1991.[27] According to its own publicity, Ashton-Drake Galleries, founded in 1985, is "the world's largest direct marketer of limited edition, collectible porcelain dolls."[28] Its parent company, The Bradford Exchange, was founded in 1973 by another colorful character, J. Roderick MacArthur, who built the firm up by producing collectible plates with American themes, such as the Lafayette Legacy Collection, and a series based on Norman Rockwell's illustrations, Rockwell's American Dream. Bradford sold half a billion dollars' worth of collectibles in 1994, a 6.6 percent share of the total collectibles industry.[29]

Lenox, a more modest producer of PCDs but a major producer of other collectibles, is a subsidiary of the Brown-Forman Corporation, originally a firm of distillers dating back to 1870 in Kentucky. A company with product interests that have ranged from luggage to credit cards, Brown-Forman's big move was the acquisition of the Southern Comfort Corporation in 1979 for $94.6 million cash. Its total net sales in 1998 were nearly $2 billion. Brown-Forman now consists of two business segments, one dealing in drink, the other in consumer durables, especially china, crystal, and ceramic collectibles. The company took over Lenox in August 1983, paying $45 per share for each Lenox share, for a total cost of $413.2 million. Brown-Forman sold off Lenox's jewelry division for $120 million cash in 1988, but the Lenox subsidiary continued to produce collectibles and to acquire other firms—for example, Wings Luggage in 1991.[30]

As the collectibles industry took off in the 1980s, bigger companies bought out smaller businesses and developed their own products on a larger scale. Such corporate expansion and takeover are evocative of that earlier boom period in the history of dolls, when the German company Simon & Halbig was swallowed up by its rival Heinrich Handwerck, and WPM was taken over (in 1886) by Ernst Kammer and Franz Reinhardt.[31] The Franklin Mint was set up in 1965 by Joe Segel (who later founded the QVC—Quality Value Convenience—TV shopping channel). The company, well known for its medallions and jewelry, was taken over by Warner Brothers in 1981 and was bought by the current owners, Stewart and Lynda Resnick, from Warner in 1985 for $167.5 million. They added the Franklin Heirloom Dolls to the firm's repertoire, and by 1995 the firm had about $800 million in sales worldwide ($600 million in the United States), and employees in 18 offices.[32]

In June 1989, Stanhome Inc., a Massachusetts firm that (as Stanley Home Products) had sold brushes and polishes to housewives since 1931, acquired the doll-producing Hamilton Group for $21.3 million. The founder of Stanhome was a former Fuller Brush salesman, Frank Stanley Beverage, who is credited with inventing, among other things, the coffee party mode of selling—a technique perfected by Tupperware. Stanhome had expanded into the giftware, memorabilia, collectibles industry, and the company acquired Enesco to produce the Precious Moments figurines, worth $10 million in sales every year.[33] In the early 1990s the company's subsidiaries (Enesco European Giftware Group Limited, Enesco plc., etc.) were trading in Britain, France, Germany, Hong Kong, Canada, and Spain.

Georgetown, well established in the production and direct sales of PCDs, was bought out in October 1996 by the L. L. Knickerbocker Company, a firm that had traded in beauty products since 1985. In addition to buying Georgetown, onetime restaurateur L. L. Knickerbocker took over the costume jewelry manufacturer Krasner Group Inc. and the gemstone sourcer S.L.S. Trading Co. Ltd. in 1996. That year, Knickerbocker's net sales rose from $42 million to $68.3 million, its gross profits from $6.8 million to $37.5 million. By the end of 1998 the company had 463 full-time employees. The value of Knickerbocker stocks zoomed from $4 to $46 in just six weeks in 1995, and Mr. Knickerbocker himself vowed, "My goal is to take this company to $1 billion in sales."[34] His aspirations seem to have fallen victim to the general economic downturn later in the '90s: a petition for bankruptcy was filed against Knickerbocker in August 1999.[35] The firm's assets were then acquired by Marian LLC, a company owned by record producer Brian Blosil and his doll-enthusiast wife, the pop singer Marie Osmond. The last we heard, Marian had turned over management of the Georgetown dolls to Ashton-Drake, now part of the Bradford Group.

MANUFACTURE

The history of doll production has a tendency to repeat itself, shifting back and forth between production on the small scale and large scale, from kitchen table and workshop to factory and international enterprise. The contemporary collector doll is no exception to this pattern. Viewed just as a physical object that someone has to make, it has some notable characteristics:

- The manufacture is divisible, consisting of several parts (limbs, clothes, accessories) that are usually produced separately and assembled into the finished product.
- Materials are relatively costly: the most visible parts are made out of porcelain, which is difficult to produce.
- Manufacture is labor intensive: it requires careful assembly and finishing by hand.
- Production is scale-elastic: dolls can be made entirely by a single person working alone at home, or by hundreds of people in a big factory.
- The added value is also very elastic: a PCD can be mass produced quite cheaply, or custom-made at great expense.

This means that if you were manufacturing dolls in a businesslike way, the parts could be made in many different places, and assembled and finished somewhere else, according to local prices of materials and labor and the costs of transport. In the present global economy the dolls are unlikely to be made where most of them are actually sold— in North America and Europe.

To get the big picture on doll manufacture in the United States, we consulted the Department of Commerce and Bureau of the Census reports which appear every five years. There, dolls in general are grouped along with stuffed toys into the commodity heading "Industry 3942." In 1992 dolls, including fashion dolls, accounted for just 10.4 percent (worth $30.3 million) of this category, but by 1997 the proportion of dolls had risen to 27 percent—$79.9 million out of total sales of $299.8 million. This increase coincides with the boom in PCDs, but we don't know with any accuracy how many of the U.S.-produced dolls are actually included in these data. It is likely that some have been grouped under other industry headings like "souvenirs" or "giftware" or have been merged with "figurines."[36]

Over the 15 years up to 1992, the number of doll and stuffed animal manufacturers in the United States fell from 231 to 209 firms and the value of production dropped from about $500 million to $300 million. The figures indicate that although doll sales expanded through the 1980s and 1990s, the number of U.S. workers engaged in doll production dropped drastically. In 1997, only seven firms employed more than 100 U.S. workers, and the great majority employed fewer than 20 workers. While their numbers have fallen steadily, to 2,500 actually engaged in production currently, their wages have improved, but they are still not well paid. In 1997, manufacturers added $194 million value to the total shipped value of $300 million (65 percent), but paid just $42 million (14 percent) in wages. (See figures 2a–2d.)

A very basic selling line for the PCDs is that they are produced—in part if not wholly—by hand.[37] The cost of the dolls and their promise of future "antique" value depends on the individual care with which they are made. The more the manufacturer resorts to machines and assembly lines, the less that promise can be fulfilled. Much of the assembly and decoration is too finicky to be done by machines anyway, and detectable brush strokes in the application of eyebrows or dimples actually enhance the value of the product. Increasing the volume of production and lowering the price, the basic tactic for developing most other commodities, would kill this particular product. For example, "Hannah's porcelain head and limbs are of a high quality fine bisque. Her hand-set, blue-gray eyes are warm and expressive, bestowing a sweet nature on her expertly sculpted, hand-blushed face." The dolls were hand-painted, -crafted, -sewn, -stitched, -tailored, and -numbered. Their eyes were hand-set, their hair cut and curled by hand. This was done "meticulously," "carefully," and "exquisitely"; *Billy* "has artfully hand-painted features and is inscribed with the artist's signature on his upper back." The word "craftsman" occurred in 19 percent of the advertisements, while a far larger portion credited the workmanship to an *artist* (alone or in various compounds like "artistry") in 68 percent. But in truth, the level of artistry required in the manufacture of the PCDs is not great. Although the work is done "adorably," "sweetly," or "lovingly," what is actually required is the careful repetition of quite simple and very precisely prescribed hand movements.

The main work is done by artisans who, according to the advertisements, "lovingly" paint the PCDs and stitch their tiny garments. In reality, the work is tedious, underpaid, and surprisingly dangerous. In

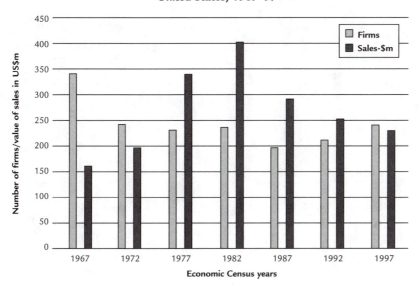

Figure 2-a: Number of doll manufacturers and total sales in the United States, 1967–97

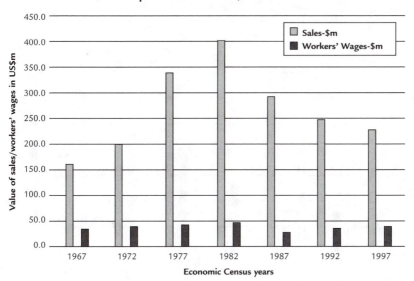

Figure 2-b: Total sales of U.S. doll firms and wages of production workers, 1967–97

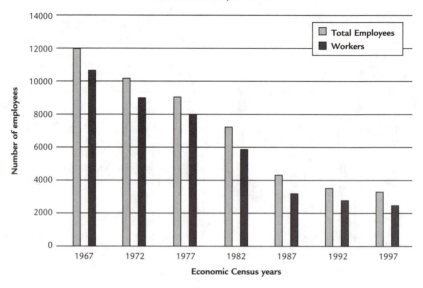

Figure 2-c: Total employees and total production workers in U.S. doll firms, 1967–97

Figure 2-d: Number of production workers in U.S. doll fims and average wages, 1967–97

the nineteenth century, outworkers (and their families) inhaled stuffing, poisoned themselves with white lead, and scalded themselves with wax; the twentieth century added many more hazards, such as solvents, thermoplastics, and polystyrene fillers.[38] All this points to the increasing "outsourcing" of doll manufacture. Now, as in comparable industries (clothing, souvenirs, etc.) most of the PCDs are being made in countries like Thailand, China, Indonesia, and Mexico. As one critic has remarked, the different worlds are brought together "in such a way as to conceal almost perfectly any trace of origin, of the labour processes that produced them, or of the social relations implicated in their production."[39] As you unwrap each little person and lift her out of her box, there is little (beyond an occasional "assembled in the USA") to betray her transnational makeup. But there is nothing particularly novel about this. For the last 200 years doll production has been on the move: from Germany and south-central Europe (Bohemia, Thüringia, Groden valley) to France and England in the nineteenth century, then on to the United States, and to Hong Kong and the Guangdong hinterland in China in the twentieth century. It was not always the complete doll that moved: in the early days German body parts were sewn into torsos and dressed in France, and today, crates of little heads, or dresses, or rocking horses converge from around the world in the creation of *Sarah* or *Harry*.

This "globalization" of production has attracted much negative publicity, and manufacturers are less than candid about where their dolls are produced. In general, the more expensive the doll, the more likely it is to have been manufactured in one place. Danbury seeks to outsource as much as possible, whereas Franklin, whose dolls cost about twice as much, prefers in-house production staff.[40] In the early 1990s, Knickerbocker (Georgetown) had eight facilities, two of which are in Bangkok (where the company has a total of 39,500 square feet).[41] Given the diverse origins of the PCD's components, there are few traces of those "Made with Pride in the USA" labels. The *Economist* says of the phenomenally successful American Girl series: "These quintessentially American dolls are made in Germany. Their exquisite accessories are made in many other countries. American Girl, meet the world economy."[42]

The names of the artists and designers mentioned on the TV shopping clubs (Y. K. Wu, C. Y. Liao) suggest that at least for the lower priced dolls, even the design stages are shifting to the East. Design is now the "front end" of the production process, the only part which is not resolutely anonymous. In the merchandising of the dolls the artists have been brought into the spotlight quite recently: not many were named in the 1980s, but they featured explicitly in 88 percent of the advertisements we collected during the 1990s.[43] Now artist names and reputations have become more important to collectors than the name of the series, or even of the manufacturer itself. Firms like Ashton-Drake now list their dolls on the Web by artist. Some of the names look a bit stagey (Bella Bambina, Lia Di Leo) but the emphasis lately has been on *real* personalities, out there stumping on the TV shows. Their appearance is revealing: they are not pale, slender young things in artist's smocks, they are middle-aged, motherly women. It is very clear that their customers who phone in for a chat feel completely at ease.

In parallel with this there has been a shift from in-house designers to relatively well paid freelancers, the "geniuses" who create the "magic" of the PCD. We have the strongest impression that the firms now recognize that the fountain of new ideas is out there among the clientele, rather than among its own staff. Ashton-Drake advertises for designers on its Web site, declaring "We pay on a project by project basis. . . . Ashton-Drake maintains an extensive Artist Resource File, which is constantly reviewed by our product development team as new doll concepts are created." Jobs are also available for wig makers, prop makers, and illustrators "that can capture realistic babies, toddlers, children, brides, fashion and religious figures." They should "have understanding of expressive posing, and realistic features and proportions."[44]

Prolific designers like Yolanda Bello, who works for Ashton-Drake, seem to have entered the collectible doll industry in the mid-1980s. The biographical sketches that have accompanied their emergence in the sales process have a strikingly similar pattern. They usually have some basic training in, or talent for, painting and sculpture. They began making dolls at home for themselves, their children, or friends.

Laura Lee Wambach has been designing dolls for 15 years: "I was just shopping one day and saw a box of clay in a craft store and someone had sculpted a little person there and I thought well if they can do it and sell it then I can too. I have always loved art and I love to draw and paint."[45] Pauline Bjonness-Jacobsen has been sculpting dolls "forever . . . 30 years, something like that":

> I was very much interested in drawing and painting and oil painting and then I made some dolls for some friends and they were cloth dolls and they were very popular and I got an order for them to go commercially. But I have always been drawing, drawing Christmas cards, greeting cards and drawing children's clothes, and dolls. So you know I have been circling in that area.[46]

Most of the doll designers are women.[47] It is interesting that women should have appeared in such large numbers in the design of the PCDs, but in fact they have always been at the heart of doll manufacture. Although the large-scale factory production has been preemptively a male domain, the influence of women through the centuries is unmistakable. From Margaret Stieff in nineteenth-century Germany to Madame Lenci (alias Elena Konig di Scavini) in early-twentieth-century Italy and Norah Wellings in England, through to Barbie's creator, Ruth Handler, redoubtable women have been a persisting inspiration for today's designers and entrepreneurs.

It is remarkable that the wellspring of the industry is still the home work of women who are, like their clients, passionate about dolls. A very typical example is Maureen Byron of Sunderland, England, who took up doll making after a bad car crash. She works at home with a nine-to-five routine.

> Her work area houses hundreds of moulds, gallons of slip—a paste used in ceramic work—and most importantly, three kilns. And of course everywhere there are beautiful dolls—large, small, old and modern. Mo does everything from casting the doll from a mould to firing it, painting it and finally dressing it. The whole process can take up to two weeks, and dolls cost from £10 to £250, depending on the finish.[48]

A talented artist can make single "custom" dolls and sell them for several hundred dollars. Her materials are typically synthetic clays and polymer resins like "Fimo," "Cernit," and "Sculpey," which are pre-colored and can be hardened at low temperatures in a kitchen oven. But none of these has the texture or the kudos of porcelain, which demands a different order of expertise and apparatus. Not many doll makers, however skilled and ambitious, can graduate to this material, and fewer still manage to scale up production and sales on their own account. Most sell their talents to the larger firms, where they bring to the commodity a passion and an immediate rapport with the consumers that are so easily lost in (male-controlled) mass production. The big firms have learned that unless they retain this link to the source, buying in freelancers and buying up small enterprises, they quickly run out of inspiration.

MARKETING

Collectibles, dolls especially, became "the definitive example of classic direct marketing" in the 1990s.[49] Middle America is very accustomed to catalog purchasing, and the graduation of direct sales to TV shows came naturally. But as the recurrent phrase "from our home to your home" suggests, there is a strong feeling that this special, almost-human commodity should move swiftly and directly from the hands of her Maker to the bosom of the Collector, unsullied by intermediaries like wholesalers and retailers. The TV sales shows conjure up this moment of private satisfaction:

> When these boxes arrive at your door, by the way, you'll be so
> delighted because the boxes are huge, the dolls are packaged
> beautifully, and when they arrive at your door, simply take them
> out, sit them on a sofa, put them on a love-seat, and fall in love
> with the believability of something like this. Make sure, of course,
> that you're going to the phones right now to choose our Tamsin.[50]

The sales strategies for the PCDs are quite different from those for children's dolls, which have to be sold to parents "through advertisements in print media based on claims for educational value" as well as to children themselves through "television commercials based on their 'badge appeal' to peers."[51] Advertising and sales for the PCDs aim much more directly at their adult targets. From the mid-1980s, advertisements for PCDs appeared in the clutter of ads for processed foods and housewares, costume jewelry, and ready-to-wear clothes which spill out of every mailbox, TV guide, and Sunday newspaper. In the 1990s they featured prominently in magazines that picked out the private, homebody clientele quite clearly: *McCalls, Country Home, Ladies Home Journal, Parade, USA Weekend, Woman's Realm* (UK). The advertisements might catch your eye as you flipped through the magazines at a supermarket checkout. "Serious" enthusiasts could subscribe to an expanding range of specialist magazines that fueled the craze and catered to all tastes and price levels. Between 1978 and 1983 *Doll Reader* doubled its circulation to 40,000, and in the mid-1990s it appeared 9 times a year for an annual subscription of $30. Its major rival is *Dolls—The Collector's Magazine*, published 10 times a year for a $49 subscription.

Product specificity is revealed in the consistency of advertising style across the main PCD firms. The typical full- or half-page advertisement consists of a very clear photo of the doll, full body or portrait, with its accessories, a paragraph or two of narrative and sales talk, and a mail order coupon inset or pasted in (see picture 2). Ashton-Drake advertising couples a paragraph of vivid description with boilerplate text giving assurances of quality and service. Full-page advertisements in large-circulation weeklies accounted for one half of the collectibles industry's $378 million of media spending in 1995. The Franklin Mint's advertising budget for that year was $90 million, $54 million of which it had spent on Sunday magazine advertisements by the seventh month. Franklin had one of the largest in-house advertising staffs in the United States—an estimated 100 employees.[52] In 1995 it was the twenty-seventh largest advertiser in the United States. Bradford's advertising budget (Ashton-Drake) for that year was $27 million, Danbury's $22 million, and Lenox's $17 million.[53]

The number of dolls in our advertisement sample peaked in 1994, as did the average price; thereafter it was downhill to the end of the

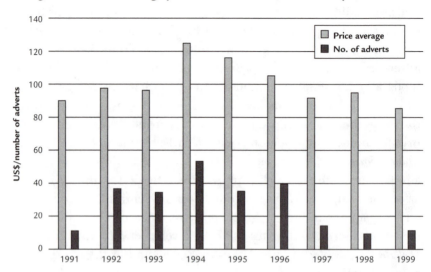

Figure 2-e: Annual average price of dolls in advertisement sample, 1991–99

decade. (See figure 2-e.) Franklin, at the top end of the PCD market, seems to have felt the pinch quite early: it laid off 10 percent of its workforce in 1995, and President Tom Durovsik resigned.[54] The problem was less with the dolls themselves than with the merchandising. In 1995 the direct sales of collectibles was, in the words of one expert, "reaching a saturation point."[55] In 1993 Stanhome started phasing out its direct sales interests, and in May 1997 the company sold its Hamilton Direct Response businesses in the United States to The Crestley Collection Ltd. for approximately $48 million.[56] Sunday magazine advertising of collectibles was collapsing: "The entire direct response area hit a wall back in May [1995]," according to the publisher of *Parade* magazine.[57] Direct sales through TV was still getting off the ground—accounting for just 5 percent of the sales of collectibles in 1995.[58] Five years later, PCD advertisements in the Sunday magazines were rare, but the TV sales shows were booming.

The Home Shopping Network began in the late 1970s as a local Florida AM radio station, graduating from local to national cable TV. Ten years later, its 24-hour programming was grossing $2 million to $3 million a day. Personal interaction with the consumer was the great innovation of TV shopping. "The people calling in talk more about the product than the show hosts do," said an HSN senior vice president enthusiastically. Consumers became members of the Home Shopping Club when they made their first purchase, becoming "like one big family." HSN sent its members birthday and anniversary cards, with gift vouchers "to complete the homey image."[59] The sales advantages are conspicuous: customer feedback is virtually instantaneous, and the pressure for impetuous decisions ("hurry—this item will be off your screen in a moment!") is followed through by extremely rapid delivery of the goods. About 70 percent of HSN's clientele are women in the 35-to-54 age bracket, and porcelain dolls were a key item from the start. The HSN vice president painted "a scenario of a woman alone at home during the day with multiple tv sets blaring from room to room. As she goes about her chores, she can keep abreast of the activity. When a new product comes on the screen, it is accompanied by bells and clapping to grab her attention." In 1999 the HSN ran three weekly doll sales programs: *Gallery of Dolls*, *The Doll Shop*, and *The Doll Cottage*. These aired during the night on Pacific time, the earliest starting at 10 P.M., the latest ending at 6 A.M. On the occasions we monitored these shows, post-midnight shoppers from Connecticut to California all sounded astonishingly lively.

Anticipating a general trend, Franklin had already been shifting its merchandising to TV, and to "museum-quality stores"—nearly 50 of them in 1995.[60] Today, there is a very visible proliferation of specialist doll shops in North America and Europe. Retail stores like *My Little People* of Wethersfield, Connecticut, also sell directly, by phone, fax, or through the Internet.[61] Yesterday's stay-at-home buyers are now out shopping, admiring the serried ranks of PCDs on the shelves, handling the dolls, and chatting with staff. The smaller main-street stores that proliferated during the 1990s have a friendly, clublike atmosphere, and many of them are reselling dolls on consignment for their regular customers. Demand still seems to be running high, and the price range is widening.[62] The low end has been well established in shops and market stalls for years. On a chilly November morning in 1995 I met a vendor setting up her stall in the marketplace of Richelieu, a small town in France. Her dolls were mostly vinyl and in the $15–$40 range (picture 3). She gave me the familiar explanation that her clientele consisted of mostly older women who say that they were deprived of dolls when they were children and who justify their collections by saying that they will pass them on to their grandchildren. A major focus for collectors in the United States is the doll fair. On California's central coast, for example, the Miller Production Group hosts 15–20 big doll shows every year. In addition to the full PCD range there are clothes ("more expensive than real baby clothes"), wigs, doll-making tools, how-to videos, furniture, and much else.[63]

These changes have favored the growth of smaller firms producing more expensive, custom-made dolls for specific retail outlets. In the doll industry as a whole, the total number of manufacturing firms increased in the United States during the 1990s, but this consisted mainly of a shift to smaller enterprises. The PCD industry has also multiplied other opportunities for new enterprises. The TLC doll company that makes accessories for the Pleasant Company's American Girls series chalked up $200,000 worth of sales in 1996, and was "growing rapidly."[64] Now there are companies providing start-up services for the small-scale producer. The Village Doll Haus supplies porcelain heads and body parts for doll makers who don't have their own kilns, and The Doll Market has everything from undressed dolls to "hair, socks, shoes, and eyes."[65]

PRICE, VALUE, AND THE "INVESTMENT"

Comparison of the PCD advertisements suggests that the product is very similar across the main firms (figure 2–f). The average price of the dolls over the nine year period (1991–99) we monitored advertisements was $106. There is much overlap in price ranges, but averages point to a vertical division of the market among the main firms that corresponds roughly with their volume of sales: average price for Ashton-Drake dolls over the nine-year period was $73, for Hamilton $104, for Danbury $106, Georgetown $124, Lenox $153, and Franklin $199.

There is no correlation between the size of the doll and the price. What matters is the quality of materials and finish, and anything that

Picture 3: Marketplace doll stall.
Richelieu, France, November 1995.
Photo by A. F. Robertson.

Figure 2-f: Price ranges of dolls by main doll firms in advertisement sample, 1991–99

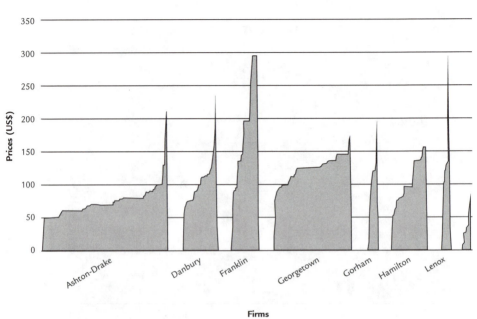

suggests individual artisanal attention rather than mass production. Eighty-four percent of the dolls came with some specified accessory other than clothes (necklace, chair, flowers, cart, dog, rocking chair, mirror, parasol), but curiously, the average price of dolls without named accessories was significantly higher ($124) than those with ($101). This may partly reflect a general tendency in merchandising for lower priced items to draw attention to features that are taken for granted at higher prices.

The dolls were also spread out fairly evenly by age category among the main firms, except that Ashton-Drake produced 21 of the 26 "infant" dolls in our sample. Infant dolls with their closed eyes, partial bodies and simple garments were the cheapest ($85 on average). The adult dolls were slightly more expensive ($109) than the average price for children and toddlers ($107). There was little difference in the price averages for dolls of different ethnicity: Caucasian dolls cost on average $105, African Americans $114, and

Native Americans $97. The two largest-selling companies, Ashton-Drake and Georgetown, produced the most ethnically diverse range. Between them they accounted for all but 1 of the 18 African American dolls in our sample.

The dolls are porcelain mainly because they imitate the antiques that doll enthusiasts can no longer afford. The hope is that they will, in the fullness of time, become *real* antiques, but like their predecessors their future value depends heavily on the fragility of the material. Every doll that gets broken adds to the worth of those that remain. Down the years, dolls have been saved from attrition by being carefully conserved. With an eye to investment, the "serious" collector keeps everything intact, from bows and shoelaces to wrappings, labels, and receipts, and must resist the temptation to make little changes to clothes and hair. Nearly all the doll owners we met were critical of collectors who put material values above emotional values. Keeping a doll boxed, with her label and price tag still fixed to her wrist, is considered inhumane. We were repeatedly assured that every doll was out on display, that all of them were loved and carefully handled, and that nobody was hidden away waiting for her dollar value to appreciate.

The manufacturers of the PCDs have to strike a delicate balance between the realism of the doll and its price. Our sample suggests that $100 is the threshold at which enough detail can be applied to the doll to make it look realistic, while producing it in sufficient numbers to make it commercially viable. Around $200 is the starting point for the production of individual, hand-made dolls. A doll by a reputable artist which has some chance of holding and enhancing its value costs more than $500. Small-scale specialist producers encounter this threshold when they expand business. Ken Shader turned his hobby making porcelain dolls into a $4 million business, Shader's China Doll Inc. Each part of each doll was signed and dated by the craftsperson who made it, a feature that recommended it to the serious collector. As business expanded, three quarters of Shader's dolls were produced on contract for other firms, leaving him in a quandary about whether to step up mass production at lower values, or continue trading up-market in his own name.[66]

Until the mid-1990s, many PCD advertisements stressed the investment value of the dolls, including little charts of the escalating resale value of previous items.

> As a leading authority on collectible dolls, Ashton-Drake is commit-
> ted to producing the highest quality of dolls at irresistible values.
> Ashton-Drake's first doll, "Jason," is legendary in the doll world.
> Designed by doll artist Yolanda Bello, Ashton-Drake offered "Jason"
> to collectors for $48, from 1985 through 1986. Since then, "Jason"
> has sold at an auction for as much as $1200 and is sold by dealers
> for $800 and more.[67]

By the end of the decade such assurances were rare, probably because a glut was already evident, but also because investment has never been the primary motive of the ordinary doll buyer. The firms do not, of course, offer any guarantees against doll depreciation, only against a lack of customer appreciation. Cash refunds are specified in 67 percent of the advertisements. Periods covered range from 30 days (42 percent), 100 days (3 percent), and a year (55 percent). "You may acquire 'Virginia' at *no risk* with our *100% Buy-Back Guarantee.*"

Collectors are less influenced by promises of the investment potential of their dolls, than concerns (especially of family members) that collecting PCDs is a waste of money. This seems to be the main reason why advertising continues to offer reassurances about the material value of the dolls. The main tactics are to stress the individuality of each doll by marking it with a number or original signature; to restrict the copies of each doll to a "limited edition"; to issue certificates of quality and award special prizes; and to have public institutions and celebrities endorse the product.

Identification marks are stamped on the back of the neck, the small of the back, the sole of the foot, and sometimes on each separate body part. Like the marks on silver and fine china, this is supposed to "authenticate" the doll in the future. "As your assurance of authenticity, Shirley Temple's signature will be inscribed in the porcelain back of your doll. You will also receive a serially-numbered Certificate of Authenticity" (picture 4).

Twenty-eight percent of the dolls in our sample were produced in a limited edition, a designation that is supposedly monitored by NALED, the National Association of Limited Edition Dealers. Precisely how the PCDs were "limited" varied: 15 percent were restricted by "firing days"—100 days is the mode (half of the cases), otherwise 45 and 365 days. The enthusiasm for firing-day limitations, after which molds were to be "broken forever," died out around 1996. Buyers seem to have cottoned on to the fact that a big company can fire an awful lot of dolls in 365 days. Nearly half the dolls were "numbered," but only a quarter were also explicitly "limited." The buyer will not know the number until the doll is delivered, at which stage there may be little point in complaining that it seems unreasonably high. Latterly the firms evidently discovered that the average customer is not much troubled by the incongruity of a "best selling" doll in a "strictly limited edition," nor much impressed by number stamps and broken molds. The word "edition" itself seemed to carry enough weight: dolls were variously in "exclusive," "artist's, " "first," "premier," or "landmark" editions.

Ashton-Drake awards its dolls certificates based on its own "uniform grading standards for dolls." We have not seen reference to anything other than the top, "premier" grade. The industry also awards its dolls and their designers prizes, which are used to certify the product in advertisements. The best known are the "DOTY," (Doll of the Year) awards from "The International Doll Academy." The two basic categories are "play" and "collectible," the latter broken down into porcelain, vinyl, artist (i.e. expensive), and direct purchase (cheap). Respectable magazines like *Dolls* and *Doll Reader* help to monitor these competitions, which are open to the smallest producers.

Manufacturers are always looking for ways of asserting the value of their dolls: *Mary* is "the first-ever heirloom porcelain doll issued under the authority of Catholic Daughters of the Americas." A well-established tradition is to link the doll to another familiar branded product. Early examples were *Dolly Dimple*, advertising self-rising flour, and *Sunny Jim* (alias "Mr. Force"), advertising Force Wheatflakes.[68] In recent years these "corporate collectibles," as they are now known, have appeared in increasing numbers among the ranks of the PCDs.

No. _____ 4677 I _____

Certificate of Authenticity

"Jennifer"

by

Jane Zidjunas

This document certifies that this
collector doll is crafted from an
original work of art by Jane Zidjunas
and an exclusive presentation of
The Hamilton Collection.

James P. Smith, Jr.
James P. Smith, Jr.
Chairman
The Hamilton Collection

QP1CA

Nº _____ 2669 Y _____

Certificate of Authenticity

"Jessica"

by

Connie Walser Derek

This document certifies that
this adorable baby doll has been
hand painted and costumed
to perfection.

"Jessica" is an exclusive
presentation of
The Hamilton Collection.

James P. Smith, Jr.
James P. Smith, Jr.
Chairman
The Hamilton Collection

NPICA

Picture 4: Certificates of authenticity for two collector dolls.

The range is astonishing: Good Humor, Goodyear, Campbell's Soup, Coca-Cola, Taco Bell, Popsicle (*Lucy Lick-a-color*). *Scootles* is the official U.S. Postal Service Doll, and Harley-Davidson sponsors *Bobby, the Little Biker Baby,* who comes complete with bandana, ignition key, diaper, and pout. The hamburger chain has had considerable success with McMemories, the "official McDonald's collectibles club," manufactured by Ashton-Drake:

> Smiling brightly, "Katie" has every reason to be proud. Her good work at school has earned a gold star, and now she gets to go to her favorite place, McDonald's! "Katie" is a new fine-porcelain collectible doll by Titus Tomescu, endorsed by McDonald's, which supports the efforts of parents and teachers everywhere to improve education in our communities. "Katie" comes with report card and a backpack featuring the McKids logo.

When Tina Berry offered a clutch of corporate collectibles to her audience one night we monitored her HSN-TV show, the response was swift and emphatic:

> Tina: "We even have shopkeepers trying to buy this little fellow that I have coming up next. It's the Goodyear Boy!"
> Caller: "I wannim!"
> T: "Did you see him?"
> C: "I *want* him! Is he too cute or what?"
> T: "Oh, he's so precious!"[69]

The benefits flow in both directions: "product recognition," the familiarity of major brands, helps to sell the dolls, and as instant antiques the dolls perpetuate the name of the product and the affection with which it is supposedly regarded. *Danny,* "The first such doll ever authorized by The Coca-Cola Company," was offered in 1995 as "a historic premiere for doll collectors!" Manufactured by the Franklin Mint, he takes us back "to the early 1900s," and comes with baggy cap and a little cart full of Coke:

Remember your first home-made toy crafted with love as the main
ingredient? Danny's scooter is created with the same amount of
love, and is equally authentic just like the ones little boys created
from real "Coca-Cola" crates in the early 1900s. Emblazoned with
the world-famous "Coca-Cola" trademark, it's his display stand, so
he can ride right into your heart!

It may be a measure of the extent to which such products have pervaded our lives that the collectors seem little disturbed by these tie-
ins. According to a program coordinator at the Coca-Cola Company,
"When people drink Coca-Cola, they associate it with family and
friends and adopt it as part of their lifestyle. A licensed Coca-Cola
product brings the product that much more into their lives. It is something that they can take ownership in. That is why we chose to license.
It is a way to get the Coca-Cola trademark to consumers around the
world."[70] More generally, the collectors seem quite capable of holding
the material and the emotional qualities of the dolls in separate cognitive compartments. The prices and installment terms, the references to glass eyes and hand numbering, and the merchandising
tricks do not seem to detract from the romance of the story line.

In the advertisements, the value of the dolls is talked up by every
means at the disposal of the manufacturer. Much play is made on the
classy European origins of the tradition, from the materials of the
dolls to the origins of the artists. The advertisements are peppered
with specialist vocabulary, much of it with a French accent: "petite"
(less than 10 inches), "soutache," "ecru," "voile," "pantalettes."
Nicolette is "exquisite European artistry at a noteworthy price!" *Becky*
was "created by European-born designer Bets van Boxel." Gudrun
Haak and Sylvia Natterer are both "renowned European" doll artists.

A big marketing challenge is putting a price tag on the dolls,
while playing up their priceless emotional value. "Let this toddler
know he's still loved for only $59.95!" (*Tommy*). *Sweet Carnation* is "so
posable and cuddly, at a tiny price" ($54.95). "Welcome 'Ethan' into
your home for only $69.95." "Cuddle her, dress her, and rock her to
sleep for just $79.95 payable in easy monthly installments" ("It's a
Girl"). "With all this wonderful detail, *Jenny* is priced at a reasonable

$119." Really expensive dolls tend to cut the sweet talk: "The price is $295" (*Lenox Christening Doll*).

But there is no great need for the hard sell. The doll firms have had one marketing asset that they have exploited to the full. These customers want more—and more—dolls. They are *collectors*, a fact which is imprinted squarely on the identity of the commodity itself. As a prelude to tackling the question why some women would want to collect these dolls by the hundred, we must first consider the more general mystery of why people should want collect large amounts of *anything*. How and why has this strange behavior become such a prevalent aspect of modern life and popular culture?

Chapter Three

The Collection Just Grows and Grows

"Peaches and Cream is certain to win a place in your collection—and your heart."

Estimates of the number of people in North America and Europe who collect things range from around a third of the population to as many as two thirds. Those who collect statistics differ mainly in their estimation of the "seriousness" of the collection: most of us *accumulate* stuff, but *collecting* indicates a conscious orderliness, discernment, persistence, and scale—a couple of items doesn't amount to a collection. "I did not realize that I was a doll collector until recently," says a chat room participant. "I had just kept accumulating dolls."[1]

Nevertheless, "serious" collections often bear a close resemblance to the stuff the rest of us spontaneously accumulate. There is simply no limit to the range of things that are "collectible." The most enduring and the most popular are stamps and coins, followed by "dolls, toys, art glass, and furniture."[2] But as Barbara Harrison notes in a *Harper's* magazine article, people also collect "teeth and toupees, skulls and cookie jars, trolley-car tickets, hair and fans and kites and forceps, dogs and coins, canes, canaries and shoes, data on Siamese twins or the Dionne quintuplets, Presley stuff and Beatle stuff and buttons and bones, hatpins and forged signatures and first editions and gas masks."[3] In the 1990s frog stuff became so popular that special shops like "Frog Hollow" in Kensington, London, catered to it.[4] "Darryl Pitt, owner of a small production firm in Manhattan, collects meteorites, traveling frequently to Africa and Asia to chase rocks that have fallen from the sky."[5] In this motley array, collecting porcelain dolls starts to look quite sedate.

Collecting is often regarded as a historically modern phenomenon.[6] The way we imagine it, there was not much scope for collecting in pre-industrial societies. In the old feudal and mercantile hierarchies, the tiny minority who collected valuables were politically licensed to do so; ordinary villagers would soon encounter the leveling pressures of superiors, neighbors, and family. Adults who accumulated worn-out tools, old crockery, or dead animals (all collectible items today) would be regarded as eccentric if not mad. But with industrialization, the expanding scale of society, and the development of new class structures, private accumulation became endemic. In this narrative of modernization, the alienation of individuals from the old communal solidarities meant that the value of people became more closely associated with the value of things—not just rich and rare things but *lots* of them. The new industrial barons bought up all the superfluous things that distinguished their aristocratic predecessors—houses, paintings, furniture. But latter-day collector mania suggests that almost anything, accumulated in sufficient quantity, may become a conveyor of social value. According to Susan Pearce, "Collecting holds the middle ground within the social system, between market and temple, where values are created out of rubbish."[7]

As a generic activity, collecting has become institutionalized. There are numerous magazines and clubs for collectors, plain and simple. People who are serious collectors of one thing are likely to collect other things—in a sense, they collect collections. One will spin off another: the step from cigarette cards to matchboxes is not so large. Most PCD enthusiasts have at least the nucleus of one or more other collections—plates, thimbles, glassware. Half of them also collect porcelain figurines like the Lladró and Precious Moments series.[8]

"My other passion is lilies of the valley," says a doll collector from North Carolina. "I collect anything with lilies of the valley—china, hankies, etc."[9]

Collecting involves specializing, and specialization—making more and more specific categories for virtually everything, including people—is what modernization has been all about. It is a compulsion to select and categorize things from the world around us, to complete or close a "series" or "class" of "choice objects," and thus to refine the identities of the collectors themselves. It is, says Pearce, an exercise in meaning-making (matchboxes have a story to tell), an attempt to give coherence to the otherwise unintelligible junk we accumulate. And it is also a "biographical urge," a way of defining ourselves (my match-boxes tell a story about *me*). Collecting is woven very tightly into the fabric of people's lives—a passion for something weird can make you a special individual—like Edna, the "Frog Lady" of Walsall, England.[10] In the alienated, depersonalized modern world, you can make your name as a collector. An obituary in the *New York Times* noted the passing of "Hugh Hicks, 79, prodigious collector of light bulbs."[11] Former commodities trader Greg Tunks, whose motto is "Something for nothing," has made a reputation collecting and dealing in used credit cards.[12] The serial murderer Jeffrey Dahmer, notes Barbara Harrison ominously, was also "a collector."[13]

Even outright trash can make a serious person of the collector. Classifying, distinguishing, curating, all make you in some degree a *connoisseur*, and if there are enough of you, you can get together and promote your collections *and* yourselves as a group of discerning people. In the twentieth century connoisseurship has been stretched to "kitsch" and "schlock," patronizing categories that for many less passionate observers would cover the PCDs nicely. Most collectibles have very limited use values: you don't strike the matches, you don't eat your dinner off the fancy plates. They are not to be not touched, tasted, or smelled, and even visual access can be very grudging: stamps and etchings are kept under protective covers, jewelry in bank vaults, dolls in their original boxes. Old musical instruments and gramophone records are seldom played, bottles of classic perfumes never opened, the 1932 Montrachet never drunk.

Their exchange value is defined by the collectors themselves rather than more general markets. Who else would know or care that this canvas is worth millions, and that canvas nothing? By collecting lots of bottle tops, or cheese labels, or Dalí prints, we hope to pack material value into a novel category of object, but without the collusion of other enthusiasts they are worth precious little. The trouble with the PCDs is that unlike stamps there are still no established rules of value other than those for antiques, and the PCD is explicitly or implicitly an imitation, or retro-antique. The collectors rarely buy PCDs from each other or swap them; they get them by mail order from the manufacturers. They have, as yet, little collective organization to define tastes, standards, and resale values, which makes investing in them very much an act of faith and hope.

The scale, range, and material value of a collection dignifies its owner, but what makes a collector "serious" is aesthetic judgment and knowledgeability in the estimation of fellow collectors. "Serious" collecting dates back to the Enlightenment, when eighteenth-century gentlemen scholars assembled huge collections of rocks, insects, stuffed animals, or "ritual objects" from exotic places, which in due course became the nuclei of public museums. One Rothschild collected albino animals and birds, another specialized in fleas.[14] The "seriousness" of these collections remains an inspiration to people today who can spend enormous amounts of time and money acquiring, classifying, shelving, filing, and curating. As playthings, dolls are at something of a disadvantage in the "seriousness" stakes, but assiduous collectors of antique dolls have quite substantial libraries, and meetings of the numerous branches of the United Federation of Doll Clubs (UFDC) are devoted to descriptive analyses of individual dolls, visits to museums, classes in repair and maintenance, and discussions of history, production techniques, and fabrics. In this elite context, the PCDs tend to be disparaged, and there is little more to talk about than their popular emotional appeal.

Current attitudes to collecting indicate that values remain ambiguously material and social. A collection distinguishes you as a person, but it is also an investment, a clever way of conveying value to virtually anything that would otherwise be junk—used stamps, old furniture, bottle tops, gum wrappers, paintings. The work of putting it in order, sifting a narrow category of objects out from the general mass, is often sustained by the promise of profit. But ultimately this depends on the assumption that someone, somewhere, will want to buy your stuff *as* a collection or *for* a collection. All established collectibles have their own dealers—books being an obvious example. A major secondhand bookseller in Britain specializes in hand-sorting container loads of books bought from all over the world. The company had, for example, accumulated more that 200 different editions of *Goldilocks and the Three Bears,* which it intended to sell to a university or private connoisseur.

The ethos of the market, of shrewd choices and competitive risk-taking, is ever-present in serious collecting. The concentration of a narrow category of objects—bottle tops, pictures of Elvis—creates the sense that they are a *limited good,* and that in this restricted market one collector's gains will be another's loss. Competition is thrilling, but acquiring complete monopoly may be a very lonely satisfaction, and may even cause the cash value of the collectible to slump. A collector may profess to being "humbled" by the distinction of owning a priceless painting, or a picture of Elvis that may be, however exiguously, defined as "unique." Ironically, the more valuable the collection, the less the collector may feel inclined to own up to it. "Texaco CEO James Kinnear does not speak to the public about his orchids; Don Petersen, the former CEO of Ford, won't discuss his mineral crystals." "It may start off as an exhibitionist thing," says Gordon Apker, an avid collector of "wheeled things," but "the more dramatic it gets, the more you hide it. You have something to lose."[15]

But for the ordinary Joe and Jane, collecting is also in part an effort to recapture a sense of belonging, something of the old lost community. Serious collectors establish clubs devoted to spark plugs, buttons, rocks, or cigarette packs. It may be a private vice, but it is also a means of making and sustaining relations with like-minded people: accumulating, classifying, discussing, and transferring objects within families, peer groups, clubs, associations, swap meets. There may be a dearth of Van Goghs, but there will always be enough postage stamps to allow large numbers of philatelists to convene in numerous associations, reaffirming the sensation that they are a nicer class of people. The seemingly infinite expandability of the whole notion of collecting is signaled by the fact that collectors of cars or guns commonly join not just one but dozens of associations: they collect club memberships.[16]

On the face of it, collecting involves lots of adult business like investing, saving, gaining prestige, making a reputation, building a legacy. And yet the mania is widely regarded as childish, something to be a bit ashamed of, especially when the objects collected are toys or trash. "Collectors share a sense of specialness, or of not having received satisfying love or attention, or of having been hurt or unfairly treated in infancy," says Manhattan psychoanalyst Werner Muensterberger.[17] Although serious collecting seems to entail the civilized business of establishing categories, rules, and order, it also smacks of a lack of self-control, of such infantile, primeval sentiments as *greed*. Almost everyone who comments on collecting invariably adverts to its wellsprings in human nature. Collecting takes us back to the thrill of the chase. It has its roots in the old-fashioned vices of gluttony, avarice, and lust. "Collecting is like sex," Barbara Harrison writes in *Harper's*. "Satisfaction creates new appetites."[18] Collectors themselves say "it's in the blood" or "all about feelings." In its advanced forms, collecting is truly a visceral passion: "My bricks are inside me, they are something no one can ever take away from me."[19]

Collectors themselves will often admit that their urge is a kind of madness. It's "exactly like a drug high," says Russell Belk, a professor of marketing at the University of Utah who has interviewed 200 collectors.[20] According to child psychologist Milton Brutten, "It's very much in my case akin to falling in love with a person." Brutten has been collecting contemporary paintings and sculpture for 25 years. "Artworks became infused with a romantic or erotic energy," he admits. "When I'm moved, beads of sweat appear on my forehead. My heart starts pounding. The artwork becomes a very rich, meaningful being that can help me resolve conflicts. I feel that life is not worth living without that sculpture."[21] Little wonder that in extreme forms the passion can lead to incarceration: Dennis Masellis is in jail in New York for stealing $7 million from his employer "to feed his uncontrollable Bakelite habit" and his collection of 400 Barbie dolls.[22] In the main, collecting is harmless, a Rutgers University psychologist and glass collector told Ehrenfeld: "You don't hear many case histories of families where someone mortgaged the house for a collection. You're much more likely to gamble away the family fortune or drink it away than use it up buying beautiful things."[23]

A comprehensive psychology of collecting has yet to be written, but it would probably dwell on five themes: childish regression, sexual urge, anality (the urge to order, categorize, and curate), the search for security, and loneliness. There is a developmental connection to be argued among them, reaching back to infancy and forward to old age, evocative of the perspective on growth we have deployed in this book. But to understand the PCD phenomenon it is also important to bring these feelings into conjunction with the recent history of collecting as a cultural phenomenon—our quest for the biohistorical meaning. In the following sections we shall begin the exploration biographically, considering what dolls mean as childish things in the lives of adult collectors, and the motivations of growth, before returning to the role of the manufacturers in producing a new commodity that taps so deeply into human feelings.

PLAY AND DISPLAY

A collection takes things out of their normal functional domains and retires them into a very restricted category of use (or "non-use"), basically "display." A vintage car may be polished and admired, but driving it around puts its value as a collectible in jeopardy. Likewise, a doll collection is unlikely to survive its ostensible function in child's play. Most objects, when they are classified as collectibles, make the transition from use to display, either as a late stage in their own individual "lives" or historically, as a category of objects. In a Spanish village recently I met a clog maker who, when he retired, sold all his tools and lasts to the village doctor, who has devoted a room in his capacious house to their display. The same doctor has a very large and possibly definitive collection of stone mortars, which will never again feel the impact of a pestle.

Today's PCD differs from its antecedents in that it has no such use
history: it is neither a plaything nor an antique, it is manufactured as
an *imitation* of a plaything *and* an antique. It doesn't actually function
like a toy or one of the nineteenth-century originals, it does a different sort of job, and a central purpose of this project has been to find
out what this job is. The dual origins of the PCD as toy and antique is
expressed in a heightened ambiguity about its function: is it for *play*
or for *display*? Little children and the senile are least likely to "display"
their dolls, and most likely to "play" with them—bathing, nursing,
and changing their clothes. Older women who want to do this are
most likely to opt for plastic or vinyl play dolls. This is probably why
the PCD manufacturers and their customers both avoid using the
word "play"—although that is what the invitations in the advertisements to cuddle, sing to, and generally care for the PCDs seem to
amount to. Within the doll trade generally, the distinction is between
play and *shelf.* Although adults "play" golf, chess, music, and so on, the
semantic undercurrent of childishness is inescapable. This attitude
persists despite the insistence of developmental psychologists during
the twentieth century that play is "not trivial," a view that has greatly
influenced progressive parenting and school curricula.[24] Article 30 of
the United Nations Convention on the Rights of the Child (1989) rec-
ognizes the child's right to play.[25] But these interpretations of child's
play remain patronizingly adult in that they are predicated on the
assumption that play helps a child to grow up, to "get serious." Serious
collectors do not "play" with their stamps or vintage cars, but where
the collectible is itself a toy, the stigma of childishness is more obvious. When she feels her adult dignity is in question, a PCD collector
is likely to revert to the chilly description of her dolls as "decorative
accents" for her home.

Webster's *New World Dictionary* tells us that "serious"—a word that
appears so insistently in discussion of collecting—"implies absorption
in deep thought or involvement in something really important as distinguished from something frivolous or merely amusing [he takes a
serious interest in the theater]." The *Oxford English Dictionary* defines
it as "having . . . earnest purpose or thought; of grave or solemn disposition or intention; having depth or solidity of character, not light

or superficial; now often, concerned with the grave and earnest sides of life as opposed to amusement or pleasure-seeking." A little observation will make it apparent that for the small children and elderly people, or for many of our PCD collectors, caring for a doll is, in such terms, abundantly "serious." The gravity of the activity is to be understood in its own context (childhood, loneliness, senility) rather than from the disparaging perspectives of other life stages or gender stereotypes. The PCD collectors translate the seriousness of their involvement with dolls into emotional words like "passion." When people are drawn into conversations about dolls, the gravity of their *own* relationships with dolls is seldom in doubt. Tales of deep emotional involvement and of life-and-death traumas make it clear that if we are to understand dolls we should never dismiss their functions as either "merely" play, or "merely" display.

The ambiguity about play and display is evident in the way people of all ages divide up the dolls they have collected. Corinna had two sorts of Barbie, the ones she played with, all jumbled up in a basket, and the ones she preserved neatly in their boxes. Isaak Volynsky, Mattel's corporate director of new technology, points out that the pricier "shelf" Barbies intended for collection and display are different: they "have to be just about perfect—with defect-free surfaces, finely detailed features, and the solid feel of a small statue." There is a corresponding concern with the quality of packaging, since the container is often used to display the doll. Much the same applies to the PCDs, whose wrappings Volynsky describes as "humongous and expensive."[26] One woman, born in 1938, describes coveting, and being given by her indulgent grandmother, an expensive Madame Alexander doll. She never played with her, but kept her "in a child's walker" in her bedroom. "I never combed her hair; I never even took the hat off. The doll I really played with and was my friend was Sally, this poor bedraggled soul."[27]

Marilyn, now in her twenties, remembers:

As a child I never played with my dolls. I thought that they looked nice, and that is why I had them. They always stayed in my pet-net, a hammock hung in the corner of the ceiling to display stuffed animals, and rested on my bed or my dresser. I named them; usually the names they came with or were assigned. These dolls were never my friends. They never played with me. I have them all today, and they are still in the same condition in which they were bought. I feared my dolls because they were strangers living with me in my bedroom. I did not know them.

The French poet Baudelaire, a century and a half ago, thought this was unhealthy. There are some children, he said, who "do not make use of their toys, but save them up, range them in order, make libraries and museums of them. Only rarely do they show them to their little friends, all the while imploring them *not to touch*. I would instinctively be on my guard against these *men-children*."[28]

We found that if children have PCDs, they don't play with them. This usually pleases the grandparents or aunts who give the doll. For little girls, porcelain dolls are display dolls: "I don't really care if you can change them or not, 'cos I just like to look at them" said 11-year-old Emily. Porcelain, fragile and clunky, is more for appearance rather than touch: it just doesn't work as a play doll, and little children prefer dolls they can cuddle and throw about. The most basic play/display distinction for many children is between the soft furry animals that are favorites at bedtime, and the fancy dolls they have been given as "special" presents.

Seiter remarks that "boys *become* their toys in play; girls take care of their toys"—which probably inclines them more toward display.[29] As they grow up, children will usually shift the function of their dolls from play to display. As they approach puberty children become more interested in the theatrical qualities of their toys, an emphasis that accompanies a shift toward Barbie or Action Man. This greater interest in exhibiting dolls is also a reflection of our increasing self-consciousness as we grow: the dolls are a medium by which we put ourselves empathetically on display. As we shall see, this self-imaging aspect is important in understanding the form and functions of the PCD. The collector can see in her dolls, stable and secure on their shelves or in their cabinets, multiple images of a self which may otherwise be fading.

Some women keep their old play dolls on a shelf in their bedrooms for most of their lives. There they sit, biding their time for a reawakening of the "childish" enthusiasm that so often comes in their later years. Thus, the play/display distinction can be a measure of the distance between childhood and adulthood: children who display are behaving like adults, adults who play are behaving like children. "Play dolls" are a very distinct, even threatening category from the serious adult collector's point of view. Playing with collectibles jeopardizes their value: "you do have to use some caution to make sure you protect your investment for future generations" cautions a Web site on doll care. "You may also want to take into consideration whether or not children or animals will be in contact with your collection. If this is the case, you may want to keep your dolls out of the reach of little hands and curious family pets."[30]

"Decor" is a function referred to quite often in the PCD advertisements: "*All Tuckered Out* will add a charming decorative accent to your home." Pat Kakassy, senior marketing manager of the PCD manufacturer Lenox, says: "People are returning to the home and returning to nesting. They are doing home decorating that does involve more collecting."[31] Robyn's grandma, Mary L., collects pretty "lady-like" dolls, with names like Peaches and Patches, Sunny and Honey, and Pumpkin. "When walking into the living room of my grandparents' home a visitor is apt to encounter close to 15 dolls," and many more in the guest rooms. "The collection is displayed in a realistic manner, with dolls seated on park benches, hiding under chairs, and quietly sitting on rocking chairs. The dolls are meant for an audience." The irony here is that while homes have become spaces for conspicuous display and consumption, they have also become increasingly private: very few of these extensive and elaborate doll displays are in any sense open to public view. Nevertheless, collectors spend a great deal of time and money on presentation, furnishing one or more rooms with custom-made cases and shelves for their dolls. A rigorous maintenance schedule of almost surgical precision is recommended, involving the donning of cotton gloves and gentle dusting with a hair dryer. A 1996 Ashton-Drake catalog offers Mylar cases with built-in stands, dust covers, and vinyl slipcovers in a range of sizes, and modular display cases with mirror backs and "velvety" linings. Some collectors arrange their dolls on shelves in dizzying ranks, but most prefer to group them into tableaux: picnics, playgrounds, tea parties, and bedroom scenes are popular. A Web page advises that "Dolls are particularly charming when they look like they are interacting with each other."[32] The modest collector with 200 or 300 dolls will arrange them in clusters all over the house, so that there are dolls everywhere you look (picture 5). When we visited Debbie, her husband was stretched out on the Barco-lounger watching TV, seemingly oblivious of our intrusion and the dozens of dolls clustered around him on the furniture, on shelves, and in cabinets.

Carol D., a Californian in her early sixties, keeps her dolls in a specially purchased hutch, or display cabinet. "Each doll has its own space, and they are never rearranged," her granddaughter reports. "Carol is very anal about keeping her dolls clean and tidy." She cleans the hutch three times a week—"Not just straightening up, but a thorough cleaning." She wouldn't display them around the house "because I couldn't stand to have dust or dirt on them." When she gets more dolls she'll just get a bigger hutch, she says. This raises the question of how the average collector can accommodate a hundred or more porcelain dolls. The simplest answer must be "in her empty nest," after her children have moved out. But nowadays the nest is not just emptier, it's bigger. Despite dwindling household sizes, average domestic space for the middle classes in the United States almost doubled since the Second World War: "Suburban homes—pictured continually in television sitcoms and magazine advertisements—were to be filled with everything the parents had not had. . . . Ranch-style houses provided separate children's bedrooms that could be filled with toys."[33] The trend continues: in California, a typical new house now measures 2,300 square feet—55 percent more than in 1970.[34] If collectors can resist the temptation to jam all available space, dolls are rotated from storage to display. Husbands who may tolerate the transformation of living rooms into overcrowded nurseries complain about intrusions into conventionally male domains like the garage. More affluent collectors put choice items on long-term display, creating the illusion of "real" babies and children peopling the home (picture 6).

Caring for such a large family is hard work. Or is it play? As adults we may smile indulgently at childish make-believe, the *work* of breath-

Picture 5: At Debbie's house—dolls everywhere you look . . .
Photos by A. F. Robertson.

Picture 6: Eva's dolls—at home.
Photos by Eva Kuhn.

ing life into a doll, caring for it, expecting much of it. On the one hand, "play" is as much an adult as a child's activity, but the boundaries are drawn differently. Things like cars and guns are well known as a man's "toys," the more so if he has lots of them. Model cars may be a male category that parallels the PCDs, though "play" (running them up and down the carpet?) may be more covert. Even though stamp collecting involves a lot of serious curatorial work, and the (ideal) product is a highly formalized display, as a "hobby" it has a pre-adult aura. It was recommended to me as a child as a way of learning geography and history and of developing a sense of order. (My mother, a serious philatelist, was also a professional librarian and indexer.)

Many serious collections are confined to store cupboards or bank vaults, but what makes doll collections seem unusually "warm-blooded" (as one woman put it) is their very visible integration into the collectors' homes and lives. These displays are much more than a "decorative accent." They are intended to conjure up whole families sharing the domestic space. The collector is very much the maternal figure, moving around the house talking, adjusting, cleaning, caring for "all the little people." It is doubtful that even the most avid philatelist could achieve quite the same domestic effect as, for example, Joan B., who has more than a couple of hundred dolls in her home in England.

> When Joan opens her front door, dolls greet the visitor, sitting on
> either side of the hallway on their own chairs. Walk around her
> house and dolls of every shape, size, type and colour fill the rooms.
> They sit on the stairs, on beds, on cupboards; they peep out
> between the bannisters. Some perch on their own special chairs;
> others are huddled together. The majority are elegant little girls
> dressed Victorian-style. . . . One or two are antique, but many are
> not worth a bean. Joan just loves dolls.[35]

THE BIOGRAPHY OF THE COLLECTION

We grow up, we grow old, we grow into and out of things, and somehow in the thick of all this our collections grow. What's the connection?

Part of the answer can be found in the frequent assertion that the serious collection is, in ideal if not always in reality, a *life's work*. It is paced by the progress not just of a personal life course, but of growth in the social, intergenerational sense we outlined in chapter 1. This way of linking our physical development and the upbringing of people in specific cultural and historical contexts provides a framework for thinking about the phenomenon of collecting and its morality. Insisting that *mortality* is an essential aspect of human growth draws attention to an irony implicit in all collecting, but which is conspicuous in the case of dolls: while the life of the collection and the collector run in parallel, we may hope that the survival of the material objects will in some measure help us transcend our own death.

In conversation, the PCD enthusiasts make repeated references to family processes, from the past to the future, and justify their often huge doll "families" in these terms. Families, like collections, grow: the one is quite a good metaphor for the other. But a collection of dolls running to many hundreds has plainly outstripped its human parallels. The irony is that while it is above all in the nature of children to grow, this is one thing a doll cannot do. And so their numbers multiply, the collection expanding relentlessly into a huge quasi-family. The result is a bizarre reversal of the historical tendency of the family to contract to its modern compact, "nuclear" mode—mom, dad, and a couple of kids.[36]

According to a 1995 survey, doll collecting is not a casual or fleeting affair. Half of those canvassed had been collectors for more than 10 years, and half of them currently had more than 100 dolls. The nucleus of collections in 43 percent of cases were dolls saved from childhood, but 42 percent began their doll collections as adults, through direct (mail-order) purchasing.[37] The fact that a collection commonly extends through many phases of a person's life largely accounts for its motley qualities. Tucked in among the array of PCDs are the odd decrepit play dolls and stuffed animals saved from the owner's childhood, which for sentimental reasons cannot be excluded from the display. Occasionally a collector will add a new child's doll that takes her fancy "to keep the others company." The relics of other passing enthusiasms also linger on, notably Barbies. A regular feature are the perennially popular "dolls of the world," small figures in various sorts of ethnic garb, that are often souvenirs of a period in the collector's life when she was traveling and taking an interest in exotic places.

Collectors like to talk biographically about these different categories, linking episodes in their own lives to phases in the development of the collection. "Well, my doll collection started when my grandmother presented me with a little troll," a visitor to the Home Shopping Network told the host of the *Collectors Day* show. "It wasn't really a doll, it was more a little coin bank. And I just thought it was lonely and it needed some company, so I started creating little collections around it."[38] For some women, the collection apparently grows seamlessly and unobtrusively as life progresses. Sandy M. of Dundee, Scotland, says: "I suppose I have a good couple of hundred, but I can't really tell you how many. The collection has just grown and grown." Sandy wasn't particularly interested in dolls as a child, preferring her brother's construction toys, and riding ponies. "Maybe I'm just making up for lost time!" Now she is moving to another house "to have enough space to arrange things properly."[39]

By far the most hazardous period in the life of the doll is its owner's puberty. If it can survive this episode of disinterest and neglect it may graduate from the play to display category. In between there is a period of hibernation, very often in the custody of the owner's mother, who, if she has passed some of her own dolls on to her daughter, has a special interest in their welfare. Later, if the owner's interest is reawakened, collecting may begin in earnest. These biographical details may in due course be inscribed in the history of a famous personal collection such as that of Angela Kellie, whose dolls became the nucleus of a Museum of the Social History of Childhood in Scotland:

> As Angela became too old to play with dolls, they were put into family storage. . . . Their role as toys of passage in Angela's childhood was over, but by the time she was an adult in the 1950s, she began to add to the collection deliberately by searching antique shops. Between 1950 and 1978, the years of her marriage and her young family, the dolls became a collecting interest occupying the

role in her day-to-day life, which collecting does by structuring
leisure time and shopping trips and, in Angela's case, by creating a
personal position and relationships through showing her dolls and
giving talks to local women's clubs.[40]

Important turning points in a woman's life are often clearly expressed
in the episodic qualities of a collection. "Angela's husband died in
1978, and the collection helped to structure her response to this
event."[41] Such events become dramatic punctuation points in the narrative that accompanies a guided tour of the collection. Anne R.'s
daughter died of leukemia when she was six years old. On the twentieth anniversary of this devastating event, she was traveling in the rural
U.S. South. "Alongside the road was a stand run by descendants of
Louisiana's free people of color, selling rag dolls called mamans, representing quadroons and octoroons. Anne stopped and bought five of
the dolls. 'Later that same week I started haunting antique shops and
flea markets for dolls of all kinds,' she recalls."[42] "Collections help to
'get us through' periods of our lives," says Susan Pearce, especially
those troublesome "periods of transition" like adolescence or retirement.[43]

An interest in dolls is often reawakened later in life by some family event that stirs up personal memories. "I have recently joined the
ranks of doll enthusiasts after an absence of about 45 years," says
Debbie in her first-ever contribution to an Internet chat room:

> I was prompted to come back when my sisters and I found the
> head to one of my grandmother's dolls and some clothing as well.
> She had no hair, no eyes and a body that is not the original. I want
> to restore her, not because she is valuable but because she was my
> Grannie's. This interest spread when my sisters and I got together
> recently and I saw one of my sister's dolls from childhood. I found
> ebay and have begun to replace my childhood dolls. I have also
> begun collecting as I find dollies at garage sales, flea markets and
> antique shops that are affordable.[44]

Joan C. came to doll collecting after selling a broken doll for £1 at a
car boot sale, while she was winding up her aunt's affairs. Afterward

she was stricken with guilt. "A childish poem came into my mind which says *'Dolly, poor dolly; dear dolly don't cry dear dolly; what a naughty boy he was to smash you.'* Which conjured up all my feelings of about my three brothers who used to take my dolls and smash them up when we were kids. So I never really had a doll from my childhood." Joan is a bit embarrassed about her big "doll family" and keeps meaning to pack them away. "I wonder what a psychiatrist would say to me?"[45]

Revived memories of dolls lost in childhood are a recurrent theme in the biography of collections. Cindy, one of our researchers, talked to Sandy K. in Santa Barbara, who said she had started collecting dolls about five years previously.

> I asked her why she started to collect dolls. She was a bit apprehensive about answering my question point blank. I told her that I was doing some research for a paper, and she asked me if she could get back to me. The next day she came in to where I work, and showed me a picture of her family. As I scanned the picture I noticed a perfectly dressed, neat and orderly little girl holding a rag doll. I asked if that was her, and it was. She then went on to explain that her doll (the one in the picture) was taken away from her by her mother when she was ten years old because it was too ugly and dirty. Sandy says that her doll was the only friend she had, and it was taken away so abruptly. Ever since then, Sandy has missed her doll, and always wanted her back. Sure, she was given other dolls but she never loved one as much as "Jenni," the one that was taken away. Now Sandy collects dolls.

GREED AND GROWTH

The shame and guilt to which some doll collectors admit and others uncontritely deny turn on the fear that others regard their passion as both regressive and excessive.[46] The paradigm is the greedy child, a prominent character in folklore and culture around the world. The infant, pumping away at its mother's breast, is a byword for gluttony, but like the adolescent who seems to feed non-stop, its greediness is justified by the need to grow. In between these two big growth spurts, children are supposed to learn how to moderate their desires in the interests of becoming decent citizens. We are expected to grow out of our beastly instincts, a painful process that modern psychology identifies as the basis of adult neuroses. "For many grown-up collectors, to pile up treasures is to stave off childhood feelings of abandonment, to erect a tangible (yet frangible) hedge against ancient anxiety."[47] Dignifying seemingly unreasonable acquisitive behavior as a "collection" looks like an adult trick, an apology for excess, for wanting and getting more of something than you could possibly, plausibly need.

Our ambivalence about accumulation turns on the fact that while it seems selfish, in some basic sense it is essential for our own survival, for the welfare of our family, and probably also for the progress of our species. Raising a family depends on acquisitiveness which, so long as it does not conspicuously harm other people, is respectable and justified. What economists and demographers have called the "family life cycle squeeze" provides a long-term, transgenerational pattern of economic motivation. In modern societies a married couple has only a few fleeting years to meet the consumer demands of their children and then to insulate themselves from the effects of their own physical decline. In their prime, parents must get a grip on productive processes, save and invest, take innovative risks, and pin their faith on any institution (ranging from bank accounts and educational trusts to lotteries and religious cults) that can offer some assurance of long-term security.

Bachelors and spinsters who accumulate to secure their own childless future are very exposed to blame. These are the Scrooges and witches on whom suspicion of avarice is most sharply focused. If they have banked on material wealth rather than human relationships they stand isolated and critically vulnerable as they approach the threshold of death. Sandwiched between gluttonous youth and avaricious age, the middle generation has a particularly critical eye for greed. The thoroughly middle-class, middle-aged "fear of falling"— the loss of income, respectability, property—has as its base the specter of *family* starvation.[48]

There is a pessimistic human tendency to see all the exchanges of growth in zero-sum terms: one generation saps the energy of the other. The Lusi of New Britain specifically attribute the weakness and senility of the very old to the fact that their vitality has been expended into their children.[49] The senior generation is expected to devolve power and wealth, but for their own continued welfare they must depend on the attentions of their able-bodied juniors. Avarice, said Immanuel Kant, "belongs chiefly to older persons (as a substitute for their natural impotence)."[50] The key to survival in old age is retaining some control over family assets in all forms—savings, land, movable capital, and the labor of the younger generations. This extends to sexual control, the planning and sanctioning of marriages which keeps the reins of growth in the hands of the senior generation.[51] This is the framework in which suspicions of senile greed flourish: an invidious concern about hoarded wealth, dwindling contribution to productive efforts, and too much consumed.

Women, at the center of the life processes of reproduction and consumption, and commonly of production as well, are most heavily implicated: "greedy institutions such as the family are hard task masters" says Coser, and the "housewife"—the domestic manager—bears an unfair share of the stigma.[52] Certainly, women's powers within the relations of reproduction have exposed them to every accusation of disorder, vice, and evil, not only from men but from the rising generation of women that threatens to displace them. Much has been written, for example, about the female identity of witches.[53] That they are so often *older* women raises again the notion of sterile growth: the woman who wants to secure her survival after her family duties are fulfilled is suspect. But if women's enthusiasm for collecting may be traced to frugal concerns for family welfare, the male stereotype of accumulative zeal—sometimes referred to as the Don Juan syndrome—is less flatteringly sexual. According to Barbara Harrison,

> Polygamists are collectors. Womanizers are collectors (and invariably melancholy). The hunger of a womanizer, who collects women as automatically as plants and animals collect food, is never satisfied; he never achieves satiety. "How beautiful they all are," said the nicest womanizer I know. We were seated at a window table in a restaurant, and the girls in their summer dresses were passing by, and he didn't even know he'd said it, sweet, sad man. His hunger is always renewed, his security always threatened.[54]

We often hear the complaint that modernization has broken down the old community morality that discouraged people from wanting more than they and their families "really" need and deserve. Today, it seems that individual selfishness knows no limits—people can go on accumulating indefinitely. Those who justify this trend claim that the progress of human society depends on it. "Greed is the Juice That Gets Things Going in U.S." reads a headline from the 1980s, widely regarded as "the greedy decade."[55] But no matter how people have tried to change its image, greed is never good. It is a resolutely negative moral judgment: somebody, possibly you yourself, reckons that you want more of something than you need or deserve. The best justification for greed is to declare that you need more because you are *growing*—especially if you want more not just for yourself but for the people for whom you are responsible (your family) in the human life process. Big businesses, nation-states, and other human corporations use the same growth justification, but in recent years this has been perceived as a ruse, an overworked metaphor that draws accusations of "corporate greed." A similar sort of suspicion hangs over a "collection" of material objects, especially if these objects do not appear to be serving any useful, life-sustaining purpose.

For accumulation to appear wholesome, it should involve the whole family. We found that an enthusiasm for collecting is very often a family affair. Parents encourage their children, and spouses encourage each other. Deb W.'s husband and sons are into gun and knife collecting. She bridled at my ill-advised suggestion that these were nastier things to collect than dolls. She explained patiently that weapons are an inextricable part of the American western traditions in which her family was rooted, and that her menfolk were sweet and gentle people who encouraged doll collecting among their womenfolk. Deb insisted that they were connoisseurs, interested only in *quality* guns and knives. I made a lame comment about my own fascination with Swiss Army knives. "There you are then," she said, "you know how it feels."

Husbands are commonly drawn into repairing, conserving, or transporting dolls, but her collection and his are usually separate enterprises. Ehrenfeld tells of a couple who collect, respectively, dolls and "wheeled things" and have found ways to collaborate: "They've decorated their home with vignettes of her dolls riding his pedal cars or pushing his toy baby carriages." Living with an avid collector can be very trying, or an exercise in mutual toleration. As his financial business prospered, Ben E. started replacing the household furniture with antiques. Now, he says, "Our house looks like a forest there's so many candlesticks around. We don't have a comfortable place to sit. We sit in wing chairs from 1710." Ben has to take time out of his busy schedule to "water" his furniture: "I have 80 little plastic saucers of water in all the hollow pieces at home," he says.[56] It is not surprising that collections often feature in divorce proceedings, which are particularly acrimonious if the collection was built up together. "It's worse than with children," declared one divorcée.[57]

We shall look more closely in the next two chapters at the way collecting reinforces and substitutes for family relationships, an important reason for its prevalence in later life. The historical increase in longevity and the decline in household sizes over the last century has left larger numbers of older people—women especially—isolated. Collecting figures prominently among the diverse hobbies that help substitute for the gratifications of work after retirement. The extra attraction of dolls is that they appear more personable companions than, say, a stamp collection.

> I have been pretty much housebound for many years and my doll collection has become my life. I know it sounds a little nutty, but if one is unable to go out into the world, one must bring the world to their world. . . . The only negative in collecting dolls is that it *never* ends. I want more and more to love. Every doll I own is out. Nobody is in a box somewhere waiting to be let out.[58]

Many collectors are dogged by anxiety about what will happen to their collections when they die. Carol D. admitted: "I am really selfish when it comes to my dolls. They are mine and only mine. I mean, when I die they will be left to my granddaughters, but I am not ready to part with them now. Besides, I am not done collecting yet." And if she had all the money in the world? "My entire house would be filled with beautiful dolls." *Why?* "Because I *love* them!"

Collecting later in life runs up against a moral precept deeply embedded in the intergenerational growth cycle virtually everywhere: as they age, people are expected to divest themselves of their assets, not accumulate more. We owe it to our parents to take care of them, but as they decline they should be letting go of what they have, not wanting more. Suspicion and guilt invade an empty nest that gets filled with goods. Accusations of greed and avarice go to and fro between the generations, as elders cling to their resources and adult offspring with growing children of their own resent their seniors' leisure, luxury spending, or sterile stockpiling of wealth. The self-recrimination of the elderly, wishing not to be a burden and dreading the lapse into second childhood, only adds to the anguish. Desolation, nostalgia, and insecurity seem to underlie the urge to surround themselves with material possessions which remind them who they are, and that they still have a viable place in the real world. They may describe their collecting as harmless play or pastime, but serious collectors usually claim an altruistic motive: they plan to bequeath something of value to their children—or more explicitly to their *grand*children.

The companies dealing in "collectibles" have latched on to this. "Heirloom" is a key word in PCD merchandising.[59] *Heirloom:* the word wraps a sense of history, family sentiment, personal possession, and material value into a neat package. Creating an heirloom is an investment, but it is also a complicated social act: it is the selection of an object by a particular person, whose identity and reputation will travel with it through time. It places obligations on the persons who have the right to receive it, marking out *who* as well as what belongs to whom. It links the past into the future: designated an heirloom, the object has already taken on the historic qualities of an *antique.* The PCD manufacturers make much play on this: *Margaret Lynn* is "an heirloom collector doll that recaptures all the splendour of winter at the turn of the century. Hand-crafted in the same tradition of master dollmaking that began with the priceless antique dolls from the Victorian era." But the essence of the heirloom is its physical presence, making relationships very palpable. Inheriting a large Chippendale commode, 50 fountain pens, or 300 dolls is a physical as well as moral burden. All these qualities are intensified by unifying such objects into a collection. This confronts the heir with another sort of choice: to respect the integrity of the collection, to keep it growing, or to fragment it among the ever-increasing ranks of descendants.

Whatever function an object may originally have had (furniture, a plaything) tends to get swallowed up by its heirloom status.

> Angela [Kellie] was born in 1930, and during her earliest years she was given dolls which had belonged to her mother and her aunt when they were children, two late-nineteenth century wax dolls by a friend of the family, and, when she was about eight, two French dolls which had belonged to her paternal grandmother. By about 1940, then, the collection spanned three generations of the family, in fact both sides of Angela's family: the dolls which were the souvenir of childhood for the adults had come together to create an heirloom collection for the little girl, a fact of which the adults were well aware.[60]

But how could a little girl bear the burden of a collection that had built up so much portentous value? Having made their way sedately down the distaff side, expanding their numbers and boosting their material value, Angela Kellie's dolls were far beyond play, and ready only for the sort of display afforded by the museum she duly established.

Heirlooms do not draw random lines between relatives through time. They are governed by rules: the rights of an eldest son, or of someone specified in a will. Some objects (guns, crockery) have selective qualities built in to them—they are more likely to pass to a male or a female heir. Even more so than jewelry, clothing, and domestic utensils, dolls are distinctively—challengingly—*female* property. Anthropologists have written a good deal about the importance of this in helping to secure women's lives in the face of male economic privilege.[61] In a patriarchal world such gendered goods have the strategic advantage of passing from mother to daughter, carrying both sentimental and material value that men cannot, respectably, get their hands on. Flo, a Barbie enthusiast, "says she views her collecting as a mothering activity, since mothers are supposed to keep things for their daughters, and her daughter and granddaughters will inherit her collection."[62]

But something more than material values are being bequeathed with the collection. It is a memorial to the collector, a lifework that affords a degree of personal redemption in a relentlessly secularized world. "If collections can create the sense of a life-history, stretching back, perhaps before the collector's own birth, they also create the sense of immortality, of life extended beyond the individual's death."[63] Deb W. told us that the older collectors she knows wonder uneasily what will happen to dolls they have "saved": will an unthinking relative regard them as "a load of old junk" and heave them out, unaware of the emotional energy that has gone into the collecting? They fear that heirs will not respect the patience, opportunism, and aesthetic interest that went into building up the collection. "We feel about our collections as if they were part of our physical selves, and we identify with them," says Pearce. "Loss of collections brings the same grief and the same sense of deprivation which accompanies other bereavements." People say, "It's a permanent record of my life," and many of them have grandiose ideas of public interest in their collections: "I've thought of putting it in a museum."[64] Judi H., who works for May Department Stores, dreams of turning a Victorian house into a museum for her 2,800 dolls.[65] The PCD advertisements make some play on such ambitions: *Catherine Rose* is "created in a tradition which has seen dolls of this [Victorian] era become priceless antiques, displayed in museums and distinguished private collections."

The precedent for this is the large museum or gallery endowed by industrial barons over the last century and a half. Art collecting, according to Oxford don Angelica Goodden, is "the greed that can be glorious." "The 'real' collector, as is well known, has an obsessive desire to possess that may be simply a different version of an earlier, less reputable, lust for accumulation." But the guilt of wealth can be expiated in "the enduring art of acquisition." According to Goodden, "luckily, the odium attached to wealth lessens when the cash is channeled into art, since art confers a kind of spiritual respectability."[66] It does so, of course, mainly because so many rich and powerful people have, for so many centuries, sought expiation in such grand public gestures for notably egoistic lives: the collection is a moral purgative when it is finally dumped in a public gallery.

"The true collector thinks he's never going to die and that if he does, he'll die with all his toys," says Harry R., a "passionate collector of puzzles." He says his biggest rival has two of the rarest items, which he covets: "I follow his health quite closely." He swears that rather than let his 4,000 puzzles fall into the hands of his competitors he'll leave them all jumbled in a huge box.[67] The perfect collection is sacrosanct, bearing the reputation of its author into the future. But the irony of this end-oriented activity is that the collection is truly alive only while it is incomplete and its author is still in pursuit of coveted items. The satisfaction of having laid claim to the last available Matisse or Elvis autograph is overshadowed by a sense of desolation akin to death. "With our possessions we weave our shrouds," says Harrison. "Everything we collect is a memento mori."[68]

On his visit to the Santa Barbara Doll club in October 1997, our investigator Frank made an intriguing discovery: "Fanny brought up an interesting point. As we get closer to the end of the millennium people tend to get crazy. They start collecting everything. There seems to be, she said, a fear in people that history will be lost in the next millennium." This may partly account for the boom in collectibles—and in stock values, consumer spending, and much else—in the later 1990s. Once again, the doll firms have latched onto this idea: "It's the Millennium Angel, think about that!" sang Tina Berry on the Home Shopping Network. "Do not wait to get this, because when you tie an event like the Millennium into a series of dolls that are already popular, imagine what's going to happen when people all of a sudden wake up and they realize there was a number one doll, that they got the Millennium doll. . . . We have it for you today. She is an absolute perfect value."[69]

PASSION ON DEMAND

"I collect dolls, primarily because I have so much joy and passion," declares a caller to the Home Shopping Network's *Collectors Day* program:

> And just the conquest of knowing they are mine. I decorate them
> and they are just wonderful creations. . . . Collecting dolls is such a
> wonderful thing because it reminds you of all the pretty things in

life. It allows you to take the time to appreciate the joy and beauty that they bring you because they are always there. They are always with you, when you wake up in the morning, when you have a lonesome day, they are there.[70]

As with any commodity, strategic information, tested in the marketplace, is vital in establishing the links from demand to supply. The process, notably in the case of the PCDs, is exploratory and collusive, the vital link being the designers who are themselves doll collectors. Marketing specialists will argue that it is essential to understand any product you are trying to sell, but there are limits to the possibility of, and necessity for such understanding. The manufacturers of porcelain dolls evidently knew a lot about their product, but the decline of the industry in the 1990s suggests that they did not always know as much as they would have liked.

Inevitably, the doll manufacturers' perception of their customers has been shaped by numbers. Early market feedback made clear to the collectibles industry generally that its "most loyal and devoted customers [are] older women."[71] Within that broader category, "serious doll collectors are predominantly middle aged, relatively well-off, and entirely female."[72] A 1994 survey in the United States by Unity Marketing found that three quarters of doll collectors were ages 35 to 64, three quarters were married, and three quarters had no children under age 18 at home.

Figure 3-a: Age of U.S. doll collectors (1994)

Age of collector	Percent of total
18–24	2
25–34	6
35–44	22
45–54	30
55–64	25
65+	15

Source: Fulkerson 1995, pp. 17–18.

According to this survey, "Serious doll collectors are likely to have grown children." They are predominantly middle class: 41 percent are still working full time, 50 percent have household incomes of at least $45,000, 55 percent have some college education, 16 percent graduated, and 12 percent have done graduate work. "Yet these accomplished women have a strong need to nurture, and dolls may fill that need."[73]

Of prime importance is the fact that this cohort of women had relatively large amounts of disposable income from their own earnings as well as from pensions and conjugal support. Half the doll collectors spent between $251 and $1,000 a year on dolls, and a third spent more than that. The dolls ranged in price up to $500, with most of them in the $100–$200 bracket. A quarter paid $200–$500 for a doll, and nearly all those sampled reckoned they would spend at least $500 on dolls in the coming year.[74] The PCD product range settled on the middle and lower income levels, the most lucrative for mass-produced dolls, leaving the top end of the market to the low volume, specialty producers. The owner of a doll shop we spoke to told us that many women begin with a few dolls of the Ashton-Drake type, graduating to the "more serious" collection of antique and custom-made dolls as their enthusiasm for quantity turns to a taste for quality. "You have to begin collecting somewhere," and the PCD industry is ready to oblige.

Defining a commodity as "collectible" is a merchandising strategy that multiplies the desire for a single object. In sales jargon it is *line extension*—offering variations on a theme that tempts the buyer to get the whole series. Mattel's Barbie may be the greatest line extension of modern times.[75] Domestic crockery is a prototype of the collectible commodity, produced more for display than use, and carried to elegant lengths by the Wedgwood and Spode potteries of England in the eighteenth century. A table service for six or a dozen is inherently a collection, the standardized patterns allowing less affluent devotees to build up a full service over long periods of time.[76] It is evidently "female property," and its scarcity value is enhanced by its fragility. It is thus not entirely accidental that companies like Ashton-Drake also deal in ornamental porcelain plates, a close neighbor in the product environment of collector dolls.

For the sales managers of these firms, there are two fundamental strategies: "Get new customers at the lowest possible cost, and retain them for subsequent purchases." Buy number one in the Rainbow of Love series, "then at three-month intervals you'll automatically be shipped the other five babies in the collection at $59.95 each." Some detective work in the early 1990s by *Forbes* magazine indicated that for a company like Danbury the cost of developing and manufacturing each collector plate was about $6 and its retail price $25. Since the marketing costs of getting a first-time customer onto its mailing list was about $50, a single sale made little sense. If the firm lines up 14 more plates and persuades each customer to buy the whole series, the profit margin on each plate could be as much as 60 percent.[77] Buying one plate or PCD often "guarantees" you the right to buy the others in a series—while retaining your name on the all-important mailing list. The promise to the buyer is that an object gains value by being part of a set: you must protect your investment against missing items.

Forty-one percent of the dolls in our sample belong in a named series of some sort: Amish Inspirations, The Children of Main Street America, Days of the Week, Connie's Adorable Babies, Faraway Friends, Gardens of Innocence, and so on. The average price of dolls in and out of series was almost the same, although there was a tendency for the most expensive dolls not to be in a series. New collections kept appearing throughout the 1990s, but the high proportion of one-off titles in our sample suggests that more collections are inaugurated than are substantially fulfilled.

Offering a collection involves establishing an organizing theme—creating more detailed subdefinitions of the commodity. But the problem is how to narrow the collectible category down (French Impressionist painting, British Imperial postage stamps of the nineteenth century) without reducing it to meaningless fragments (Yolanda's Precious Playmates, or Barely Yours, or Blossoming Belles—"She's just as sweet and lovely as a blooming rosebud!"). The collectibles firms are ready to experiment, because people collect lots of different things, and one of the merchandising tactics is to link these. In 1998, Mayfair (Georgetown's alias in the United Kingdom) made an interesting offer: "Now for the first time ever . . . Images

from the *exclusive* Mayfair Doll Collection are available on thimbles."
There, in a little wooden display case, are dainty porcelain thimbles,
each with a picture of *Caroline* or *Apple Dumpling*. "The final thimble
in this collection of 24 will certify you as the registered owner of the
whole collection . . . it will bear your name as the registered owner."[78]

It seems that collectors themselves are ready to play this game.
Nancy, a caller to the QVC home shopping channel in November
2001, reported that she had just bought *Annette* and *Roquelle*, but had
a request for the featured guest doll designer Pauline Bjonness-
Jacobsen:

> Nancy: "Um . . . would you ever think of doing the 12-inch dolls
> that are dressed like the Little Women?
> PB-J: Oh yeah, yeah, yeah. I know those books.
> Nancy: I would love to see some of the little dolls. You could come
> out every month with one of the Little Women dolls in the 12-inch
> [size]. Until you got all seven, I think there are seven.
> PB-J: Four, I think there are four.
> Nancy: Oh maybe there are four.
> PB-J: But we could make seven. The ones who live next door to the
> Little Women. Bring them all in.[79]

"It's neurotic," an aficionado of African sculpture and early-twentieth-century American paintings said of his own collecting. "It's lim-
itless. The next object turns you on as much as the last one. Money is
just a scorecard."[80] It can hardly be counted as *rational* in the sense
that the neo-classical philosophers of the marketplace have proposed,
which is probably why the manufacturers of collectibles have never
been able to come fully to economic terms with their products. But *all*
market transactions are loaded with feelings (consider a Wall Street
feeding frenzy, or the visceral thrill of a new house or car, or buying
of a basket of fresh strawberries). Imitating real bodies, the PCDs con-
struct an unusually close link between visceral feelings and wants as
they are traded in the marketplace. The problem is, we have been
taught to believe that markets are rational, not passionate places.
Believing that it's the rationality that makes them "work" allows

traders to keep the books and make stock predictions. But we also know that economics alone can't explain why I buy stuff in the super-market that I don't want, or buy more before lunch than after. Nor can it explain why someone wants 300 dolls when one or two would seem to be enough.

This ambiguity is amply expressed in the sales talk for the PCDs. The material inducements ("attractively priced," "prime value," "great investment") are clearly stated, but emotional values are always woven into the advertising copy:

> "*Michelle*" is sure to become one of your best-loved possessions. Possession that brings endless pride.

> *Tiffany* "is an adorable Victorian treasure" and her "costume has been lavished with loving detail too."

> *Victoria* is "a turn of the century treasure. . . . Her dress is sheer white voile with over a yard of lavish lace trim."

Variants of the ambiguous word "treasure" appear often in the adver-tisements. The dolls are "rich," "lavish," and "sumptuous"; they are "coveted," their value is "irresistible." Their aura is described as "golden." *Angelica* is "lavishly gowned in rich velvet, shimmering taffeta, and sparkling gold lame." *Amy*, a "magnificent collectors' mas-terpiece" is "brilliantly crafted of the very finest hand-painted porce-lain bisque and lavishly costumed in sumptuous ensemble!" One of the key words in selling the PCDs is "precious." Weaving together both material and emotional values, the word is used in a fifth of the PCD advertisements, and is of course the title of the immensely suc-cessful Precious Moments series. (See Appendix A.)

The porcelain collector dolls are the product of a quite complicated interplay of demand and supply, between the desires of the women who buy them, often in large numbers, and the commercial oppor-tunism of the firms that make them. The manufacturers' concern that the women should have more and more dolls engages with the passionate urge of the women to own not just one, but many of these exquisite objects. In this chapter we have viewed collecting as a symptom of the urge to accumulate, which is essential to the cycle of human growth. In the next chapter we shall draw the biographical and the historical lines more closely together, putting the lives of the women who now appear mainly as distinct cohorts of collectors into the historical perspective of the twentieth century.

We keep returning to the oddity of this commodity: the objects collected are perceived ambiguously as things and as people. Whatever dispassionate observers may imagine, they are bought, and sold, as *lifelike*. Accumulating people is what growth, both in the sense of human reproduction and social expansion, is all about, but in every human society how this is done is subject to intense moral regulation. Until it was outlawed in our societies, slavery, the private appropriation of people, was positively sanctioned; and paying money for adopted children or human embryos remains morally contentious. The dolls circumvent these restrictions: you can pay for and possess not just one, but hundreds of these "real" little people.

The ambiguity of these lifelike dolls allows the collectors to carry to extravagant lengths an urge for family growth which is, at heart, profoundly normal. These women are childless, some permanently so, others mostly in the temporary sense that their children have already gone or have not yet come. Quite a few have real children of their own at home, but have room in their lives for more. They often talk about their boundless love, and it is hardly surprising that the modern marketplace has allowed the suppliers to fulfill their desires. It seems that the urge to buy more and more dolls will always and ultimately be a fruitless search for a missing, abundantly real child. And yet, for many of the collectors we met there is something absurd about that possibility: asked if they would swap all their dolls for a real living child of their own, they usually gave some variant of this surprised response: "Well, for a start, I'd have to be a whole lot younger!"

Chapter Four

The Doll That
Needs You

"Hannah needs a hug."

Selling many sorts of commodity means identifying people's wants and persuading them that these are more urgently *needs*. There is a vacuum in your life which our product (bread, beer, a car) must fill.

"Timmy's realistic pose elicits a nurturing feeling." There are lots of products that we, as potential consumers, could be said to need, but there are not many products that could plausibly be said to *need us*. Doll manufacturers make much play on the happy coincidence that this little porcelain or plastic person "wants" you as much as you want it. Their products are represented as orphans, waiting in limbo (a warehouse in Niles, Illinois) like puppies in a pet store for someone to take them home (picture 7). "Welcome a wonderful visitor to your home—to stay with you always" (*Shannon*). "Charming little *Hans* is looking for a home, and he is waiting for an adventure. He's adorable, and ready to celebrate, with you."

Some doll advertising has taken this neediness to great lengths, emphasizing "helplessness, crying, shivering, trembling, hunger, and need for a diaper change." One advertisement for a play doll runs: "'Don't shiver, Newborn Baby Shivers, my love will keep you warm.'"[1]

Picture 7: Waiting for you to take her home.
Photo by A. F. Robertson.

This sales tactic, evidently aimed more at the doll-purchasing parents than children themselves, has drawn some grim comments from Nancy Scheper-Hughes and Howard Stein, who see a "darker, more obsessive side of the adoption/rescue/infanticide fantasy":

> The Cabbage Patch dolls, fetus-like in appearance, are advertized as abandoned (can we think they are possibly aborted?) infants in search of good homes and the 'right kind' of parents. The dolls are extravagantly expensive to adopt, so that poorer families can shelter a cabbage patch kid only at great personal sacrifice. The dependent dolls come with "authentic" adoption papers and with a proper name.[2]

The PCD advertisements play on an emptiness in the life of the collector that can be resolved by the act of purchase: "Share the love in her heart. Send for *Grace* today." "Let *Annabelle* fill your heart with her gift of love." Key words in the emotional vocabulary are "adore" and "adorable," used in a quarter of the advertisements. Similar words are "delightful," "charm(ing)," "enchant(ing)," and "captivat(ing)." Overflowing with affection, the dolls may sound better than the real thing to women who have been through emotional deserts with their own teenagers. Over the last half-century we have been tormented with ideals of parenthood and childhood that are very hard for both parties to sustain. The dolls represent a second chance, an assurance of *undying* affection. "Taking care" of dolls is a very long tradition, and can be a lifelong commitment extending from infancy through to old age. It can be therapeutic but it can also be a little stressful, like real child care. The more beautiful and realistic the doll, the greater the responsibility, and the more acute the guilt of failing to look after something so vulnerable and fragile.

The PCD is not simply the cynical commercial exploitation of older women's susceptibilities. It responds to real enough needs—witness the fact that so many dolls have been designed by women who have experienced the vacuum themselves. The creative endeavors of Elena Konig di Scavini, alias Madame Lenci, one of the most successful doll manufacturers of the early twentieth century, "were fuelled by

her disappointment at not having children."[3] Like so many of the
PCD designers today, she had a visceral understanding of how to
make a *thing* that could substitute for a missing person more effectively than any other thing.

NEEDS, WANTS, AND DESIRES

Do the women who buy the PCDs, often in large quantities, need the
dolls? Or do they merely want them? The distinction between needs
and wants is a very old and troublesome one in the history of Western
philosophy. It is predicated on an even older and more radically troublesome distinction between body and mind. In modern usage, it is
generally assumed that needs are rooted in the body, while wants are
mental, choices over which we exert some voluntary control. We *feel*
needs, we *think* wants. This is usually illustrated by the urgency of my
"needing a drink of water" (or I may die), and more selectively "wanting" a Pepsi or a martini.[4] The point is driven home by saying that if I
"need" a martini, I am probably an alcoholic—the "want" has become
an abnormal and involuntary bodily requirement. And after strenu-
ous exercise I may likewise "need" the revitalizing sugars and salts in
the Pepsi, rather than plain old water. Moral assessments of what we
"deserve" turn on this judgment: people generally explain that *greed* is
"wanting more than you need."[5]

Since classical antiquity, scholars have argued endlessly about
these categories. If "needs" are basically common to human bodies
everywhere, surely they can be spelled out biologically (in terms of
calories, temperatures, hours of sleep, etc.). Generalizations of this
sort do not satisfy those who find the historical and cultural relativity
of values much more interesting. Of course we all need a drink, but
what matters is why we drink one thing rather than another—the
options of tea, kava, Pepsi, or whatever. This has the effect of relin-
quishing discussion of our basic human needs to the natural scien-
tists, and confining historical and cultural discussion to our infinitely
variable and expandable wants. Clearly, you cannot satisfy, or express,
or even know about a particular want if history, culture, and language
have not put it there. Napoleon needed helicopter gun ships to turn

the tide of events at Waterloo, but it is unlikely that he specifically "wanted" them, whatever fantasies he may have had about strategic air strikes. Porcelain collector dolls are now wanted with great avidity, and history has obliged by getting them out there into the market-place.

But this does not imply that the collectors do not need the PCDs, however exotic and extravagant they may appear. Rather, it suggests that we (scholars) have no clear and reliable ways of understanding and expressing what those underlying needs are. A passionate desire for *Caroline* or *Billy* cannot—yet—be reduced to bodily indices like calories, glandular secretions, or genetic predispositions, but it is also very difficult to find words that do justice to the powerful motivation to buy them. Wants are easier to express than needs, because wants are "in the mind" rather than "of the body": we can talk about them. As David Berry remarks in his book on *Luxury*, "While it makes little sense to say that individuals can want something without knowing they are so wanting, it is sensible to say that individuals can have needs of which they are unaware."[6] Until children can say what they want, parents are left guessing about what they need. This presents us with a problem of interpretation: to explain why people need things like dolls, we may not find out all we want to know simply by listening to what they say. It is likely to be much more important to try to divine what they *feel*, which implies a more empathetic connection with their bodies. And as we all know, the deeper our feelings, the more difficult they are to put into words.

Contemporary academic interest has fixed on *desire* as a mediating term that seeks connections between the cultural and historical contexts of wanting and of bodily needing. However, it does so with a particular set of biases that have notably adult, sexual undertones. Children need things, and their wants must be regulated, but if they say they "desire" something they sound precocious. In the doll advertisements, *Hannah* needs a hug, and *Kaitlyn* wants a kiss; neither of them "desires" these lit-tle gratifications. The latent erotic connotations of "desire" seem to have purged the word from the advertisements. We found only two traces of it: one referred to an explicitly adult doll, the buxom *Cinderella*: "Passions flare as the clock strikes twelve, and desire ignites a young girl's heart." The second was *Sophie*, a little girl in Victorian button-up boots: "Everyone needs someone to love. . . . And Sophie has found her heart's desire." But it turns out that what *Sophie* desires is not hugs or kisses, but a doll of her own, which puts her acquisitive urges directly on a par with those of the collector herself: "Little Victorian girls used to fall in love with beautiful dollies every bit as much as we do today. And Sophie had her heart set on one of her mama's dearest treasures . . . the famous Victorian doll known as the Bru."

Because the word "desire" seems inapt in doll talk, I have side-stepped it in this book, talking instead—like the collectors them-selves—about *passion*. This powerful word shifts our attention back toward bodily feeling, going beyond desire to evocations of both agony and ecstasy. It helps us to identify a wider range of sensations through the lives of the collectors, as these have unfolded in particu-lar historical circumstances. As we got to know more about doll col-lecting, two distinct biohistorical categories emerged: the women who were experiencing, respectively, the agony of the "empty womb" and of the "empty nest." The two categories are not mutually exclusive: a woman who has never had children has also in some sense an empty nest; and a woman whose children have left home may have very direct empty womb cravings for another baby. But the distinction is a substantial one, about bodies in time: the ticking clock of female fer-tility on the one hand, and on the other the cyclical pattern of family growth that shifts children out of the parental household to establish parental households of their own. The empty nest and empty womb present significant differences in the motives for acquiring the dolls, different expectations of their functions, and different preferences in design. And they are by far the most common and the clearest expla-nations that the collectors themselves offer for their passion for dolls.

THE EMPTY NEST

"I need a child beside me to fill my heart," says Aunty Nabou in Mariama Bâ's novel about women in Senegal, *So Long a Letter*. "I want this child to be both my legs and my right arm. I am growing old. I will make of this child another me. Since the marriage of my own children, the house has been empty." Her sister replies: "Take young Nabou, your namesake. She is yours. I ask only for her bones." Satisfied, Aunty Nabou packs her suitcase with all the country goodies which are expensive in town: dried couscous, roasted groundnut paste, millet, eggs, milk, chicken. "Holding young Nabou's hand firmly in her right hand, she took the road back to town."[7]

All around the world, past and present, children are on the move. Sorting out which kid belongs to whom is one of the many complexities of doing anthropological or sociological surveys of households. In the African villages where I did my fieldwork, old people seemed to have an abundant supply of real grandchildren, nephews, and nieces to comfort and assist them as they aged. And in Europe in past centuries young people moved from one household to another as foster children, apprentices, or housemaids, balancing the tense equation of food, work, and accommodation in the life processes of the wider community. The tight little nuclear family of our modern industrial world seems resistant to such a flow. Children are moved, but usually in the agony of some sort of failure—divorce, destitution, delinquency. The kitchens of complex households formed by second and subsequent marriages often feature flow charts detailing where each child is supposed to be, week by week. When, inevitably, kids extricate themselves from the emotional vortex to get on with their own lives, the loss is felt all the more keenly. For the great majority of mothers who do not continue to foster other needy children, now may be the time to buy a dog—or a doll.

The big difference between the empty nest in other places and at other times is that in the industrialized countries today the void lasts so much longer. Here are some of the most significant demographic facts for the U.S. population:

- Over the last 200 years, a woman's life expectancy has *doubled* to about 80 years.
- Over the last 200 years, a woman's actual *childbearing* span has dropped from 17 to 10 years.
- A woman born in 1951 could reckon on having 52 years of life ahead of her after bearing her last child.

- A woman born in 1951 could reckon on having 28 years of life ahead of her after rearing her last child.
- Two hundred years ago, the average woman died *12 years before* the birth of her last grandchild.
- Now, the average woman can expect to live *25 years after* the birth of her last grandchild.
- Between 1900 and 1980 the proportion of people older than 65 tripled, to 12 percent.
- Since 1940, the proportion of people over 65 who live alone has quadrupled.
- Women today can expect to live nearly 10 years longer than men.
- Widows now outnumber widowers by about 11 to 2.
- Over the age of 65, women are twice as likely as men to be living alone.[8]

The PCD phenomenon must be seen both in the context of this historically new and much extended life span, and of lives lived in particular historical circumstances. What is so interesting about the dolls is how they link a very early and a much later phase in the woman's life: they are objects that tie their experiences as children in one historical period to adult experiences in a historical period some half-century later. The PCD boom was timed for the 1990s, and for women in their fifties and sixties. If their enthusiasm for dolls has anything to do with their own experiences as children we have to reach back to the 1930s. And there we encounter a generally unhappy period in the history of the industrial countries, remembered mainly as the Great Depression.

The older women collectors we talked to nearly always made some sort of reference to the lack of toys in their own childhoods—mostly in the 1930s and 1940s, the years of the Depression and World War II. Many of them also talked about the loss of childhood itself, and the need for some sort of compensation in later life. The recollections of so many women testify to how traumatic the disappearance, mutilation, or other loss of a doll can be. A century ago, a thoughtless mother burned her little daughter's doll when it had deteriorated almost beyond recognition. The child wept for a week, and years later reproached her mother: "Why did you burn it, I loved it so, and she loved me. She is in God's house and sometime I will see her."[9]

Nancy G. lost her dolls in the Depression. "My dolls were up there on the shelf, and then one day, when we had to move, they just disappeared. Some, my brothers broke—not on purpose. I guess I always wanted to have my dolls back." Nancy wanted *those* dolls, not just *any* dolls, and when she could afford it she became a serious antiques collector. Nancy never married—"I am a single person"—but had a successful career in local government. Raised in Connecticut, she came to California with her mother 30 years ago, after her father died. She likes cats, is a wood carver, walks everywhere, and was about 80 when I first met her in 1994, at a doll fair. She was minding the local club's display, a big chipboard doll house filled with an assortment of "serious" dolls. She was cradling a new purchase, a nineteenth-century china-faced German doll that cost $700. It was small and rather plain, the face about three and a half inches in diameter, with yellow hair molded onto its skull. It had a simple white dress with a bit of embroidery, and pointed leather boots on limp tubular legs. The doll was one of a pair of "twins," and her friend—a fellow Club member—bought the other. Nancy said she keeps her collection in drawers and chests. "You have to keep them covered, because the clothes deteriorate." Her pleasure is to unpack them, undress and dress them, and then carefully put them away again.

If we want to know more about the women who experienced childhood during the Depression, we have as an excellent source a psychosocial study of 167 people born in 1920–21 in Oakland, California. They were white, mostly Protestant kids from middle- and working-class homes, selected from fifth- and sixth-grade classes in 1931. Their life experiences were tracked through to the early 1990s, supplemented by a slightly later sample from the Berkeley area.[10] They form a valuable reference group for our own California-based project—they represent the grandmothers of our student researchers. Although we have no record of how many of them actually collected dolls, their circumstances are indicative of those who do.[11] During the PCD boom of the 1990s they were in their seventies, very much part of the target clientele. The detailed monitoring of these people's lives gives us a pretty clear view of who would be likely to collect dolls later in life and who would not.

In the 1930s, when these people were adolescents, the Oakland research was heavily preoccupied with psychosocial testing and the "objective" reports of parents and teachers. Today they would probably be observed much more directly, with more attention paid to their own understandings and activities. More account would also be taken of their relations with other family members, especially grandparents, which the study "unfortunately overlooked" (there were, after all, rather fewer of them at the time of the study than now).[12] Nevertheless, the children's family circumstances emerge quite clearly. Their parents were in their late thirties and early forties at the depth of the Depression (the first months of 1933), and Oakland was an area of relatively great deprivation in national terms. That year their median family income dropped 40 percent to around $1,900.[13] A third of the families sought public assistance during the 1930s.[14] The study explores the relationships between these Depression kids and their parents, and notes the difference between them and their own children: a "sharp contrast in childhoods, one marked by scarcity and the other by affluence."[15]

Their adolescence was severely curtailed—"there were no 'teenagers' in the Depression."[16] Inevitably, for the children who were sent to school with cardboard in their shoes to cover the holes, toys were a very low priority on the family budget. The two survival tactics—cutting expenditure and supplementing income—meant children worked much more, inside (girls especially) and outside (boys) the household, and thus had less time, as well as money, to spend on toys. It is also likely that if the toys they had were not actually sold, those of any value went into the display/save category, rather than play. Children made do with rag or clothespeg dolls and tin-can cars. If the better-off children felt most deprived, it was probably because toy manufacture had boomed in the first two decades of the century, and expectations had been raised. In parallel with this, new middle-class ideals of child rearing were stressing the value of toys and play in the experience of childhood.[17]

As part of the "downward extension of adultlike experience" for the more deprived children especially, half of the Oakland boys and a quarter of the girls had part-time jobs, and they contributed their earnings to the family budget. Economic hardships took boys outside the household, and as they grew up they became more outward-oriented and socially independent. Girls were even busier, but had lower cash earnings, especially in the most deprived households where mothers worked outside the home or there were siblings to care for. In such households chores were allocated to even the smallest children.[18]

The Oakland children experienced great anxiety in relation to their parents, especially to their un- or underemployed fathers:

> In the area of family relationships, mother's centrality as decision maker and emotional resource is the primary theme among deprived households. Severe economic loss increased the perceived power of the mother in family matters within the middle and working class, and diminished father's social prestige, attractiveness, and emotional significance, as perceived by sons and daughters.[19]

The intensification of girls' work and responsibilities at home brought them into closer contact and alliance with their mothers, and thereby into greater conflict with their fathers. They were "generally described as emotionally sensitive or self-conscious (feelings easily hurt, cries easily, etc.) by their mothers, and tended to underestimate their social standing among classmates."[20] When grown up, the girls were much more likely to value family ties positively than the boys, but also to perceive conflict more acutely and be critical of parental conduct. Although households could be described as "matricentric," many children developed a critical view of mothering. The girls often complained of a maternal "martyr" syndrome—"Remember what I gave up so that you could have good clothes and food?"[21]

The "surprising" conclusion for the Oakland researchers was that the deprived kids of the Depression grew up resilient and adaptive, not debilitated and demoralized. "What young Americans in the 30s lacked was opportunity, not desire or ambition."[22] The Oakland study found that whether the parental family was seen as a passive victim or as a tight little problem-solving team, the effect of the Depression was generally to give the children a commitment to what we would now call "family values."[23] For girls especially, "exposure to conditions which made rewarding, secure relationships difficult to achieve and therefore scarce" fostered a lifelong commitment to the notion of the family as a haven in a heartless world.[24] If in later life the Oakland girls were trying "to undo the 'psychic disruptions' of Depression and war," they may indeed have felt more keenly the "empty nest" phase, and a need to make homes for dolls as family surrogates.[25]

The Oakland women married during the war, typically at age 20, close to the national norm for the time, and "had their first child shortly thereafter in a period of relative affluence."[26] They were unlikely to be encouraged to go on to higher education. A quarter worked only until marriage and childbearing; a third interrupted their careers to rear children and then returned to work; 8 percent worked only after child rearing; and the rest worked intermittently or not at all.[27] The period between school and marriage was typically hectic for a girl. Most had at least a year of work and were largely preoccupied with finding a husband, on whom a young woman's own life and social status depended. Marriage meant sacrificing personal autonomy and a career, but offered an escape from the parental home and "a legitimate context in which to satisfy needs for sexual relations, childbearing, status, and love."[28] In 1984 (by which time they were in their late fifties and sixties) 57 percent of the women were still married to their first husband, 12 percent were divorced and unmarried, 19 percent were remarried, 9 percent widowed, and 4 percent had never married. In the final study, when the women were in their seventies, 20 percent of the women were widowed, nearly all of them living alone.[29] The normative progress of a woman's life during this period has been summarized thus:

> She is expected to move from birth and home-centered childhood
> into school attendance for a time sufficient to find a husband, but
> not so long as to waste valuable youth on knowledge used only for
> a short time. The next appropriate stages are work before and
> after marriage, giving birth to a limited number of children, rear-

ing children, caring for the retired husband, widowhood, and death.[30]

The Oakland study indicates that while childhood deprivation may have provided a spur, it did not determine a way of life. Adaptations were mostly in the *timing* of life events: the Depression kids showed a capacity to catch up, reproductively, socially, and materially. Collecting dolls is one small piece of this program—if you didn't get them before, you can get them later! The study reckoned that "some disciplines practiced in the 30s—frugality, conservation, and so forth" would become ingrained in the Depression kids and passed on to the next generation.[31] However, it is interesting that the children of the Great Depression did not generally carry a sense of grievance with them throughout their lives. Some may have pestered their own children about wasting food or being careless with possessions, but mostly they seem to have been indulgent parents and grandparents. The follow-up studies in the 1980s, when it was proving increasingly difficult to keep tabs on the original Oakland sample, found that "neither men nor women felt that the Great Depression had had much effect on their lives. A third of the women and more than half of the men said they had been essentially unaware of it."[32] In their forties, very few people in the Oakland sample felt that they had known themselves at all well during their high school years.[33] Time mellows our memories—the same people had complained of deprivation earlier in their lives. "Clearly, awareness is not a necessary condition for an event or set of circumstances to have had a strong influence on aspects of the life course."[34]

In our own inquiries, however, we found that the collectors' sense of deprivation was much more clearly focused. Although not inclined to dwell on their miseries in later life, they remembered the lack of playtime and playthings, most notably dolls for the girls. These feelings were evoked not so much by the logic of what "really" happened earlier in the course of a long and eventful life, but by a second, parallel sense of loss, the departure of children and the death of a spouse, an encounter with the solitude of the empty nest. "'When I was a little girl we didn't have the means,' said Debbie Kay, mother of six. 'But now that I am a grownup little girl I can afford what I want.'

Having a lifelike doll in the house is a nice way to sublimate the need to have a baby around. 'And this way they won't grow up and leave me,' a laughing Debbie Kay said."[35] Women who have devoted their lives to child rearing may feel particularly keenly the sense of emptiness when the children leave home. Doll collecting can start with the early onset of this process, a solace to Mom as teenagers become absorbed in their own affairs. We might imagine that a woman who has raised five or ten children would regard their departure as a welcome respite, but we hear repeatedly that such "supermoms" make the most avid doll collectors. "As the last of nine children in the blended family of Carol and Dennis Larsen left home, the dolls arrived." The Larsens farm 2,500 acres in Iowa; Carol has taken computer classes and deals with the business side. She collects and now makes her own porcelain dolls, "learning from other artists and by reading." Carol's creative energy is a reminder that the empty nest may also harbor sensations of the empty womb. The domestic space vacated by the children has been taken over by display and workshop areas, sewing tables and kilns. "Can't we ever eat supper without a naked doll on the counter?" complained the youngest Larsen, who now works the farm with his dad. Dennis has taken up carpentry and makes dolls' furniture, and he and Carol sell their wares at 20 weekend shows a year. "We work well together," says Dennis.[36]

The dolls that cluster around the older women are an antidote for loneliness and the sense of purposelessness, the great agonies of modern times. A more elaborate study than ours would have paid close attention to numerous older women who do *not* collect dolls. Our intuition is that a woman living in close proximity to her grandchildren and actively involved with them simply has no need for surrogates—she lacks the time, space, and inclination. But the geographical mobility and social encapsulation of the modern "nuclear" family has greatly increased the segregation of older people. A significant reason why they are less likely to live with their children "is simply that they have fewer children."[37] The extent to which contacts between children and older people have been eroded is a major tragedy of our times. Sylvia Ann Hewlett reminds us that "children infuse the end of life with comfort and help mute its terror."[38] But very much the same could be said of the role of older family members at the beginning of our lives. The dolls in the advertisements declare that children need the affection and guidance of the older generation, as much as the adults themselves need the solace of children. And that, in its simplest terms, is what the history of human society, and the regeneration of culture, is all about.

THE EMPTY WOMB

The interests and experiences of doll collectors who have never had children are somewhat different from those who have. Women in the middle years of their lives (35 to 45) may be drawn to doll collecting as an antidote for the emptiness that goes with postponing childbearing until it may be too late. The demographic pattern underlying this tendency is all too familiar to those who decry "the demise of the traditional family":

- The birthrate halved during the twentieth century, from about 28 live births per thousand people in 1920.
- The postwar baby boom, which peaked in 1958 at 25.3 live births per thousand Americans, was followed by a "baby bust," with a birthrate of 14.8 per thousand in 1976.
- Since 1960, use of woman-controlled contraception (the Pill) and medically approved pregnancy termination (abortion) has increased.
- Since 1960, women have been delaying marriage until they are on average about 24 (men until they are 26).
- Americans are now much more likely to get divorced: rates have risen steeply from an annual rate of 1.6 per thousand Americans in 1930, to 4.7 in 1990. There is now a more than 50 percent chance that a marriage will end in divorce.
- The proportion of women who work outside the home rose steeply, from about one in eight in 1940 to one in four in 1976 and one in two in 1987. By 1990, 56 percent of married women in the United States were "out to work."
- Household sizes dropped from an average of four persons in

1920 to 2.7 persons in 1985; many more younger people were living alone.[39]

In a general pattern of declining fertility, parenting has been postponed and reorganized, occupying less of a woman's life course, and being less rooted in the domestic institutions of marriage. In the 1940s women went out to work to help support the postwar surge in babies, and thereafter had to reckon the advantages of a career and personal earnings against the traditional role of housewife, at home raising children and dependent on a husband's earnings. In 1975, women in the 34–39 age group produced less than 4 percent of American babies, compared with 10 percent in 1945. In the 1980s and 1990s, magazine articles picked up on the "baby craving" of women who were now close to or past menopause. More affluent women had recourse to the new birth technologies, notably the implanting of their own or a donor's fertilized egg. Adoption agencies were overworked, and scandals about the "buying" of babies from poor countries proliferated. The baby shortage raised the temperature of debates about abortion, clashes between "pro-life" and "pro-choice" parties turning on the issue of whether or not women should be socially obliged to sustain a pregnancy. As for so long in the human past, too many of those who are pregnant now don't want to be, and too many of those who aren't pregnant want to be. Life is not fair.

Sylvia Ann Hewlett has provided a valuable profile of "baby hunger."[40] Her study was initiated by her own "battle for motherhood," and proceeded to inquiries among her own college cohort 25 years after graduation. This inspired a larger study of "high-achieving" professional women, the "breakthrough generation" most susceptible to childlessness, now ages 41–55, and their peers in the age group 28–40. At age 40, a third of the women with incomes in the $55,000–65,000 a year range were childless, the rate rising to a half at the top end of "ultra-achievers," those earning more than $100,000.[41] According to Hewlett, childlessness for these women was not a choice, it was force of circumstance. Women who have overcome career pressures and have raised children are justifiably outraged about accusations of "greed"—wanting more out of life. "Darn it," says 35-year-old

Cindy, "I'm talking about the basics: love and work. What sane person doesn't want that?"[42]

Hewlett uncovered "a range of complicated emotions. Some of these women blamed career, some blamed men, many blamed themselves. Some were seriously in pain, others had come to terms with a different kind of life. All wished they had found a way to have children."[43] Kate, 52, is an academic medic: "Looking back I can't think why I allowed my career to obliterate my thirties. I just didn't pay attention":

> I'm only just absorbing the consequences. I was looking at some
> data the other day and it hit me: If I reach age 65 in good health,
> the likelihood is that I will live for another 19.1 years. That's an
> awfully long time to be on my own without the crutch of work. I
> don't know why it didn't occur to me before, but since I don't have
> children I also won't have grandchildren.[44]

At least women who had concentrated on a career rather than child rearing were likely to have the disposable income to seek some sort of solution to declining fertility. Hewlett cites Mayo Clinic figures that show women's fertility dropping from its peak between ages 20 to 30, to 50 percent at 35, and 5 percent after 40. "The basic problem is that women run out of eggs." In-vitro fertilization (IVF) extends a hope which Hewlett feels is overrated. It costs a lot—$10,000 to $100,000—and its effectiveness declines steeply with age. The proportion of live IVF births is still tiny—only 25,582 babies out of 3.9 million, or 0.6 percent, born in the United States in 1998.[45]

Hewlett does not mention dolls as a way of assuaging the agony of baby hunger. Of the three women we met who were buying dolls at the top, custom-made end of the doll range, two were childless high achievers with incomes to match. They were inclined to disdain the run-of-the-mill PCDs, which provided solace for women with lower disposable incomes. Judi H. of Portland, Oregon, is an executive with a division of the May company, and "gets a high" buying dolls. She has 2,800 of them, which she reckons are worth around half a million dollars. She has hopes of establishing a museum to house them in the future. Fiftyish and never married, Judi confides that the dolls have "fulfilled a tremendous maternal need. I could never mother 3,000 children and be a CEO." Of her dolls she says "I know what every one of them is doing. I know if a cleaning woman has moved one." They regularly receive the professional attention of a seamstress, who hand-starches their costumes. She says her doll family lightens her heart when she comes home at the end of a long day. Only one of them accompanies her to the office, but is kept hidden away to avoid adverse comments about what Judi calls her "ultrafeminine hobby."[46]

Although we lack statistical evidence, there are strong indications that women in the 35-to-45-year-old, empty-womb category are particularly attracted to newborn and infant dolls, like "Homecoming":

> When you cradle this delicate porcelain newborn in your arms,
> you'll experience the warmth, the pride, and the love all parents
> feel when they bring their brand-new baby home. Acquire
> "Homecoming," first issue in the *Baby's 1st Celebrations* collection,
> by Brenda Conner. Here is the miracle of a newborn, sculpted in
> fine porcelain with a mother's tenderness and affection . . .
> Reserve your newborn today!"

This doll might be a good match for Sarah J., 45, who works as an account manager for a large, Atlanta-based insurance company:

> I found it excruciatingly painful to even be around my brand-new
> niece. One of the few times I held little Lucy she rooted around in
> my neck and as I felt her unbelievably soft, newborn skin the physi-
> cal craving to hold my own baby became almost unbearable. . . .
> This whole experience stirred me up. I guess I was forced to recog-
> nize that children are a big deal, that I had missed out on some-
> thing huge.[47]

One PCD advertisement has an inset picture of a woman, apparently in her late thirties, hugging the infant doll *Good as Gold*. One of our child commentators, eight-year-old Anna, drew our attention to it. "Is that a parent?" she asked. "That's interesting," she mused. "A parent playing with a doll."

The agony of the empty womb should not be underrated. "It sounds crazy, doesn't it?" says one such woman. "How can an imagined child provoke such deep grief?"[48] The pain is more poignant when the doll is a memento mori for a stillborn child. Carol H. dropped a bombshell during a conversation with one of our researchers, Cindy, her granddaughter: "She said she had four miscarriages, all girls, before she successfully gave birth to two boys." This was the first Cindy had heard of it. "She mentioned it so nonchalantly, it threw me off guard." In her otherwise extensive collection, Carol has only one boy doll. Cindy wanted to know why, and Carol explained "that she was looking for the perfect little boy." At this point in the conversation Carol is overcome emotionally. "She gets up and pours herself another glass of wine. She looks at me for a while, almost right through me like I wasn't there." Then she tells Cindy about "her boys":

> When Dan was born the only feeling that was in my mind was pure joy. It was the exact same feeling when Tony was born. I tried to have children; it was the only thing I ever wanted. It was the happiest time in my life. They were, and are, the light of my life. I love them the way I never thought possible. If God meant for those [miscarried] children to be born, they would have been born. Instead, He sent me Dan and Tony, the two most perfect children in the world. For a long time before they were born I couldn't understand why He took [the others] away from me, then Dan and Tony were born and I understood why. When I look at the dolls they remind me of that time when everything was so perfect. They were perfect little angels, but now they're grown up and on their own. I liked taking care of them, I miss taking care of them. I think that is why I take such good care of my dolls, they never have dust on them, never a hair out of place. And they are always young.

Clinical perceptions of these problems, and the use of dolls in relieving symptoms, have their roots in Freudian psychology.[49] We came across three cases of women who were given dolls on medical advice to help them through traumas associated with childbirth: depression because of infertility, the loss of child by miscarriage, and a death in infancy. Since the patient may go through an extended period caring quite intensively for the doll, children's play dolls may function better, but some anatomically correct details are also desired. A likely candidate is The Doll Factory's "Original Newborn Baby" which, though less than half life size, has a genuine "soft spot" on its skull. He/she (there's a choice) has a hospital identification bracelet, a birth certificate, and "acrylic eyes, non-moving."[50] Regarding other therapeutic uses for dolls, we should put in a good word for Barbie who, we learn, has helped at least one woman through the trauma of mastectomy.[51]

A forerunner of the therapeutic doll was the "Bye-Lo Baby," designed in the 1920s by Californian art school teacher Grace Storey Putnam and marketed by the George Borgfeldt toy company. "Eager women consumers lined up outside toy stores just before Christmas 1922 in order to purchase the 'Million Dollar Baby.'" One described it as "so soft and warm and lifelike in texture and coloring, that you would think that you were holding a living, breathing infant." Putnam wanted the doll to be "a little wobbly—as real babies are," but the manufacturers preferred bisque to rubber. She noted that "men did not like it at all," complaining of its "unattractive realism," especially its half-closed eyes. She reckoned this was because the Bye-Lo was "too like their own babies. . . . They do not care for their own babies until they are old enough to smile at them."[52]

Dolls have for long been used as instructional aids for prospective parents. This has become increasingly necessary as families have fragmented and household sizes dwindled, inhibiting the flow of essential advice and information between the generations.[53] Early in the twentieth century Martha Chase produced her famous "Sanitary Dolls" for use in hospitals and pre-natal clinics to instruct women on child-care practices. A latter-day variation on this theme is "Baby Think it Over" for teenage girls, especially those suspected of having a precocious and persistent urge to be mothers. These $200 dolls have to be "tended" at the usual awkward times, as a daunting test of maternal endurance. Designed by aerospace engineer Richard Jurmain, the doll wails at random intervals and provides digital information to the supervisor about how much rough handling it has received. With sales worth around $5 million in the mid-1990s, these cautionary dolls come in white, black, Latino, and Asian versions, and both sexes. They are used mainly in high schools. "Teachers say that a few students have stabbed their dolls, hurled them out of windows and ripped the electronic circuitry out in order to quiet the crying. These students flunk the assignment, of course, and are usually recommended for counseling."[54]

We noticed that collectors visiting the various Web chat rooms frequently refer to the therapeutic function of the dolls in relieving stress. Tending them has a calming effect, absorbing emotional energy:

> I get particularly stressed out when I can't use my dolls or sewing
> for dolls to relieve stress, as is the case right now when I'm trying
> to prepare for a big family do at thanksgiving and have no room or
> time to set up my machine and ironing board. So I've been sewing
> little doll things by hand: yesterday, in odd minutes, I made Alex a
> nightie, a bikini, a shawl and a matching purse, all by hand."[55]

Chapter Five

Dollification

"Now you can bring this beautiful child into your life."

The objects in our lives that we wear, eat, work and play with are all loaded with meaning. Our relationship with these things is two-sided: we give meaning to them (cars, kilts) and they give meaning, directly or indirectly, to us (drivers, Scotsmen). By the same token, the things around us can become important aspects of our relationships with one another. To a large extent, we know who we and other people are by referring to the objects around us. Cars and kilts remind us how we should behave toward certain people, and what we in turn can expect of them.

Some things (wedding rings, uniforms) can become powerful expressions of our relationships, in that we make important connections (marriages, armies) with one another through them. However, our relationships with certain things can get very personal. They are more than just symbolic links with other people: we give them identities and draw them into our social relations as if they themselves were persons. We have the ability to imbue almost anything, from pebbles to whole mountain ranges, with personality. Things like houses or cars which get intertwined with our lives can become like family or friends—and occasionally enemies. Such objects can even substitute for "real" family and friends if our social relationships are sparse.

The PCDs have all these personable qualities. The manufacturers send them out into the world as virtual persons with names, clothes, roles, and basic identities. They are then drawn into the lives of the collectors as embodied memories of children who have grown up, surrogates for grandchildren who live far away, dreams of daughters or sons who were desired but never born, and evocations of the growth of the doll collector herself. And not incidentally, they are also little people in their own right. Yes, they really are. Look at *Jenny*: "Show her how much you care. Mail your order today."

In this chapter we piece together how this transformation of things into persons happens, examining how the doll acquires its personality ("Sarah"), how it stands in for real persons ("my daughter"), and how it involves its owner in relationships with others ("grandma," "collector"). We shall pay a lot of attention to the advertisements for the PCDs, since they provide the most graphic evidence of the manufacturers' collusion with the collectors in these elaborate acts of social invention. In the chapters that follow we shall try to detect how the work of the women in creating "real little people" finds expression in the physical form of the dolls *as things*, thus closing the circle with the work of the firms in designing and manufacturing a saleable commodity.

Children are very good at personalizing almost anything that falls to hand, and in doing so they apparently invented the doll. Reporting on their pioneering survey more than a century ago, Hall and Ellis noted that a "doll" can be almost anything on which a child confers the qualities of a person: pillows, sticks, corn cobs, toothpicks, half-burned matches, newspapers, glasses, forks and spoons, flowers, vegetables, "a piece of Porter house steak," a hitching post, chickens, cats, *other children,* and even the child's own hand. Victor Hugo's heroine Cosette "dressed, hugged and put to sleep a naked sword."[1] If we include the child's capacity to make playmates who are completely invisible to the rest of us, we might even say that a doll can be *nothing*.

"Dollification," according to Hall and Ellis, "always involves ascribing more or less psychic qualities to the object, and treating it as if it were an animate and sentient thing." The imputed personality may actually be more important than the materialness of the object itself: in their survey Hall and Ellis found that "if a doll has its head replaced it usually retains its identity." "Children are often under a long delusion concerning the material of which dolls are made. Even long after it is *known* that they are wood, wax, etc., it is *felt* that they are of skin, flesh, etc." To help sustain the illusion, broken dolls are mended in "hospitals," not "workshops." Finding sawdust or kapok oozing out of their dolls, little children may simply assume that they themselves are like that inside. The eventual discovery that this is not so can be terminally disillusioning for the child—the end of a relationship with dolls.[2] This break is encouraged in our societies as part of the process of growing up, but as the PCD phenomenon testifies it is not always actually completed.

Curiosity is vital to a child's growth, and learning to discriminate among persons and things is an essential social and psychological skill. Sooner or later a child will be struck by the ambiguity of the doll as a person/thing. Curiosity is piqued: if the outer shell is palpably plastic or porcelain, maybe the "real" person is hiding inside? This rang bells with our student researchers, who remembered unstitching their dolls and popping their heads off. Down the decades, wicked brothers, motivated by envy or malice, have been a grave threat to the precious illusion, exposing, dismembering, destroying. "The overriding desire of most little brats" said Baudelaire a century and a half ago, "is to get at and *see the soul* of their toys, either at the end of a certain period of use, or on occasion *straightaway*." The child attacks, tears the toy apart. "*But where is its soul?* This moment marks the beginnings of stupor and melancholy."[3]

As they grow up, children are expected to learn how to restrain their imaginative relationships with things. A failure to do so becomes, in an adult, the psychic disorder of *fetishism*.[4] "When detected 'dollifying' very intractable objects children often show signs of self-consciousness and even shame." Hall and Ellis viewed this disappearing magic with some regret. "The rudest doll has the great advantage of stimulating the imagination by giving it more to do, than does the elaborately finished doll. It can also enter more freely into the child's life, because it can be played with more freely without danger of being soiled or injured."[5] The impression we get is that this childish inventiveness has been curtailed by the mass-produced, washable, bashable plastic dolls of the twentieth century.

As we grow up there is an interesting shift in our understanding of "doll": from any thing on which we may confer the qualities of a person, to a particular thing whose basic quality is that it looks like a person. This comes through clearly in the (adult) dictionary definitions of the doll: "a child's toy, puppet, marionette, etc. made to resemble a human being."[6] Children may be content with a doll that looks like almost anything, but for adults it is important that a "real" doll actually look like a person. This is especially important for adults who take more than a casual interest in dolls. We might even say that the older you are, *the more like a real person you want your doll to look.* At the age of 70 or 80, petting a shoe or "a piece of Porter house steak" would be a convincing symptom of senile dementia. Playing with any doll, especially if it looks like a *child's* doll, is at best a bit shameful. The most dignified way of representing yourself is to put the dolls on *display* and say you are a *collector.* But this little trick need not detract from your belief, deeply rooted in childhood experience, that the doll is in fact a special sort of person. "Dollification" is a game that modern advertisers know and play very well. They use it to help us form warm relationships with such unlikely products as pastry dough and car tires by giving them friendly human faces.

As the anthropologist Margaret Mead pointed out long ago, we become in many respects *more* rather than less adept at mystification as we get older.[7] There is something ironic about the adult urge to make dolls look more explicitly like real people so that they can look more explicitly like real dolls. But for outsiders, making the PCDs look more and more *lifelike* only makes the discrepancy with real children more obvious, and the fetishism more apparent. For their part, the collectors are at some risk of seeing the resemblance between dolls and children a little too clearly, becoming susceptible to the old shock of bereavement when they are forcibly reminded that they are "just things" (the shattered porcelain, teddy losing his stuffing). People can get very attached to all sorts of collectible objects (thimbles, knives, bubblegum cards) but their "thing-ness" is usually more obvious and less troubling. The PCDs are not simply collected as clever porcelain artifacts, they are collected because they are like real children. But for the most part the PCD enthusiasts and the doll makers have evidently learned to deal with the ambiguity. The advertisements play up the "person-ness" of the dolls for all it's worth, but when they draw our attention to their material value or details of their manufacture they can bring us back to their "thing-ness" with a jolt: *Billy* comes to us "brimming with personality" but unlike your own son he "is inscribed with the artist's signature on his upper back" (*ouch!*).

PERSONIFYING THE COMMODITY

NAMES

Realism depends not simply on appearances, but on fleshing out a personality with which the purchaser can identify. The most obvious starting point is the name. Naming dolls is a long-established merchandising practice, as the "Fifis" and "Janes" in any nineteenth-century doll collection will testify.[8] Sixty-eight percent of the dolls in our sample have unambiguous, conventional, gendered names like *Allison* or *Jonathan*. The importance of the name is signaled by the frequency with which it is repeated in each advertisement—nine times in the case of *Stephanie*. The main doll companies have worked hard to differentiate this aspect of their product, virtually exhausting the supply of familiar names, and spellings of these. The range in our small sample is impressive, nevertheless there are four *Heathers*, three *Hopes*, and three *Julies*.

A further 13 percent of dolls in our sample have circumstantial names like "*Cherry Pie*," or "*Mr Mischief*." "She's so sweet, so dainty, so enchanting that there was only one name we could give her . . . '*Peaches and Cream*'!" says designer Dianna Effner of this Ashton-Drake doll. "Her name is Peaches & Cream," insists designer Ann Timmerman of a rival Georgetown doll.

The remaining 19 percent have narrative titles rather than names: "Tickled Pink," "Roly Poly Harvest," or "First Communion." The newborns and infants are more likely to have titles than names: "It's a Girl," "Homecoming," or "Good as Gold." For these, an explicit selling line is that the doll needs you, the purchaser, to give it an identity, much as you would your own baby. The few dolls whose gender is inexplicit are in this age category. Ashton-Drake's "Special Deliveries" series allows the purchaser to choose name and birthdate as well as clothes and accessories—the only visible gender distinction. "Your baby will have its own, personalized Certificate of Originality and Wrist Tag, with your child's name and birth date!" The package in the mail has something of the gender-neutral pregnancy, the unwrapping being akin to a birth, followed by the discovery: "*It's a boy!*" or "*It's a girl.*"[9]

Birth certificates (for infants) and adoption papers (for children) were offered until the early 1990s, when the practice evidently faded. While some purchasers welcomed the official assurance that their "children" were legitimate, others were more interested in product documentation, the certificates of authenticity and guarantees of satisfaction which vouched for the doll as a commodity rather than as a person. Combining both sorts of document in the packaging could be an unwelcome confusion.

ROLES AND RELATIONSHIPS

Tilt *Stevie*'s "fully poseable head, and it looks as if he's just discovered Mommy is watching." To be satisfactorily lifelike, the dolls must "do," as well as simply "be." Picking flowers is a favorite activity for the girls, readily elaborated with accessories. Text and titles spin a yarn: "Mommy I'm Sorry," "My First Tooth," "Caught in the Act," "Playing Footsie," "Tickles." Sometimes the tale is very familiar—Little Bo Peep, Red Riding Hood, Jack and Jill (there are tears and lost sheep, but no wolves or broken crowns). It helps if the doll is already a known character like Shirley Temple or one of the girls from *Little House on the Prairie*. The pose and the advertising copy work together to build up the sense of involvement: "Julie's wishing so hard, it feels like she'll burst. She wants to wear that pearl necklace more than anything else in the world. Mommy just has to say yes!" "Today is

Grandma's birthday, and Annabelle can't wait to give Grandma her special present!"

For many collectors, the dolls offer the certainty of stable, unconditional, "affectionate" relationships, and the advertisements labor to establish the character of the doll in these terms. A rich vocabulary lubricates the process of bonding with the dolls: they are adorable, darling, sweet, affectionate, enchanting, delightful, tender, heartwarming, beloved, charming, and so on. The mishaps and tantrums, the unfurled toilet rolls and scratched knees, only serve to underscore their sweetness. "Don't Have a Cow Mom" says *Becky*, a very successful doll from the Hamilton Collection, "created by European-born designer Bets van Boxel":

> Who's that spunky little girl in her "udderly" adorable new "cow" dress? She's "Becky" and she's sure to win your heart with her sassy charm and bubbly personality. This spirited little girl, with her hands on her hips and the exasperated tilt of her head, is simply irresistible. "Becky" has silky blonde hair that bounces with each hop, skip and jump. Her blue eyes are as merry as can be and her rosy cheeks simply glow with happiness. Crafted of fine hand-painted bisque porcelain, this adorable doll is hand-numbered and accompanied by a same-numbered Certificate of Authenticity.

"All children talk to their toys" said Baudelaire.[10] The advertisements draw the purchaser into dialogue with the dolls, and thus into specific identities and relationships. Mommies are, of course, the stars. *Timmy* ("A tender childhood portrait at a captivating price") has been "quietly playing in his toy-filled room since dinner. As his eyes become heavy with sleep, he decides he better go find Mommy. He pitter-patters down the steps, finds her in her favorite chair, then says in his most concerned voice, 'M-o-m-m-y, I'm sleepy.'"

A whole series titled I Want My Mommy is "a heartwarming collection of porcelain dolls that portrays the early relationship between toddlers and their 'Mommies.'" One of these is in trouble:

> Even though Mommy had said "no playing in the living room,"
> Tommy kind of . . . well, he forgot . . . Then (oops!) the ball

knocked over the planter and the fun sort of stopped. So, when bedtime arrives, he can't help saying with heartfelt sincerity, "Mommy, I'm sorry . . ."

Quality Craftsmanship at a Remarkable Value!

Little Tommy's sweetly sculpted face, pouty chin, and hand-painted lips convey the whole story at a glance. His pleading hand-set blue eyes beg for forgiveness under raised brows. His fine bisque sculpted fingers "clasp" behind his back.

Will Mommy ever forgive him? You bet. Her indulgence knows no bounds. She has dressed *Bobby* up "in a clown costume of his very own, and Bobby's adding a few finishing touches—with Mommy's lipstick!" "Mommy has lovingly put a bandage on *Kayla*'s boo-boo." She scratched her knee, but "wiping her tears away with a chubby hand, she will soon be on her way again." *Kayla* is "crafted of fine, bisque porcelain and expertly hand-painted. With her turned down lips, button nose and big blue eyes, this adorable pigtailed toddler is irresistible. Make this precious little girl with her sweet-but-sad expression your very own."

Both sellers and buyers work hard to weave the dolls into the web of family relations. Now that there are a lot more grandparents around for a lot longer, their importance in family networks has increased. Critics have recently complained that Freudian psychology has made too much of the triangular relationship between parents and children, and has paid too little attention to the emotional and practical importance of the third (and increasingly even the fourth) generation.[11] "No moments are more precious—or more warmly remembered—than those shared between grandmother and grandchild" says the advertisement for *Susan*. People need grandchildren (and vice versa), and if her own children are not cooperating, dolls help fill this next period of emptiness in a woman's life. If being a grandparent is, as one of our informants put it, "parenting without the mess, pain and responsibility," the dolls can be an effective substitute for the real thing. Some of the PCDs are directly represented to her as a granddaughter seeking her affection, wisdom, and indulgence. "Nothing could be more dear than Grandma's special love. *Annabelle* loves her grandmother more than anyone." Occasionally, grandma herself makes an appearance in the display, as in this "heart-warming moment between grandmother and granddaughter, sensitively captured in fine bisque porcelain" by Danbury:

> Cuddled safely in Grandmother's arms, little Susan listens intently to her favorite fairy tale. . . . The sweet expressions of both grandmother and child are astonishingly lifelike. Artful hand-painting makes little Susan's face radiate with joy, and brings a glow of contentment to Grandma's rosy cheeks. The dolls' posable heads and arms, as well as their lower legs, are handcrafted in fine bisque porcelain. The ottoman, fairy tale book and Granny's glasses are included at no extra charge.

Grandma may not feel the need for dolls if she is warmly attended by real grandchildren—until they in turn grow up. Bernice, from Washington, has just bought *Mandy* on a TV sales show: "She reminds me so much of my granddaughter. My granddaughter is nine months old. Her little clenched fists, and open hands. Darling. I babysit her and so I am with her all day. And when she is all grown up and I don't get to baby-sit her any more I will have Mandy to remind me of her."[12]

These days grandparents commonly provide a great deal of material and emotional support to the hard-pressed "nuclear" family. During the twentieth century many aspects of grandmotherhood have been expanded and redefined. Nevertheless, it seems as far as the PCDs are concerned older women still hanker to be *mommies,* and the advertisements recruit them in this role. Grandma is more usually evoked indirectly as an important figure in the family environment of the child, but she has the wisdom to keep a discreet distance. There are even hints of rivalry:

"I want my mommy!"

> Nicole has been very good for Grandma—almost the whole afternoon. But after a while, there comes a time when a little girl just wants to go home. Biting her lip . . . hugging her Teddy . . . she

bravely manages not to cry. And everyone's happy to hear
Mommy's footsteps coming up the walk. Don't make her wait any
longer. Give your heart to Nicole today. After all—she just wants to
go home—with you!

In a similar way, other family members who are unlikely to be
direct marketing targets are evoked by the dolls and their scripts.
Blackberry Blossom "is having her portrait painted by her grandfather,
whom she adores." Some collectors may like to imagine themselves as
aunts, but they are mentioned in only three advertisements, and in
each case the doll is a *visitor.* "Mama has brought Clarissa to visit Aunt
Emily, who gave her the fancy dress she's wearing. Now Clarissa
reaches to be picked up, so she can thank Aunt Emily in her own way.
. . . Let little Clarissa come calling at your house." It seems that the
dolls are drawn into the idealized family network as extensions of
Mommy's relationships. Daddies appear quite often, evidently as the
sorts of people mommies think daddies really ought to be, rather
than as potential buyers. Karen T., who owns a daddy doll rocking and
feeding his baby, feels that the figure "amazingly resembles my husband and baby girl and brings back loads of memories from our
daughter's infancy."[13] Little girls are skilled at drawing this at times
elusive parent into the emotional web. In one advertisement it's
Mommy's voice that urges *Shannon* to "smile big for Daddy."

> [Daddy] calls her his "Peanut," and indulges her every whim.
> "Peanut," designed by Jeanne Singer, is the first issue in the *My
> Heart Belongs to Daddy* doll collection, capturing the love between
> little girls and their doting fathers.

> "Daddy's Home!" . . . The words "Lindsay's" been waiting to hear
> all afternoon. Breaking into a great big smile, she reaches for him
> to pick her up. "Lindsay" knows that in just a moment, he'll sweep
> her into his arms and lift her high over his head. . . . "Lindsay" pre-
> mieres an irresistible new collection of *Daddy's Little Girls.* . . . As
> her owner, you will have the opportunity to acquire each doll in
> the collection. . . . Dressed in her adorable romper sprigged with
> flowers and trimmed in eyelet lace "Lindsay" is just waiting for you

to pick her up and bring her to your home today! "Lindsay's" very special pendant tells everyone she is "Daddy's Little One."

Sibling relationships are rarely referred to in this matricentric fabric of relations. Paired dolls are occasionally portrayed as siblings, usually twins, but more often they are sweethearts, posed kissing or holding hands. Even when they are arranged by collectors into larger displays, the dolls are imagined as friends and playmates rather than siblings. It is certainly hard to imagine why an adult woman might want a surrogate baby brother or sister, rather than a son or daughter, or why manufacturers would emphasize this in their sales talk. By contrast, dolls designed for children are often explicitly sold as substitute siblings. In an interesting twist these make an appearance with quite a few of the PCDs—dolls with dolls:

> It's Megan singing a lullaby to her baby! The day her baby sister came home, Megan got a new baby, too. At first, she didn't know what to think, but now she's proud to be the big sister. And like Mommy, she's rocking her baby off to sleep singing "*Lullaby and good night.*" She hasn't even noticed Mommy's peeking in! Share in the sweetness of this tender young mother.

This theme emerges strongly in the characterization of Grandma, drawing a line through *four* generations, the doll marking the granddaughter's own "child." "When 'Amber's' mother brought home a new baby, her Grandma knew that this was an important time for 'Amber' to be reassured that she was indeed a very special person. So Grandma made 'Little Amber'—a doll that looks just like this wonderful little girl, and even made matching dresses and hair ribbons!" The doll with a look-alike doll of her own was a popular motif around the turn of the twentieth century, recapitulated in many PCDs today. This points to an intriguing involution in the way the collector is drawn into relationships with her dolls: *Megan* is acting the role of Mommy with her doll, just like the collector herself. The tableau is a demonstration both of what a good mother *and* a satisfactory relationship with dolls should be. *Amber* carries the refraction further, with sisterly, motherly, grandmotherly relations all converging in

"Little Amber," the doll's doll. This image of a child carrying an image of itself is surely a very curious notion: the three levels of representation must pose quite a challenge for the designer. Although *Amber* declares triumphantly "I Have a Doll That Looks Just Like Me!" of course it does not—it looks like a doll. But why *Amber*, or the collector herself, would want a doll that "looks just like me" rather than somebody else is an intriguing question to which we shall return later.

Unlike most real children, dolls will be and do whatever you imagine. They have the capacity to be completely submissive, acting out the little roles the manufacturer and the collector devise for them, absorbing affection and admiration unconditionally. But the relationship with any doll is not without its anxieties. Because people trust their dolls and extract so much comfort from them, there is always the muted fear that they might be disloyal, untrustworthy, malicious. This, says one of our researchers, Marilyn, is "like the tension of a love affair: many have an actual fear of commitment because they are afraid of betrayal." If dolls have a life, they may also have a life of their own. "One look at *Sweet Strawberry* and you have entered her world . . . you wonder, what's she thinking of now?" In the daylight hours they sit there oozing charm but—a recurrent neurosis among doll owners young and old—who knows what this little gang gets up to at night?

BOYS AND GIRLS

In the PCD range there is a very marked preference for girl dolls—81 percent of our sample, counting those in the eight boy-girl pairs. Apart from the traditional association of dolls with girls, there are several reasons why women may prefer feminine symbols of, and substitutes for, "real" relations in later life. As the Oakland study indicates, the mother-daughter bond was particularly important for the Depression and wartime generation. As they age, women depend increasingly on their daughters and value their company. And insofar as the collectors see the dolls as reflections of *themselves*, the preference will obviously be for girls.

Gender is discriminated quite clearly in the design of the dolls and in their accompanying texts. Looking through the advertisements, it is easy to get a feeling for the distinct ways in which boy and girl dolls are presented. Girls are portrayed as beautiful, pure, dainty, serene, precious, adorable, innocent, elegant. Words that suggest passive femininity seem to jump out of the text: wait, daydreams, sweet, hopeful, fresh, sweet-natured, delicate beauty, soft loveliness, wistful expression, imploring, tears. According to our student observer Susie, "the tone of their advertisements is more euphonic and the flow of speech is gentler and slower." Poses and dress are explicitly nostalgic, evoking values of feminine prettiness, childish docility, and timeless dependability, which hark back to the Depression years and beyond. If they are active, girls gather bouquets, make tea, play with pets. The very few who are "working" are picking or selling fruit or flowers, like *Annie* the Victorian lavender girl, or *Nalo* the African market girl.

"Come into the garden . . . " invites an advertisement for the Georgetown Collection's classic *Caroline* (see picture 2), "and dream your cares away."

> She spent the morning gathering flowers in Aunt Martha's beautiful garden. But now, the sun is so wonderfully warm and the flowers smell so sweet . . . she can't help stopping just for a bit and letting her thoughts drift far, far away.
>
> Caroline is the very first in an elegant and extraordinary collection, "Sweethearts Of Summer" ™. Created by acclaimed doll artist Pamela Phillips, the collection celebrates the special beauty of old-fashioned girls—and the charm of classic country gardens. . . .
>
> Keep the enchantment of a summer garden in your home forever. . . . Send for Caroline today!

This role modeling came in for stern criticism from our student researchers. Advertisements that try to insist on the little accomplishments of girls were especially mocked, like the black doll *Shawna* who has "just learned to stack her blocks all by herself," and Beautiful Dreamers, "a doll collection portraying little girls who aspire to the fine arts." The several "first day at school" dolls were viewed cynically, especially one with a product tie-in: "Smiling brightly, 'Katie' has every reason to be proud. Her good work at school has earned a gold star, and now she gets to go to her favorite place, McDonald's!" Nor were the students greatly impressed by attempts to make the girl dolls look feisty, like *Erin—Up at Bat* ("A real winner") or *Julie* (a "mischievous girl") or *Jo*, from "Little Women" ("passionate and independent"). The boisterous behavior of "The Little Girl With a Curl," scowling, strutting, and stamping her foot around the broken flowerpot, did not cut much ice. Tantrums just reinforce the gender stereotype.

Scanning the advertisements, we find boy dolls represented as busy, active, noisy, naughty, messy, but entirely lovable: "Bobby can't help but grin in his hand-tailored blue-jeans with rainbow-colored suspenders, bright-yellow boots, and junior Fire-Chief hat. He 'struts' with a garden hose in hand and a stuffed Dalmatian pup beside him. Brown, handset eyes shine with mischief and little-boy plans." Some characteristically boy words are: mischief, trouble, antics, grin, charm, decide, plan, explore, steal, animated, rambunctious, impish, scamp, attentive, thoughtful, earnest. However, our student critics were quick to point out that the boy dolls were not exactly portrayed as macho. The tendency to infantilize them is suggested by the fact that 45 percent of them are babies or toddlers, compared with 21 percent of the girl dolls. For all the boy talk in the advertisements, they clamor for caring, cuddling, and reassurance.

> Elke Hutchens combines both mischief and innocence in Christopher's adorable features. Who could say "no" to such a cute little boy? With that mischievous grin, those deep blue eyes and incredible dimples, Christopher can get away with just about anything—including stealing your heart!"

> Billy is the cutest little buckaroo . . . brimming with personality and boyish charm, from his sandy blond hair to his pudgy fingers and toes.

Dirt and the need for a motherly wipe down is a recurrent theme. So too are references to the toilet: *Stevie* "holds a miniature roll of 'toilet paper,' which you can unwind to display any way you please." *Brian*, absorbed in a "special moment in the life of a little boy," sits pensively on his potty, drawers down round his ankles. "I'm a big boy now," he insists:

> There's nothing more appealing than a young child trying to be grown up. Sometimes it takes every ounce of determination a little tyke can muster . . . but it's worth every bit of the effort just to see Mommy and Daddy so proud. . . . The minute you see Brian's winsome face and the wishful expression in his big blue eyes, you'll recognize Elke Hutchens' magical ability to evoke the innocence and sweetness of young children. Just look at the way he's sitting, with his little mouth set and his chin cupped in his hands.

Although scanning the texts gave a strong impression of gender distinctions, we spent a lot of time analyzing the advertisements to get a "more scientific" picture of the differences in language and style (see appendix B1, B2). We began by sorting out the most frequently used words into eight categories: those referring to personal *qualities, actions, relations*, the *body*, and *touch*; then words that dealt with the dolls as a *commodity*, the *techniques* of their production, and their *realism*. We discovered that big, countable differences were not as significant as we had imagined. Predictably, the sales and technical vocabulary was much the same for boy and girl dolls, and for dolls of all ages.

On "qualities" the girls were definitely more *beautiful* than the boys, the word occurring in 32 percent of the girl doll advertisements, compared with just 7 percent of the boys. The difference between boys and girls emerged more clearly in the less frequently used words, confirming our impression that for gender differences the range of the vocabulary is more telling than the frequent use of particular "code" words. Counting "quality" words that appeared in at least 10 percent of the advertisements, girls were distinctively *precious, charming, exquisite, innocent, gentle, enchanting*, and *angelic*; they also *sparkled* and *inspired*. Boys were *proud, captivating, mischievous, happy*, and *cute*; they were twice as likely to have a *future* than the girls. At this 10 percent-plus level, the language of "body" and "touch" was much the same, except that girls were more *delicate.* On relationships, the boys were about three times more likely to have a *mommy* or *daddy,* and more than twice as likely to have a *personality.*

There was much gender overlap in the "action" words. The boys had more *fun* than the girls, but rather to our surprise they *slept, dreamed,* and were *cuddled* more. This again points to the infantilization of the boy dolls. We were tempted to imagine that notwithstanding all the boy-talk the boys were being *feminized* as well as infantilized. However, it does seem that both collectors and manufacturers want their boys to be recognizably boys. Our student researchers remarked that the boy dolls generally "look more real." In contrast, it was the girl dolls (which dominate the PCD range and thus give it its general identity) that "looked distorted"—somehow "more feminine" than one would ever expect a real child to be.

We broke our sample up into four age categories:

Infant: up to one year (usually prone, held, or propped up).
Toddler: one to three years (often sitting—the soles of their feet typically turned inward).
Child: over three years to puberty.
Adult: past puberty.

We later found this roughly matches the Ashton-Drake sales categories of "babies, toddlers, children, adults and brides."[14] We classified two thirds of the girl dolls in our sample of advertisements as "children." A significant proportion, a little more than 10 percent, looked older that this, and we classified them as "adults," but not without much discussion, because of their often ambiguous appearance. Half of them were dressed as brides, a long-standing tradition in doll making and a souvenir of happy times in the collector's own life. We found no "adult" male PCDs (although men make an appearance in the expensive, custom-made range), and nothing remotely resembling a male adolescent. "Teenagers" as we would clearly recognize them are absent from the PCD range. This fits what we know about family life over the last fifty years: while many mothers put a bright face on it, the teenage phase is the most stressful and the least rewarding emotionally for parents.[15] Family photo albums that burgeoned with childhood snapshots become extremely skimpy at this stage, with more scowls than smiles. When asked, collectors say frankly that they have no interest in bringing "all that" back into the empty nest.

It seems that adult collectors who are nostalgic about this adolescent life phase gravitate to Barbie, the teenage icon. Whatever vices Barbie may have, mothering is not among them (a brief experiment with "Maternity Barbie" was not a success). Rebecca, one of our researchers, commented:

> Barbie is independent in every sense of the word. She relies on no
> one to take care of her, and in return refuses to take care of any-
> one. Instead, Barbie is a solitary individual, missing ties to both
> past and future. Existing without a navel, Barbie lacks even the
> most basic universal connection to her mother. . . . Barbie does not
> give any indication of stooping to marriage, let alone having chil-
> dren of her own. Barbie's boyfriend Ken and little sister Skipper
> are mere accessories, and her relations with them vague and insub-
> stantial. Barbie switches roles and identities with breathless ease,
> astronaut one minute, doctor the next, all with a change of
> clothes.

A COMMUNITY OF DOLLS

Encouraged by the manufacturers' designs and texts, collectors build relationships among the dolls, much as children piece together Lego. "I just love the little ones. I put them all together in poses and put them with the little watering cans. And I have one holding up a tiny basket of apples. Little baby bunnies. And it just brings them to life. They are so beautiful."[16] Family life is strongly implicated in these projects: "School is over and 'Laura' is anxious to be on her way, for she eagerly anticipates one of Ma's home-cooked meals. After dinner, Pa will fiddle a few merry tunes before bedtime. It looks like another happy night for the family that lives in the little house on the prairie!" It's Mommy who holds the whole community together. However, if the object is to build a whole surrogate family, the effect as we see it in larger displays can be bizarre: dozens of sons and daughters in various sizes, shapes, and accouterments, with an invisible circle of daddies, grandmas, and the occasional aunt, hinted at by the children themselves.

Abundant motherly love can embrace the whole collection. Although it is very much a private world, it ranges quite freely in time and space, drawing in characters from exotic places and from history. The neo-antiques dwell on fin de siècle Paris or London, revisiting the workshops of Jumeau and Bru Jeune. This is history viewed through rose-tinted spectacles—it is startling to see "Dickens's London" described as "a gentler time and place" (*Annie* the lavender girl). *Dara* is from Thailand and the series "Faraway Friends." She comes with a kite and a packet of pen-pal letters. To meet *Serena*, you are invited to "fly off to a far-away place on the wings of your heart." She is "the first issue in the Passport to Friendship collection . . . your introduction to life in a small village near Nairobi, Kenya. . . . Her basket with several 'fresh vegetables' is included."

Native American dolls are popular exotic visitors to the PCD range. *Meadowlark* is an "authentic portrayal of a young native American toddler of the Chippewa tribe." Although we have only 14 Native American dolls in our sample, the distinctive vocabulary is apparent (see appendices B-3, B-4). *Proud* and *dream* are high on the list. The advertisements are more than three times as likely to use the word *tradition(al)*. *Tales* loom large, and qualities like *timeless, forever* feature prominently. Their homelands range from the Southwest to the Arctic: "*Tulu* of the raven hair. Daughter of Teremuit. Her dark eyes gleam like jewels in the firelight. Tonight the sun will never set. Her people will hold a midnight feast. And Tulu will ask a great favor of her father, holy man of the Eskimos . . . for she yearns to keep an orphaned baby seal." Their customs are likewise charming and picturesque:

> It's a special day for a little Pueblo boy . . . today he will perform
> the sacred Eagle Dance for the first time! Draped in a splendid
> feathered Cape, he darts and circles, sweeping his arms skyward in
> tribute to the powerful eagle. Now, inspired by this proud Native
> American tradition, award-winning doll artist Elke Hutchens has
> created a unique porcelain collector doll, Little Eagle Dancer.

These characterizations are "reverent," but even the dolls that are designed by tribally accredited artists are oriented to the romantic fictions of *non*–Native Americans, rather than to any plausible ethnic reality, past or present.[17] "*Morning Song*'s authentic Cheyenne wedding attire was designed by Lady Scarlet Whirlwind—a direct descendant of the great Chief Sitting Bull, and a leading authority on Native American customs." Well-known ethnic accessories play a large part in authenticating these dolls. *Golden Flower* by Carol Theroux ("who celebrates in her work her own Cherokee heritage") shyly steps up to meet the medicine man for her "naming ceremony." "An authentic Osage pattern decorates the ribbon on her skirt. Her medicine bag will protect her as she grows."

> "Sleeping Bear" dreams the proud dreams of his people! Tucked into his cradleboard, laced and beaded, "Sleeping Bear" is the pride of his family . . . and his people. His sweet, sleeping face is bisque porcelain, beautifully hand-painted. His cradleboard is soft, faux chamois, trimmed with faux fur . . . and a tiny "dreamcatcher" above his head guarantees good dreams! He's first in the Precious Papooses collection.

Anyone fantasizing about traces of Native American blood in her lineage may be attracted to dolls in this "ethnic" category, no matter how kitsch and infantilized they may appear. But it is extremely unlikely that people living on Native American reservations today are in the market for these dolls. The price of dolls in all ethnic categories is similar: $114 on average for African American dolls, $105 for Caucasian, and $97 for Native American ($106 for the whole sample). This points to the uniformity of the market—there is no evidence that the ethnic minority dolls are being priced up or down for a distinct clientele. Although the buyers and the dolls are preponderantly white, they are not exclusively so: African American women, too, are avid collectors. The market is more obviously defined by level of disposable income, and our studies indicate that white women commonly include some black dolls in their collection, and black women include white dolls.

The manufacture of black dolls for white children is as old as the industry. The tradition has been attributed to the role of black women in raising middle-class white children in the United States, and similar European experiences of colonial family life.[18] In recent decades black dolls have been treated with great anxiety by liberal parents: whatever comfort the Golliwog may have given to children down the years, he has now been banished for his caricature features and dress. The mass of "black" dolls are simply white dolls painted over. Walterhausen Puppenmanufaktur produced "The Dolls of Four Races" between 1890 and 1910, but they are the company's standard bisque socket heads with different colored glazes, hair, and eyes. Likewise, the African American Barbies that Mattel began manufacturing in the mid-1960s were cast in the same Caucasian mold.[19]

Our researchers had little difficulty identifying the 17 "black" or African American dolls in our sample of advertisements by their dark color and hairstyle, but opinions varied greatly about whether they were "genuinely black": no more than seven were admitted to this category. Predictably, the non-white students were most critical of the "blacked-up-white" dolls. They "perpetuate the notion that white, and only white, is beautiful," said Roya, who is of Iranian descent. She attributes her deep-seated disgust for all dolls to the blue-eyed, blond-haired stereotype that dogged her childhood in the almost exclusively white community in Arizona where she grew up. Where, she asks, "are the [ethnic] facial features of these dolls, and why isn't anyone complaining? . . . We need the features! We need the hair and eyes and nose and lips." But the older doll collectors seem oblivious to these complaints, and evidently content with their dusky but reassuringly familiar features.

Manufacturers are well aware of the problem of ethnic representation and how easily they can be wrong-footed in their efforts to address it. *Kenya* "is the doll she'll love for all the right reasons. . . . Best of all Kenya comes in three natural skintones, so your girl is bound to feel pretty and proud."[20] However, although they accentuate the facial features that Roya feels are missing, self-consciously "appropriate" or "anthropologically correct" black dolls have lacked popular appeal. Some up-market African American designers have worked consciously in the long-standing tradition of "character" dolls, with effects that others have found grotesque. Yet it is mainly through the efforts of such designers that both the child and adult markets have been able to offer more convincing and pleasing black dolls. But PCD design remains conservative in this regard: the exotic should be, at most, skin deep and in all other respects comfortably familiar. That also means conforming to stereotype: in the advertisements the black dolls tended to be *joyful, happy,* and *innocent,* and were twice as likely to *sing* and be *angelic* as all the rest.

Latino dolls and doll collectors are, given the rapid expansion of this ethnic category in the U.S. population, conspicuously absent. The only example we have is *Marisa*: "It's market day in a tiny Mexican village, and Marisa's too excited to sleep. Rising long before the rest of her family, she brushes her long dark hair to a radiant lustre." One of our Chicana researchers, Jennifer, addressed this gap in the PCD range, concluding that Latinas lack the disposable income and earning opportunities of their "Anglo" sisters. Nor do they have an obvious empty nest or empty womb motive for collecting dolls: they bear children earlier, have larger families over longer periods of their lives, they don't live as long, and a smaller proportion of those over 65 (22 percent, compared with 31 percent for whites and 35 percent for blacks) live alone.[21] Nor are they likely to have had the same Depression experiences that boosted the collector doll boom in the United States. As more Latina women become more prosperous, however, and changing family patterns expose them more to loneliness and alienation, perhaps they, too, will start collecting dolls.

THE COMMODITY AS PERSONIFIER

If she has truly found a place in the collector's home, the doll does not simply sit passively on a shelf, a pretty concoction of porcelain and lace. She embodies much socially creative energy. She has an identity and a personality, she has relationships with other dolls in the collection, and she is drawn into the collector's own circle of family and friends. She substitutes for children who have grown up or who were perhaps never even born. She is kept busy on Mommy's account reminding the daddies and grandmas and children how they should behave. Displayed prominently at home, or despatched to the front line as a personal gift, she can play a very active role in fostering warm relationships among these people. Above all, she is constantly at work on the identity of Mommy herself, repairing and remaking relationships eroded by the relentless processes of family growth and change.

The identities that are built into the dolls are important in spinning these webs of relationship. Women are given, or buy, a PCD that bears the same name as, or "looks just like" a child or grandchild, expanding the collection as more children arrive. A century ago, Hall and Ellis noted that most children said their doll was named after a real person, usually a friend, while "a small number took the owner's name."[22] Old habits die hard. "A lot of you out there shared with me that you buy the dolls based on name," says a TV doll show presenter. "A lot of you of course tend to get all of the names for your children."[23] Patricia, talking to doll designer Pauline on one of these shows, has a particular suggestion: "Shawna Viane. S-h-a-w-n-a, that is my youngest daughter's name. Oh, I love it, she was named after my grandmother. And I would love to have a doll with the name Shawna. And I don't think anyone could do my Shawna justice but Pauline." Patricia has another of Pauline's dolls which is a ringer for her great-niece: "Oh my Lord have mercy! If the doll was smiling a little bit more it would be Andrea." Matching names and identities in this way is quite common, especially in dispersed families, and several of our student researchers remarked on the oddity of finding themselves and their siblings in a cabinet round at Grandma's house. One of them wondered whether painted portraits and photographs originally had the same faintly disturbing impact.

GIFTS AND HEIRLOOMS

Dolls are often on the move. They are given by family or friends to people who are thought to need them. Someone recently bereaved will be given a doll or a cuddly toy. A daughter leaving home to go to college or work will entrust her own dolls to her mother's care. Birthdays, anniversaries, and Mother's Days become the excuse to give more dolls, helping to establish the reputation as a *collector*. At least to start with, the recipient may be unenthusiastic: Beth, raising a teenage son single-handed, keeps getting PCDs from her mother as "pointed gifts"—"something to add to your collection." When it becomes a gift, virtually any commodity acquires some extra, personal qualities. This makes it more difficult to sell or throw away—which may be why unwanted trinkets and keepsakes so often are given to other people or to charity. If the dolls are intended more for display than play, children may find themselves with a collection on their hands regardless of their feelings. Jamie's grandfather gave her a "good" doll every birthday and Christmas, some of them PCDs that she would never have chosen herself. Although there could be no question that they were all in the family, accommodating the whole mob is awkward now that she is at college.

Columnist Ann Landers received a telling letter from a new mother who signed herself (with her husband) "Not Doll Lovers in Dixie." Her "sweet and thoughtful" older sister bought the baby a porcelain doll, promising another one for each birthday in perpetuity, and insisting, "They will make a beautiful collection." But this couple protest that they are "not into collecting things, especially breakable dolls." The child would not be able to play with them, or even touch them, until she is older. "I don't want to insult my sister by storing these dolls and not displaying them. She would be terribly hurt." So, should she tell her sister to get the baby something else? Ann Landers opined that "a gift is whatever people choose to give" and should be accepted unconditionally. Even if the child can't play with them now, the dolls will be "considered treasures when she is older." Accept the gift graciously, she advised, because she is going to have "a priceless collection down the road."[24]

Gifts are messengers in the making of relationships, but masquerading as "real live" intermediaries, the dolls go a step further than chocolates or flowers. In case the point should be missed, you can buy a special "Messenger Doll," like the 23–inch angel designed by Joanne Claire Schneider, which has a "patented time capsule" built into her back, a "cache" into which the owner or giver can insert messages or memorabilia. Joanne tells Home Shopping Network viewers:

"With Mother's Day coming, the beauty part of it is a daughter could buy it for her mother, or a mother could buy it for her daughter and put their own personal treasures in it." The recipient could then return the doll, with new stuff inside—"and keep that going for year after year." The doll even comes with a "keepsake registry" to keep track of these transactions. "I hope that everyone that buys her and opens her up feels all the love, joy, and peace that we felt when we created her," says Joanne.[25]

A gift that moves through family networks, marking out special relationships between parent and child, or between very close friends, has the special qualities of an heirloom. Kathleen's grandma was born in 1906 "in a small pioneer town in Idaho." Since "she was always on the road" she had few toys as a child, and as an adult started collecting girl dolls because her two children were boys. "My dad remembers as a boy my grandma displaying the dolls in her room and the rest of the house." She passed them on, one by one, to her granddaughters, including Kathleen:

> We were too young, so most of the time they were lost, sold at
> garage sales, poked in the face with thumbtacks, or colored on.
> Now that I am a young woman at the age of 23, I have taken on
> the responsibility of preserving what is left of my grandma's
> remaining dolls. I sometimes, very briefly, show them to my five-
> year-old niece, and then I hurry and put them back where they
> belong [in a big blue suitcase] out of fear they might just get dam-
> aged. I always knew how sacred these dolls were to her because
> they were a huge part of her life history. . . . I will eventually pass
> them on to my children and grandchildren because to me, they
> symbolize a sort of family history and large piece of my grandma's
> life.

Passed on from one generation to the next, dolls come bearing moral messages as well as material and emotional values. In the late nineteenth century girls were encouraged to practice needlework, dress decorum, good manners, and so on with their dolls in preparation for "true womanhood."[26] The didactic tradition continues, notably in the American Girls collection, from the Pleasant Company of Middleton, Wisconsin (now owned by the Barbie manufacturer, Mattel). In the late 1980s, there were four dolls, each with a matching book, depicting four fictional nine-year-old heroines: *Felicity, Kirsten, Samantha,* and *Molly.* Sales were exclusively through catalog, which described *Felicity,* for example, as "a spunky, spritely colonial girl who lived a life in Williamsburg, Virginia, during the Revolutionary War." Pleasant Rowland, a former teacher and founder of the firm, says that the American Girls collection "was designed to teach young girls about American history and give them a sense of pride and self-aware-ness of traditions in growing up female in America."[27] The company's aims are to "reinforce positive social and moral values": "The girls we inspire today will become the women who make a difference tomor-row." But unlike the Victorian dolls, the American Girls are more con-cerned to prolong childhood than promote adulthood. "Basically, what we're saying is that it's okay to be a little girl," says a Pleasant spokesperson.[28] The American Girls are great favorites with grand-mothers, who buy these dolls in phenomenal quantities (sales in 1994 rose to $152 million, and the company tripled its workforce to deal with the seasonal demand). The success of these dolls is that their highly modalized features and dress appeal to little girls, but they also contrive to convey Grandma's nostalgic yearning for a new generation that will conform to memories of perfect children long ago and far away. Take *Kit Kitterege,* described in the company's 1999 catalog as "a clever, resourceful girl growing up in 1934, during the hard times of the Great Depression": "It is a time when many people lost their jobs, their money, and even their homes. Kit's stories describe how this smart, freckle-faced girl responds when the hard times hit her family. With spirit and determination, Kit keeps their hopes up through the Depression's darkest days."

Our student commentators were in no doubt that the PCDs, as gifts, were delivering similar gendered propaganda, immortalizing childish innocence and docility rather than offering preparation for a career and modern womanhood. *Claire,* an angel doll, comes with a little book that delivers a pointedly self-interested message to the lit-tle children in Grandma's life. It's "about love and how to respect other people's property and how, when they did something wrong, how to repair it, how to say I am sorry":

> It is a story about two children going to visit grandma and grandma tells them, you know, the house that she has isn't big enough for growing boys and girls to play in but if they do play to be very careful and to not knock her shelf off the wall. And it has all the treasures that grandpa had given her over the years. . . . Well of course, like all children, they were rambunctious and they knocked the shelf off the wall and they broke grandma's treasures.[29]

Lest we imagine that all is sweetness and light in the society of dolls, let us consider the plight of James K., now in his twenties, who developed a special fear of porcelain collector dolls. He was an only child and his mother encouraged him to form intense relationships with his own dolls. He alternately poured affection on them and punished them savagely, and spent fearful nights worrying that they would gang up on him and kill him. His mother was already collecting PCDs when James was in his preteen years. Although he was not supposed to touch them he would sometimes take them out of their display cabinet and hold them. One day, one of them came to pieces in his hands. All the others in the cabinet stared at him, but he could not tell from their bland faces whether they were angry. For years after, he would heap the bedclothes up around himself at night, hoping that the sharp little porcelain fingers would get entangled before they could dig into his sleeping body. "Bad emotions are better than no emotions at all, and angry friends are better than angry strangers," he told us.

A COLLECTOR COMMUNITY

Adults who collect dolls *know* they are a bit odd. There are feelings of guilt and shame about the extravagance and clutter, about playing with toys, and about substituting things for real people. The vice is a very private one for many collectors, its full extent hidden even from their immediate families. Many have dolls that they have kept since childhood, have retrieved from their own children, or have been given.

Not all of them would welcome the label "collector," with the sense of purpose and obsession which that word implies. But for those who "come out," the experience can be liberating, exhilarating. "I turn 40 this coming feb 23 2001. What a great feeling to know a lot of people like playing with Barbie as much as I do."[30] The community of doll collectors has gained impetus from the Web. The Internet chat rooms have been busy with people exchanging information about designs and repair, favorite artists, and above all the relief of discovering that there are so many like-minded people "out there," and building a sense of solidarity. For example, VirtualDOLLS.com is "a virtual community and ezine publication—'Where Doll Collectors Gather.'" Links from these pages will introduce you to collectors in your state, and incidentally help you track down other relationships, like who was in your high school class.

Older people who lack access to the virtual forums still have more familiar media through which they can connect. The magazines that carry the PCD advertisements also have articles and correspondence columns on dolls and their collectors. The range of custom magazines for enthusiasts—many of them available on local book stands— is astonishing: *Dolls, Antique Doll Collector, Doll World, Doll Crafter, Contemporary Doll Collector, Soft Dolls and Animals, Doll Reader, Doll Artisan, Doll-Making, Doll Castle News, The Cloth Doll* . . .[31] Later in the 1990s, the TV sales shows on channels like the Home Shopping Network or QVC provided the first live interactive opportunity for many collectors. Running for several hours at a stretch, often in the middle of the night, these shows draw shoppers into conversation with the hostess and her studio guests. Callers phoning in orders for dolls are intercepted and encouraged to talk about themselves and their collections—a valuable source of information for our researchers. Some are initially embarrassed, but most warm to the occasion, treating the opportunity almost as a religious confessional. The sheer number of dolls that these night-birds have accumulated is astonishing: thirty dolls is barely a collection, two hundred or three hundred far from unusual. The mood is often electric, the anxiety of missing a purchase (little monitors on the screen tick away the surviving number of dolls) merging with the anxiety of buying too much too fast. For people who fear their ability to resist temptation, there are even help lines and Web sites offering counsel in the manner of Alcoholics Anonymous.

The TV networks have encouraged this clublike atmosphere, and now give air time to callers who are not actually making purchases. An invitation to talk opens the floodgates:

> Kim (the host): Fewer than 50 now remaining as we welcome in
> Anne in California. Hi Anne.
> Anne: Hi.
> Kim: What do you think about little *Inesse* here?
> Anne: Well, I think she is absolutely gorgeous. I love her hair. The
> minute I saw the hair I went oh, I was trying to talk myself out of
> buying her actually but then I couldn't resist, she is absolutely
> beautiful. And I was really surprised, I didn't realize the dress was
> purple at first, I thought it was black, but it is just absolutely amaz-
> ing. It is a wonderful choice. She will stand out in my collection. I
> love the hair, it just looks like so much fun. *Beautiful.* She is just
> going to be so much fun. I have quite a few dolls, I have to say this
> is my second doll of yours. I have one of the tiny babies of yours
> that I got last year. But part of the problem is as I watch you I am
> trying to make up my mind about which one I want, and by the
> time I decide they are usually sold out. So I get very frustrated. You
> are so popular and I just love this doll and I know I am going to
> enjoy her. Bye.[32]

Increasingly the collectors want to chip in ideas about design and names, and requests for *bigger* dolls have become more insistent. The main constraint on air-time is competition from other sorts of collector mania, conspicuously jewelry and plates for women, knives and sports memorabilia for men.

The "real" as opposed to "virtual" clubs for doll enthusiasts are still mostly the domain of long-established "serious" collectors of antiques. The United Federation of Doll Clubs (UFDC) is a strictly adult organization devoted mainly to "offering members a variety of educational opportunities about doll collecting." At the affiliated clubs we visited we found the aficionadas took a clinical interest in our PCD range, though usually conceding that anything which boosted a broader enthusiasm for dolls was probably a good thing. They tend to be dismissive about mass-produced, kitsch, low-value dolls, although they will admit to having "picked up" or "been given" one or two PCDs because of some specific personal interest. However, they find themselves increasingly brought into contact with PCDs at fairs or in the specialty shops where "dollers" of all levels get together.

Though lacking the cachet of the antique dolls or the passionate rivalries of the rich collectors who frequent the auction rooms, the PCD world already has its heroes and demons, its ideals and taboos. Celebrity collectors like Roseanne have given the community a boost. Demi Moore is a "serious" doll collector, with her own full-time agent, Mr. Hinkle (in 1996 correspondents in *Dolls* magazine complained of his aggressive buying). Marie Osmond collects dolls and sells her own designs through her own company, Marian LLC, and (since 1991) through the QVC channel.[33] But the high priestesses of the PCD world are, without a doubt, the "artists" who design and make the original casts. They feature in the advertisements, magazines articles, and the TV shows, and they have graduated from shadowy craftspersons in the early days to full-blown artist personalities today.

The Ashton-Drake Web site offers biographical details of its regular artists. Cindy McClure was born in Southern California and now lives in Washington. She has five daughters, loves cookies, and has designed for Ashton-Drake since 1987. "You Need a Hug, Pooh" was "a tremendous popular and critical success," nominated for an industry Doll of the Year (DOTY) award in 1998. Cindy "taught anatomy and physiology in college," where she once forgot to wear a skirt to class. She would like to be a doctor if she were not a doll artist. She herself collects "bunnies, candle holders, thimbles, prints . . . perfume bottles and juicers."[34]

Yolanda Bello lives in Des Plaines, Illinois. Her first doll for Ashton-Drake was *Michael* (1991). She has five children and collects "dolls, miniatures, J. Fred Muggs items and monkeys." Kathy Barry-Hippensteel, designer of 15 dolls in our sample, "has received widespread acclaim for her sculptural mastery." She is "one of Ashton-Drake's most enduring and popular artists because of her instinctive insights into the experience of childhood. She says . . . 'If I can make a doll that hugs somebody's heart and makes them smile, then I've done what I set out to do.'"[35]

The TV shows provide a rare opportunity to meet the artist-stars, like Pauline Bjonness-Jacobsen, selling a batch of her dolls on QVC with the help of the host, Kim:

> Kim: Oh, we have a caller on the line, Dina. Dina welcome and meet Pauline.
> Deanna: Hi, this is Deanna. How are you? Hi Pauline. Oh, I just love your dolls. And this particularly beautiful one, Mandy, she is so cute. She is lovely. I have some of your other ones too, and they are just gorgeous. They are all gorgeous . . .
>
> Kim: We are going to talk to Linda. Hi, Linda.
> Linda: Hi.
> Kim: Tell me now, about your Pauline collection, or tell Pauline.
> Linda: Hi Pauline, I had to call and tell you how wonderful your dolls are.
> Pauline: Oh, thank you.
> Linda: Absolutely wonderful, I have probably thirty of them.
> Kim: Is it the detail that keeps attracting you back to Pauline's dolls?
> Linda: It is, I just love the beautiful detail on the dresses and the faces are so serene, they are so peaceful they are like pieces of art in my home. . . .
>
> Kim: Patricia is also calling in, and I think she has a couple of your dolls. Let me be nosy and ask her. Patricia how many of Pauline's dolls do you have?
> Patricia: I have between 25 and 30.
> Pauline: Uh, oh. That's a lot.
> Patricia: No, uh oh. Joy, joy, joy . . . Pauline, they are just beautiful.

> I got Mandy today tonight. I love your vinyl baby dolls and I am
> looking at Lucinda in my curio [cabinet] right now. . . . I talked to
> you last October 19th and I was so nervous I even stuttered.[36]

POLITICS

Because of their direct resemblance to human beings, dolls have been
recruited to political causes of all sorts. As effigies they have been
paraded, burned, and dismembered, and as symbols of innocence
and vulnerability they have become part of the standard apparatus of
public demonstration. An anti-abortion protester outside the
Supreme Court in Washington is pictured with an armful of black and
white dolls and a placard: "President George Bush won because our
lord Jesus wants the babies to live."

As the adult market for dolls expands, and as collectors become
more aware of each other's identity and interests, a new political motif
is emerging. Much of the adult doll collector's sense of shame has
been put there by the very passionate critiques of modern femininity,
of which no woman we talked to was unaware. Modern feminists have
consistently attacked children's dolls as embodying the worst sorts of
conservative, patriarchal ideal. Miriam Formanek-Brunel lays most of
the blame for gender stereotyping on the tendency of businessmen to
"appropriate the dolls they marketed as symbols of an idealized feminine domesticity."[37] She complains that "scholars have overlooked the
struggle waged by women and girls for the cultural control of dolls as
representations of their gender identity":

> Dolls continue to be typically misunderstood as trivial artifacts of a
> commercialized girls' culture, static representations of femininity
> and maternity, generators only of maternal feelings and domestic
> concerns, hindrances to the development of girls as individuals,
> creations of socially conservative dollmakers, and products of a sin-
> gle national culture.[38]

Barbie has been the prime focus of onslaught. Perhaps if she were not
such a big seller this subliminally sexual figure would not have
become such a monster, vamp, fem, or dyke.[39] Barbie was modeled on

Bild-Lilli, a German doll created in 1952 by Hausser-Elastolin, which was in turn modeled on wartime pinup posters. Ruth Handler, a native of Colorado and long-term California resident, bought Bild-Lilli for her toy firm, Mattel. Recast and named Barbie after Handler's daughter, she sold 350,000 in her first year. Since she was "born" in 1959, more than a billion Barbies have been sold in 150 countries.[40] Sales topped $1.8 billion in 1997, and have been sustained mainly by product diversification into clothes and accessories, and by an increasing emphasis on high-priced collectible Barbies.[41]

Every year more than a thousand enthusiasts get together at the National Barbie Doll Collectors Convention, not just to saturate themselves in Barbiana, but to *become* Barbies. The 2002 convention, held in Ruth Handler's hometown, Denver, had "Rocky Mountain Mod" Barbie as its theme, to which the "mostly middle-aged and up and mostly women" participants responded with a flurry of "tie-dyes, go-go boots and bouffants—8 to 10 costume changes per attendee over the four days." Up there on the catwalk, "For one brief, glorious moment, Joane Baumer was a living, breathing Barbie doll—'67 Beautiful Dress Blues Gift Set Barbie." Contrary to expectations, Joane is, like so many of the conventioneers, a career woman: a physician in a major public hospital in Fort Worth who has raised a family of her own. Dr. Baumer is well aware of the heavy feminist critique of her behavior, but is uncontrite: "We were really active in the feminist movement. But it tended to ignore sexuality, which was kind of silly."[42] If Barbie helps some women to recapture teenage joys, complete with the sauce of rebellion, the PCDs are doing a different sort of job. So far, they have escaped the very public criticism to which Barbie has been subjected, perhaps because they are less conspicuous, although the women academics to whom we have introduced the dolls are often appalled.

Although the gender composition of the big PCD companies is surely as male-biased as most other enterprises in the United States, and although men are selling the dolls and profiting from them, there is no doubt that this is very much a commodity constructed for women by women. Male entrepreneurs have clearly ceded the design of the dolls to women—many of them exactly the same sort of person as the firms' main customers. The tendency is not new. Women like

Beatrice Behrman, alias "Madame Alexander," began making dolls at the kitchen table for themselves, family, and friends. Quite a few seem to have come to the job with art school, sculpting, and dressmaking backgrounds, like so many of today's PCD designers. Biographical details suggest that far from being mere victims of patriarchal ideology they were vigorously and explicitly concerned with making dolls "as representations of their gender identity." Those who established larger enterprises are often recorded as bringing their husbands into the business as managers, and possibly "front men." It is interesting to see these husband-and-wife teams working the stalls together at local doll fairs today.

If dolls are at odds with modern feminist ideals, it signals a political gap between different generations of women, rather than between women and men. It is the middle-aged, college-educated cohorts that seem most hostile. The attitudes of older women might be dismissed as "old-fashioned," but during the course of our project, the sympathies of women in their late teens and early twenties were often strongly articulated. As Maria Cristina, one of our researchers put it, the PCDs express a femininity that collectors "may feel that our current society is losing due to current trends and the women's movement": "I feel that porcelain doll collectors do not collect dolls because of their monetary value. I believe that they collect them as a replacement for a family that they once raised and because it represents ideals that are rapidly disintegrating." An emerging counter-critical theme is that if the enthusiasm for PCDs seems bizarre or even erotic to some of us, the collectors should be accorded the same tolerance for "otherness" that properly underlies contemporary political attitudes. The new electronic and TV forums bring very explicit relief from the doll collector's hitherto very private sense of guilt. The collectively induced boost in confidence is reminiscent of, and indirectly builds on the shift in political values engineered by gay solidarity over the past three decades. Engendering passion in some observers and disgust in others, the PCDs are evocative of what has become known among cultural critics as "queering"—an allusion not simply to homosexual interests but to something that "looks weird" to others.[43]

ENDING THE AFFAIR

As objects that become persons, and as agents in the making of personal relationships, the PCDs have moral power. The manufacturers know how to put this quality of their product to work. You don't *buy* one of these dolls, you "apply" for them, "reserve" them, or "commission" them. "Submit your reservation for '*Kayla*' today."

Having "invited the doll into your home," established her personality, and fitted her into your social scheme, it is unlikely that you, the collector, will reject her or feel happy about despatching her back to her maker. Gentle conversational probing makes it clear that this thought is as disturbing and alienating as seeing teddy come apart at the seams, or Dolly lying with her head cracked open. While offering sterling guarantees for their product, the doll manufacturers are cruelly matter-of-fact about the dreadful translation of the little person back to the status of an unwanted *thing*. If you are dissatisfied, they will *buy it back*, a gesture that reminds you that your doll is "just a commodity" and that you are not just wantonly forgoing its investment prospects, you are killing her.

There's the carrot and the stick, hanging over the delightful picture of *Becky* in her cow frock: "Of course your satisfaction is assured with our 100% Buy-Back Guarantee!" But even if *Becky* fails to lay claim to your heart, your feelings about sending her back to the Hamilton depot in Jacksonville, Florida, are a little more complex than your decision to return a faulty toaster.

Chapter Six

More Than Real

" . . . an enchanting young lady with blue glass eyes."

Realism is the big selling line for the porcelain collector dolls. The designers work very hard on the illusion, and the enthusiasts are deeply complicit in breathing life into the commodity. The starting point in the modeling of many dolls has been a real child, from the granddaughters of Simon and Halbig in the 1880s, through the sons and daughters who became *Sasha* or the Dreamkids in the 1960s and 1970s, to the young friends and offspring who inspire the PCD designers today. But the result is always something that goes beyond reality as less passionate observers would see it. How does this life-giving process work?

As we have seen, children make dolls by imbuing almost any object with life and personality. The younger they are, the less demanding they seem to be about physical cues, and the more ready to introject human qualities. To satisfy adult urges, "real dolls" have to look more explicitly like "real children." The PCD owners put the power of their imaginations to work on the artistry of the dolls, animating the inert body. The manufacturers know this very well, and within the limits of price and technique, they build every possible cue into the form and appearance of the doll, seeking to lock their product into the imagination of the purchaser. The collusion of designers and collectors in the quest for realism is largely lost on those who are not party to the pact. Even in adulthood, skeptical males still pose a threat: "It's only a doll," growls Eileen G.'s husband. Eileen cuts back "'It's only a doll?' Whaddya mean '*Only*' a doll?"

In this chapter we shall take a close look at the dolls' bodies, comparing them with real bodies to get a better idea of what, physically, is being manipulated in the making of the PCDs.

BODY FORMS AND FUNCTIONS

The most obvious, and yet the most readily suppressed unreal aspect of the collector dolls is their size: on average just over 14 inches in our sample of 267 dolls, in a range between 8 and 24 inches. It follows that infants are most easily reproduced to scale, which has the odd effect of making these dolls look larger than those modeled on older children. Life-size toddlers and young children bring corresponding increases in cost which puts them outside the PCD range. The effect is also rather disturbing—more of an effigy than a doll.

According to Hall and Ellis in their study of dolls a century ago, "Smallness indulges children's love of feeling their superiority, their desire to boss something and to gain their desire along lines of least resistance or to vent their reaction to the parental tyranny of anger."[1] A massive stuffed animal from FAO Schwarz may be more intimidating than fun. "Little" is plainly a useful emotive word—it is used at least once in 61 percent of the PCD advertisements. But it is also a cautionary statement of fact: the advertisements are careful to state height or length, although they also emphasize that the dolls are "shown smaller than life size" or are "larger than illustrated." Nevertheless, we may wonder how many women, having absorbed the real-talk of the advertisement, are surprised by the diminutive form of the actual product when it emerges from its wrapping. But it is, after all, *only a doll . . .*

The elaborate detailing of the PCDs relates directly to the desire for clearly individualized appearances and personalities. By contrast, children's dolls are highly standardized once a successful design has been established, and the finishing process is mostly mechanized. The sameness of Barbies, Sashas, or Cabbage Patch Kids is very obvious. The American Girls series goes to great lengths to distinguish the identity and biography of each of the dozen or so dolls in the collection, but like every other successful, mass-produced child's doll, the manufacturer has stuck rigidly to a stylized basic design (picture 8). This is usually characterized by a significant deformation, like Barbie's tapered hips and legs, the extreme width of the Cabbage Patch face, or the dimpled toothy mouth of the American Girl. The mass-produced faces look empty when compared with the detailed brushwork of the PCDs. Children are more concerned about functionality in play (bathability, the removability of clothes) than mere prettiness. For them, torsos and limbs matter at least as much as recognizable faces, which may be why children around the world and throughout history have cherished dolls with cuddly bodies and very rudimentary facial features.

At least from a parent's point of view, if you've seen one Cabbage Patch Kid, you've seen 'em all. Little girls seem undisturbed by the swarming clones of Barbie, mainly because they are much less concerned with abstracting identity and personality from the dolls than with projecting their own fantasies onto the mannequin in active play. The clothes and accessories get swapped around from one Barbie to another, and are at least as important as the doll itself. This is in marked contrast to the PCDs, where detail and distinctiveness are all-important. Adult collectors who have dozens of Barbies would never consider buying more than a single Ashton-Drake *Danielle*, unless they were gifts for other people. Unlike Barbie, *Danielle* has to take the initiative, communicating her own personality vividly to her owner's gaze. In advertisements, the PCDs are always photographed solo, graphically detailing individual identity, whereas Cabbage Patch Kids can be illustrated in cuddly heaps. Designers of the PCDs tread a fine line between developing a recognizable product line or collector series within the broader definition of the commodity, and giving each doll its essential, distinctive appearance. Manipulating one of the main proportions (cheek width, eye spacing) is risky, although

Picture 8: Two American Girl play dolls, and the collector doll *Gwendolyn*.
Top left: American Girl Samantha.
Top right: American Girl look-alike doll, supposedly modeled on a real child.
Bottom: *Gwendolyn* (Delton Collectibles).
Photos by A. F. Robertson.

there is ample scope for individuality in detailed molding, brushwork, clothes, or accessories.

Although in display the appearance of the doll may be very convincing, touch may quickly betray the unreality. The shock of this disjunction lurks in the advertising copy: "the porcelain is smooth to the touch—just like a baby's skin" ("Cute as a Button"). But the tragedy of porcelain is that while it allows such marvelous *visual* representations of human flesh, the material itself has a deathly chill. This is counteracted in the advertisements with frequent use of words like "soft" and "warm" to describe complexion. Visually, no other material—gutta percha, vinyl, various sorts of "composition"—can approach the subtle matte texture of fine bisque. With skillful application of color it can capture the quality of "baby skin," which seems so fundamental to perceptions of female beauty and is the holy grail of the cosmetics industry.[2] "His face, arms, and legs are skillfully crafted in fine porcelain, then handpainted for a look of luminous realism" ("You Deserve a Break Today"). "Delicate," occurring in 19 percent of the advertisements, is a useful word implying both fine artistry and fragility. "Untouched" is another rather ambiguous evocation of innocent beauty in the advertisements. But as often as not the advertisement invites buyers to make contact: "cuddle him, dress him, and rock him to sleep" ("It's a Boy").

True to the play/display distinction, the Santa Ynez "Doll and Teddy Bear Tea Fair" in southern California distinguishes categorically between "collectibles" and "huggables." Separating material and emotional values in this way can put doll buyers in a quandary. The "partial" or "porcelain-beanbag" doll is a compromise: the head, hands, and feet may be fine bisque, but the torso has the cuddly resilience and heft of a "real" baby. Although body composition was not mentioned in nearly two thirds of the PCD advertisements, one third were explicitly "partial," and over a quarter of these were also described as "posable." *Amy*, for example, has "porcelain hands, feet, face and eyes, generously stuffed cottony-soft body and life-like combable golden blond hair." "Beanbag" or loosely stuffed torsos and legs can be pushed into poses quite easily, and have a more cuddly, relaxed heft than the pricier all-porcelain dolls: "Her beanbag body makes her posable in so many lifelike ways. Cuddle her just a little, and she'll win your heart forever!" (*Sweet Carnation*).

Two thirds of the PCDs we surveyed are designed as set pieces, in the process of doing something (teatime, playing baseball, visiting grandmother) or acting someone (*Little Bo Peep, Laura* from "Little House on the Prairie") rather than simply "being" a Native American or Shirley Temple or a sleeping infant. One advantage of this is that the doll may not need much further manipulation to display it. Recumbent dolls, 15 percent of our sample, are obviously easiest to display, and very much more likely to be infants. Thirty-six percent, almost all of them children and toddlers, were either sitting or kneeling. Fifty-one percent, including all but one of the adults, were shown standing. Most of the fully upright dolls need supports, usually a rod behind their backs, which can look cumbersome.

Poseability is a virtue mentioned in 16 percent of our sample, but articulating joints convincingly is one of the designer's oldest challenges, especially in full-bodied porcelain dolls. Cords, springs, and rubber bands are needed to hold the members together and allow a little movement, but all of these are liable to some sort of mechanical failure in childish hands. Necks or wrists have to be set in insulating material like felt or plastic to prevent them squeaking or grinding. Advertisers tend to make it very clear if the doll is all porcelain, and thus more valuable and "genuine."

With her stiff articulated joints, a "100% porcelain" doll like *Lil' Punkin* needs a little extra massage from the copywriter. She is "so incredibly real, you'll want to sweep her into your arms! For little babies, every day is full of discoveries! There are chubby toes to explore, tiny fingers to examine, and a cute round belly button to locate. Look . . . there it is! This 'Lil' Punkin' is proud—she's found her belly button for the very first time!"

For all this body-talk, the dolls are "hyperreal" for what they *don't* do. Most obviously, of course, they don't move. It seems that women have never hankered after creepie-crawlie, walkie-talkie dolls. Mechanization is an enthusiasm of male doll designers, and doll museums testify to their ingenuity, especially around the beginning of the twentieth century.[3] But manufacturers have resisted the temptation to mechanize the PCDs. Complete passivity is preferred to jerky movements that are more likely to disrupt than enhance the illusion of reality. One or two dolls (usually ballerinas) rotate slowly on their plinths, but only older children, not the collectors, seem much interested in this sort of animation.

The PCDs are also free of other unwanted body functions. Here is Daniel Harris's disenchanted and characteristically male view of the matter:

> Behind the pleasure we take in the bodies of such cartoon heroes as Kermit and Snoopy is the fear of another sort of body altogether; the distasteful subtext of our plush toys: the excreting bodies of real live babies which, far from being clean and dry, are squalling factories of drool and snot. Our unenviable role as the hygienic custodians of children, whose dirty bottoms we must regularly wipe, noses we must blow, and soiled underwear we must launder, has led to a recurrent parental fantasy, that of the diaperless baby, the excretionless teddy bear, a low-maintenance infant whom we can kiss and fondle free of anxiety that it will throw up on our shoulder as we rock it to sleep or pee in our laps as we dandle it on our knees.[4]

It is clear that even the most motherly of PCD collectors is not interested in such "real child" traits. In this respect, realism in children's dolls runs along a very different axis. In their survey in the late nineteenth century, Hall and Ellis found that play dolls had voracious and indiscriminate appetites—they were served liberal dinners of mud, water, and other substances. One informant remembered that "in my doll weddings, something nice to eat was the chief thing." Some children persevered with the illusion of a full belly to the extent of sewing stones into their doll's clothes.[5] Apart from the odd lollipop or cup of tea, the PCDs are quite abstemious. Piddling dolls gratify little girls' inexhaustible enthusiasm for diaper changing, and if that is not enough there are quite a few dolls which extrude pulp. ("There is a hole in the bottom of each doll's torso," explains doll specialist Audrey Vincente Dean helpfully.)[6] Close inspection of one such pee-poop doll reveals that the holes, one large and one small, are indeed set in the base of the torso, in a shallow boxlike structure that positively shrieks *this is not an authentic body part!*

A few dolls in the PCD range emphasize the wrinkles, pouchy eyes, and splayed legs of the newborn, and clearly respond to a particular sort of maternal craving. In addition to its range of weepy, wetty, drooly dolls, the Peterkin company of Leicester, England, has an Early Moments neonate with a newly healed belly button and chunky, uncircumcised genitals. These may appeal to women in the "empty womb" phase, but the PCDs are overwhelmingly children, and we know of no PCD that possesses what we primly call "private parts." With today's extreme anxieties about pedophilia, few manufacturers are prepared to cater, however innocently, to the wrong market. Any explicit sexuality is conveyed by the extremities of the doll, its face and also its feet, but not the palpably sexual trunk. In the advertising copy, many of the PCDs have "hearts," some have "tummies," but none has bowels or a bladder. Our average porcelain doll collector's enthusiasm for "realism" does not extend either to precision about genitals or to the excitement of plural incontinence. The nearest we get is *Brian* sitting demurely on his potty and a couple of other little lads waving toilet rolls. If you have spent many years dealing with these messy aspects of motherhood, this is one feature of the child you may be happy to forgo. The PCD, immortalized in porcelain, has triumphed over death and its Freudian analogy, feces. The only reference to body fluids we could find in our PCD sample is to tears, as with the "tiny teardrop" of crystal that "rolls down" *Little Bo Peep*'s cheek.

The PCDs emit nothing more disturbing than pleasant odors and tunes. Quite a few of the "angel" dolls play carols and hymns (*Angelique* "doesn't just have the voice of an angel—she has the heart of one too!"), but very few of them actually talk. This may be because technically this is still very difficult to "get real." Around the turn of the twentieth century there were numerous attempts to give dolls voices. This usually involved pulling and releasing a string which made the dolls croak "mama" or more elaborate phrases. Bellows produced bleating noises, and one model screamed shrilly when disturbed. Although very elaborate voices are now put into toys (the various *Elmo*s and *Furbee*s) the PCDs are above this sort of vulgarity. The poet Rainer Maria Rilke recalls being enraged as child by his dolls' reluctance to converse with him, but more receptive owners have always enjoyed their whispered confidences.[7]

We all know the mysteriously primeval, evocative power of smells. A dog's nose tells it whether you are really there or not.[8] Odor is a subtle medium for the PCD manufacturers. Babies and little children have a distinctive smell, very perceptible to childless adults if not to the parents themselves. Homes at this broody stage are pervaded by this milky-poopy odor, which seems to resist efforts to dispel it. So far the doll firms have shown no interest in capturing and synthesizing it with a view to enlivening their product, the way auto manufacturers spray leathery smells into new cars. It is certainly important that dolls should smell right when they are unwrapped. Delicate perfumes are used, mainly in the tissue or accessories, to mask commercial odors like glue. *Caroline*, for example, carries a fragrant bouquet. The most common olfactory additive to the PCDs is baby powder: *Meagan Rose* is "a porcelain-beanbag baby who's truly Heaven Scent. . . . Arriving from a special garden up in heaven, this newborn beauty looks as if she is about to break into an enchanting baby giggle. And the fluffy 'cloud' she lies on bears the fragrance of sweet baby powder."

FACES

"The face," says doll dealer Debbie Madrigal, "is where the money is." For the connoisseur, a cracked leg or loose arm is as nothing compared to a small abrasion on the cheek. How faces look and how they change matter a great deal to humans. Facial expressions, along with gestures and other "body language," play a major part in our communications with each other. Our features are flexible, and we are continually manipulating them to convey a mood, an attitude, an identity. We narrow our eyes shrewdly to look older and wiser, or widen them ingenuously to look younger. "Human perceivers are sensitive to age-related changes in facial appearance and can readily judge the relative age of different faces shown in photographs."[9] We react badly to faces that give us the wrong age and sex cues. In men, "babyish" features are perceived in psychological tests as warm, weak, and naive, and in some contexts wicked (those gangster characters with names like "Babyface" Molloy).[10] Faces are always being scrutinized for information that is conveyed unintentionally as well as intentionally: hence the unfortunate effects for a child of having a face whose layout is "older" than its age, and which therefore has more expected of it and less given to it, and is more exposed to abuse.[11] The "beautiful-is-good" stereotype is hard on us plainer folk, and downright dangerous to the ugly.[12]

Despite differences in facial structure and culture, human beings around the world make remarkably similar judgments about how strong or submissive, sexy or frigid, fickle or trustworthy a person *looks*. Such basic distinctions were as perceptible to the sixteenth-century physiognomists as they have been to experimental psychologists in the late twentieth century.[13] Biologists have assumed that our ability to "read" faces in this way is one of our important evolutionary adaptations, essential to the social as well as the sexual intercourse on which our species depends. A positive, caring response to the infant face is vital to our survival both individually and as a species, and perceptions of youthful attractiveness are important in finding a mate.

The concern with realism concentrates on the head and face of the PCD. A century ago, heads were often sold separately, German artistry in porcelain merging with French expertise in couture to produce the perfect complete doll. Heads were also sold to private purchasers who added bodies and clothes of their own design. It would be very hard to infuse a headless doll with life and personality, much easier to empathize with a doll with a missing leg or hand. Especially in antique dolls, hands and feet have been tiny in proportion to the head. The attention paid to the head is understandable, not least because little children do have proportionately bigger heads than adults. This is linked to the expansion during the course of human evolution of our brains, which outgrew the pelvic capacity of our mothers and now have to achieve more than three quarters of their size outside her body. In its first year after birth the brain doubles in weight, sopping up half the body's available energy, and continues to

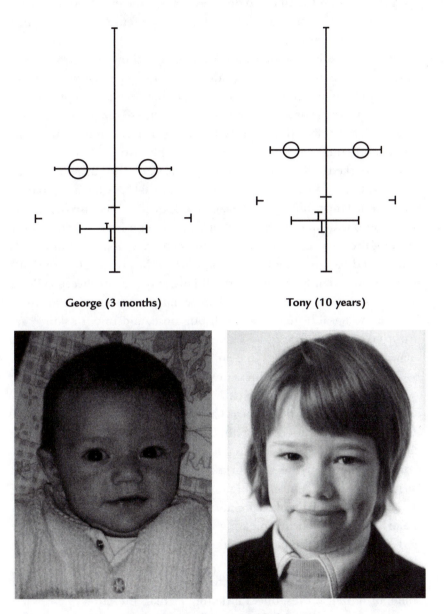

Figure 6-a: Development of facial mask
George, age 3 months, and Tony, age 10 years.
Photos by Elizabeth Stanger.

grow throughout the first two decades of life. One effect of this is that after birth we continue to look a lot more like fetuses than do other closely related mammals.

We have devised some simple diagrams to show as clearly as possible the distinctions between older and younger male and female faces, and how different bits of these faces have been manipulated to make the PCDs. (For an explanation of how these diagrams are composed, please refer to appendix F.) Between birth and early adulthood, both the shape of the head and the layout of the features change markedly. Relative to the size of its skull, the "facial mask" of the infant is very small (see figures 6-a and 6-b). After a couple of years the balance shifts, and the facial proportions increase relative to the cranium. By about ten years of age, the cranium is nearly adult size, but the face continues to grow and change well into adulthood.[14] "Compared to a mature adult, a baby's face has relatively large and wide-set eyes, dainty eyebrows, small jaws, a more concave profile, a small mouth with short lips, a relatively large and protuberant forehead, a low nasal bridge, a smallish pug nose, and smooth skin."[15] As growth is completed, adipose tissue is lost, hair color and distribution change, wrinkles and bags appear on the skin. At this stage we look back with envy at the prettiness of youth (see figure 6-b).

Capturing the distinctive early features of growth is very important in the design of dolls. Most basically, you can make a head look more childlike by increasing the size of the skull, expanding the cheeks, contracting the features toward the center of the face, and dropping them on the vertical plane (see figure 6-c). By contrast, shrinking the skull, emphasizing the chin, nose, and ears, and moving the features upward makes the face look older.[16] If the intention is to make it look aesthetically pleasing rather than "characterful," the left and right sides of the face should appear symmetrical. The PCDs all play safe on this, but the expensive custom-made dolls often do outrageous things with asymmetry to assert "personality"—a crooked smile, or quizzical eyes, one a little higher than the other.

Since the attractive qualities of infantile features were noted by Charles Darwin, they have been the subject of study by biologists, most notably Konrad Lorenz. The assumption is that the more pleas-

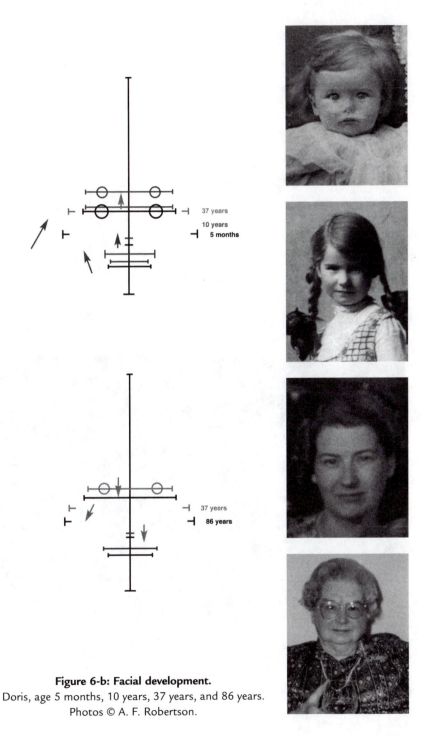

37 years

10 years

5 months

37 years

86 years

Figure 6-b: Facial development.
Doris, age 5 months, 10 years, 37 years, and 86 years.
Photos © A. F. Robertson.

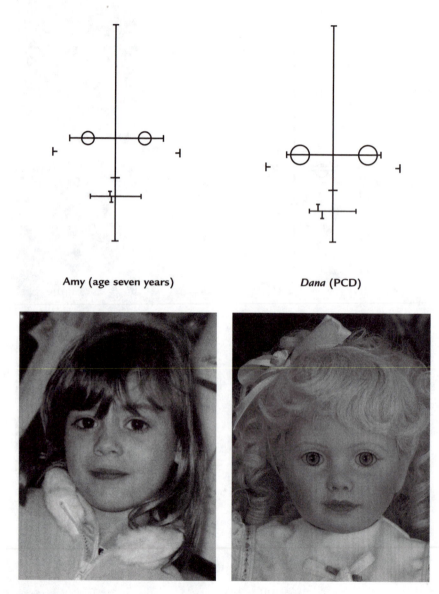

Amy (age seven years)   *Dana* (PCD)

Figure 6-c: Infantilizing facial features.
Amy, Photo by Elizabeth Stanger.
Dana, Photo by A. F. Robertson.

ant we look to our long-suffering mothers, the less likely they will be to abandon us. We evolved physical signals on the infant's side, and receptivity to them on the mother's, which strengthened the bond. Mothers respond affectionately to infant eyes, mouths, and cheeks, and to some degree fathers, too, are drawn into the nurturing conspiracy. Lorenz's summary of these traits in animals seems a little clinical: "a relatively large head, predominance of the brain capsule, large and low-lying eyes, bulging cheek region, short and thick extremities, a springy elastic consistency, and clumsy movements."[17] These features, and the psychic chemistry that is at play, are at the heart of doll design. (It has been argued that over the centuries they have also been bred into lapdogs.)[18]

The evolutionary scientist Stephen Jay Gould points out that "market researchers (for the doll industry in particular) have spent a good deal of time and practical effort learning what features appeal to people as cute and friendly."[19] Biologists have noted an interesting quirk in design: over time, dolls tend to "evolve" along the same axes as the development of humans, but they tend to do so "backward." They begin with more adult shapes, and track back to more attractive infantile patterns. The most famous example of this is the historical development of Mickey Mouse, who appears as a rather nasty pointy-nosed mature rodent in his earliest manifestations, and develops into the chubby-cheeked, wide-mouthed, bug-eyed, chinless megastar we know and love today. Hinde and Barden measured teddy bears in the Cambridge Folk Museum and in a Cambridge store, and found that over time they became decreasingly bearlike and more emphatically babylike. Their heads became rounder, their snouts smaller and shorter, and their eyes dropped lower down their faces. As with Mickey, the effect of this infantile regression was to make them less stern and more lovable.[20]

According to Dunbar, the market is what exerts the "evolutionary" pressure here. The designers themselves are not genetically programmed to make imitation babies—that's why they so often start out with adult forms. "It seems likely that as the design team sits down to consider next year's production models, they opt for those lines that have sold best the year before. They themselves need have no preconception about how bears should look: they merely try the designs that they think people will buy, some of which sell and some of which get left on the shelves."[21] The doll aficionadas would be aghast at such cynicism: doll design is not hard science, not a matter of identifying and replicating infantile forms. Of course dolls, like all successful commodities, are moulded by their commercial niche, but we should not underrate the creative artistry of the designers themselves.

There comes a point when making the doll's face look younger no longer adds to its appeal. The fetus is *not* cute: "Makers of horror movies often design aliens that look like fetuses. . . . With startling regularity, the fetus has been regarded as dangerously anomalous, a symbolically charged entity."[22] If evolutionary design is at work, this repulsion is possibly a disincentive to expending costly mothering effort on premature babies. In tests, pre-term infants are regarded as much less "cute," and hospital staff have to be reminded that they need to be touched and caressed. Perceptions of baby "cuteness" peaks at 9 months for girls and 11 months for boys. The cuddliness ratings of 6–month to 2–year-old boys are much higher than for the new-born.[23] This dangerous fetal threshold may be why "cuteness," especially its commercialization, has recently taken a critical beating. It is, says Daniel Harris, "closely linked to the grotesque, the malformed":

> Cuteness, in short, is not something we find in our children but something we *do* to them. Because it aestheticizes unhappiness, helplessness, and deformity, it almost always involves an act of sadism on the part of its creator, who makes an unconscious attempt to maim, hobble, and embarrass the thing he seeks to idolize, as in the case of "Little Mutt," a teddy bear with a game leg that a British manufacturer has even fitted with an orthopedic boot.[24]

Nevertheless, many cute doll designs, such as the Precious Moments series or the famous Kewpie, look decidedly fetal. Kewpie was the creation, around 1909, of Rose O'Neill, who was twice married but childless, and adored children. She was enraptured with her baby brother Eddie, and devastated when he died at age two. The Kewpies began as magazine drawings based on Eddie, often making serious social observations, and mutated into three-dimensional doll form. The original Kewpie was a naked androgynous "he," which became more infantilized and feminized in the hands of the market and the manufacturers.[25]

A problem about the infant face, from the designer's point of view, is that it is not very characterful. Here's the technical explanation:

> Those of us who are parents imagine all sorts of facial expressions in the young neonate. Actually, observing the infant objectively, we must admit that the expression is often rather blank. The reason is that the facial muscles are busy being used for the massive efforts of mandibular stabilization during infantile swallowing. Eventually the mandible becomes controlled and stabilized more by the muscles of mastication, particularly during unconscious reflex swallowing, and the delicate muscles of the seventh cranial nerve become truly "muscles of facial expression."[26]

Up to puberty, "real" girls and boys are quite similar in physique and physiognomy. Except for the genitals, babies are virtually indistinguishable. Two of the advertisements present newborn PCDs with no reference to gender, and two others encourage the buyer to make her own choice. The difference is the clothes: apart from their pink and blue jump suits the two newborns "It's a Girl" and "It's a Boy" are identical dolls. But from toddlers upward, the older the doll, the more emphatic the gender distinctions. The advertisements are peppered with personal pronouns, so important in the humanizing of the dolls, making it abundantly clear that 81 percent of our sample are girls, 19 percent boys (counting those in the seven boy-girl pairs). Only when the copywriter is deeply in technical mode (jointing, firing, numbering) is the doll referred to as "it."

Gender differentiation in real kids is very much a matter of upbringing—naming, dressing, role training, and so on. If nature is not much concerned to inscribe gender differences on the human body before puberty, it seems that doll designers feel they must. One way of characterizing the effect is to say that while all the dolls should look *cute*, the girls have to do better than that. Psychological experiments have shown that "girls are expected to be cuter than boys, so their cuteness is judged more stringently. Thus, a particular infant will be perceived as cuter if he or she is believed to be male since the standards for cuteness in boys are lower."[27] In the PCDs, and probably in real children too, the implication is that to look better than cute, little girls should also look *attractive*, a notion with strong sexual undertones, which finds expression in the physical design of the doll. We shall explore this in the next chapter, but the effect, stated very bluntly, is to make many of the boys look more babylike, and many of the girls more adult.

EYES

Let us look a little more closely at the various components of facial design. Eyes are how we fix on people—we gaze with them, and we gaze at them. They are, we are told, the window to the soul. They can burn, sparkle, dazzle, they can quench and dim, and they can scare you to death. As the ladies of his local Doll Club got to work on the skeptical Frank, plying him with cookies and juice, he began to get a feeling for the "reality" of the dolls clustered around the participants. "I stared into their eyes. It was as if I was staring at another person. Perhaps it was the ambience of the event but the eyes sparkled, and looked very natural and real."

The aficionadas agree that "the eyes are the most outstanding feature on a doll's face."[28] They are of central importance in the design of the doll and the imaging of reality, and are the most vital signal in attracting or repelling a prospective purchaser. Imagine substituting *Nicole's* "deep brown eyes, framed by feathery eyelashes" with a pair plucked from a Cabbage Patch Kid. With such treatment *Viola's* "sweet, allusive look" would surely vanish. Eyes are mentioned in 40 percent of the advertisements, more than any other body part. We found that there is a more than even chance that anyone, young or old, will refer to the eyes when asked to comment on a doll, and they mention eyes more than any other feature of the face or body.

Jenny is "wide-eyed and eager to please." Our attention pivots on the eyes, and they seem to change, both momentarily with our moods and more durably as we get older. The notion that little children have much bigger eyes is something of an illusion. The size of our eyes does not change much as we grow, but their proportions and position in relation to other facial features do. During the first 15 years of life they *seem* to get smaller as the jaw lengthens, the cheeks get less chubby, and the cranium becomes proportionally smaller in relation to the whole "facial mask." Accentuating the illusion of sweet, wide-eyed childish innocence in doll design is more a matter of tinkering with cheeks, chin, and brow than simply blowing up the eyes themselves (see figure 6-d.) To do so produces gross effects that may please some but can easily look grotesque. Children examining the PCD advertisements were quick to spot the general tendency to exaggerate the eyes (Emily: "too big, too wide . . . too many lashes . . . she has a funny look"). By comparison, play dolls usually have quite small and unostentatious eyes, and baby effects are achieved mostly by expanding cheeks and foreheads and reducing chins.

The eyes of most PCDs are acrylic, which is cheaper, more easily molded and colored, and can look more convincing than glass, which is preferred in antiques and higher quality PCDs. Technical references to the eyes have a particularly alienating ring (*Peanut* has "big blue glass eyes"), and there is something about repeated use of the phrase "hand set" that induces a wince (*A Friend in Need*'s "hand set brown eyes are tender and warm").

Nearly all the dolls' eyes are set centrally, presumably because they have the virtue of returning the gaze directly. However, there is no doubt that part of the striking success of Georgetown's *Caroline* is her meaningful sidelong glance. In the early 1920s Simon & Halbig made a doll with "flirty" eyes, capable of sidelong movements, but none of the PCDs have eyes that move.[29] Nor do any of the PCDs have mechanical eyes that open and close. While this is important in children's play dolls, adults find the recessed, clacking eyes distractingly unreal, and unnecessary if display is the prime function. Liza, now a grandmother, said she never liked mechanical eyes, mainly because the eyeballs rolled down drunkenly as the lids descended, and they tended to jam. To release them involved screwing the head off the doll and poking

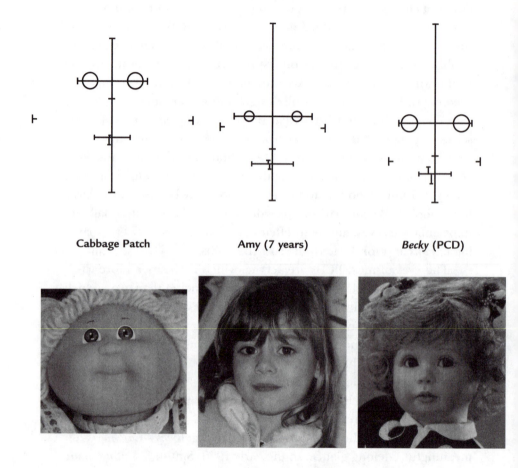

Cabbage Patch   **Amy (7 years)**   *Becky* (PCD)

Figure 6-d: Comparison of doll face forms.
Play doll—Cabbage Patch, photo by A. F. Robertson.
Real child—Amy, photo by Elizabeth Stanger.
Becky, © 1992 The Hamilton Collection, Inc. Bets Van Boxel, Artist.

around inside. Nearly half of the neonate and infant dolls in our sample had closed eyes, the advertising copy drawing attention to other features like the "Soft folds of skin under his eyes." The dolls with permanently closed eyes were disliked by children—for play they must wake up. While many people point out that the fixed stare of the porcelain doll can be disturbingly unreal, our suggestion that they might be equipped with an intermittent blink was greeted with amused horror by adults and children alike. Realism has its limits.

Of the dolls with open and clearly visible eyes in our advertisement selection, half had blue eyes, two fifths brown, and one fifth green. The preference for blue partly reflects the Caucasian bias of our sample (86 percent), 60 percent of which had blue eyes; and partly the fact that the iris and sclera of even dark-skinned children may appear blue when they are very small.[30] As with hair, the color darkens in the first two or three years of life. Of the 71 (26 percent) that we classified as infants or toddlers, nearly a third had closed or indistinct eyes; of those we could see, 64 percent were blue, and 29 percent were brown. While this roughly corresponds to what we would expect of real children, we noted that the blue in the PCDs is very bright and limpid, not the rather dull hue of the newborn.

There's more to a doll's eye than a glass marble or acrylic chip. Eyebrows and eyelashes are very important in the modeling of children, probably because as they look upward at us as adults, their eyes widen, and their eyelids and brows are raised.[31] "Looking up at you with his bright blue hand-set eyes, he's sure you'll take him home to love" ("You Deserve a Break Today"). Eyelashes are proportionately longer in children, which is why adults have to exaggerate them cosmetically to recapture this youthful appearance. *Cinderella*'s "enormous blue eyes are framed with real lashes." They are of course synthetic, probably nylon or "Kanekalon."[32] In the antique or high-priced dolls they are made of fine bristle or animal hair.[33] On the other hand, eyebrows are much finer on small children, thickening after puberty, so we have to pluck them later in life to keep that innocent look. Advertising copy for the PCDs stresses the delicacy with which they are painted, and there's no doubt that bushy eyebrows would look unappealing, or scary, on a doll.

MOUTHS, LIPS, TEETH, CHEEKS

In studies of facial attractiveness, the mouth is second in importance only to the eyes.[34] The formation of the mouth may be a decisive difference between dolls for play and the PCDs. But once again, the facial environment of the mouth matters at least as much as its specific size or shape. Cheeks therefore loom large in the calculus: "When children are very young, their cheeks are puffed out with 'sucking pads.' These fleshy areas on either side of the face elicit a powerful emotional response in adults, particularly women."[35] A byproduct of plump cheeks is the dimple, most visible when the facial muscles are pulled into a smile. Babies can be persuaded to smile quite readily, doubtless because it encourages us to reward them with our attention.[36] This reinforcement may be related to the capacity of dimples to signal prettiness into adulthood, and (on the principle that girls have to try harder to look cute) for the observed tendency for dimples to last longer in girls than boys.[37] However, as the proportions of the face mature, pudgy cheeks look much less attractive. In tune with the lengthening of the adult face, aesthetic interest seems to switch to the "height of the cheekbones." Hollywood gossip about facial modification among the stars has it that "In order to create the caved-in facial look that was uniquely hers, Marlene Dietrich had her upper rear molars removed early in her career."[38]

Cheeks are mentioned in 12 percent of the doll advertisements, lips in 7 percent, and teeth in just 1 percent. Prominent pink cheeks are an assurance of health, a matter of obvious maternal interest. With their full, flushed cheeks and clear translucent eyes, the PCDs lose no opportunity to signal the bloom of youth. *Stevie* is "hand-painted to highlight his look of glowing good health." *Alicia* has "cheeks all aglow with a hint of blush." In the nineteenth century new materials and production techniques allowed manufacturers to pursue more exact realizations, especially in skin texture and color and the luminosity of the eyes. Today, only the most expensive "character" dolls look pale, skinny, or misshapen.[39] This is probably a "runt of the litter" stimulus designed to elicit a protective or nurturing response. One student observer felt that PCDs took images of health to the point of deformity: with their "swollen legs, stubby fingers, and bloated cheeks . . . their bodies appear defenseless and dejected, begging for our attention."

There are some marked differences in the mouths of antique, collector, and children's dolls, and real live kids (see figure 6-e). The nineteenth century bisque and parian dolls have vast cheeks and tiny cupid-bow mouths. Designers of children's dolls also inflate the cheeks, and the relative unimportance of the mouth is suggested by the thinness of the upper lip, and minimal attention to details of texture or color. Some are distorted with a circular hole to take a feeding bottle. Highly stylized dolls like the Cabbage Patch Kids have vastly exaggerated cheeks and rather mean little lips. By contrast, many of the PCDs have very mature-looking mouths. The inflated lower lip is often suggestively wrinkled and may be picked out with artful brushwork in two or more colors: *Hannah*'s "hand-painted lips are softly puckered, a rosy peach to match her cheeks." "Pouty" is a word which recurs in the advertisements and TV sales shows.

The mouths of many antique dolls were executed very perfunctorily: a sketchy cupid's bow, a simple split line, even just a red dot. The breakthrough came around the middle of the nineteenth century when dolls started to smile: "The effect was enhanced when two bisque teeth moulded in a block were pasted into the mouth behind the upper lip."[40] Upper teeth seem to have been considered prettier than lower teeth—though one classic German doll has an open laughing mouth with two lower teeth and a protruding tongue.[41] Toothy effects are not always pleasing, though they appear quite often in play dolls (for example the American Girls series). Although mouths loom so large in the PCDs they are usually shut, smiling or not. Representing teeth and the moist inside of a mouth convincingly requires careful modeling and painting, and is thus more likely in the expensive dolls. Realistic representations of children must also confront the awkward problem of "mixed dentition" in five-to-nine-year-olds, the "ugly duckling" stage with its concatenation of baby teeth, gaps, and emergent "big teeth," which can look quite scary in a small mouth. Adult teeth help to give the jaw its heavier, grown-up appearance, and without them the older face can seem to collapse into an unpleasant caricature of an infant. Perhaps because we associate

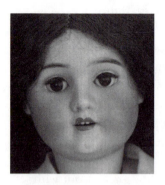

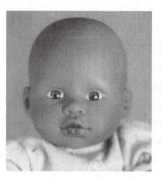

Doll by Schoenau-Hoffmeister. Antique c. 1906; 33 inches, bisque head, cloth body. Photo by A. F. Robertson.

Gabrielle: vinyl doll, 18 inches. Max Zapf, Rodental, 1997. Photo by A. F. Robertson.

Hannah ("Hannah Needs a Hug.") © 1992 Ashton-Drake Galleries. Theo Menzenbach, Artist.

Hilary © Dianna Effner

Alba (four years old) and her doll. Photo by A. F. Robertson.

Fig 6-e: Mouth forms.

tooth loss with aging, toothlessness is not generally considered attractive, even in a neonate.[42]

NOSES AND EARS

The cartilage of ears and noses continues to grow slowly throughout life, which may be why these appendages never loom large in dolls, unless they are adult caricatures.[43] In the European traditions from which the PCDs emerged, the aesthetic preference has been for daintiness. The modeling of the ears is a good indication of quality and price, and they are prominent only in the more expensive "character" dolls. The PCD designers have not gone to great lengths to replicate those strange whorls, folds, and flaps of skin. In cheaper dolls attention to the ears is minimal, and they are occasionally entirely absent, especially if they are covered by hair or headgear.

Ears may be tucked out of sight, but it would be hard to avoid the nose, sitting as it does right in the center of things. "Every doll has a nose, however minimal its indication."[44] Noses are mentioned in just 5 percent of advertisements, usually accompanied by the word "dainty." *Tiffany* "is lovingly hand-painted right down to the sprinkling of freckles across her pert little nose."

HAIR

Hair, on the other hand, is the crowning glory. On the cheaper dolls and on infants, hair is lightly molded on the skull and painted, or simply brushed on with light color. Representing "real" hair is a major technical challenge. The wooden dolls of the seventeenth and eighteenth centuries often had wigs nailed to their heads, and the later wax dolls had hair painstakingly inserted into their scalps, half a dozen at a time, with hot needles. With the nineteenth-century concern for realism, elaborate wigs of human hair or mohair were pasted onto the scalps of the pricier porcelain dolls.[45] Although rarely specified, the hair of all dolls in the PCD range is clearly synthetic. To get real human hair you have to move up several hundred dollars to the expensive custom-made range.

Hair is important for rather different reasons in play dolls and the PCDs. Children like to work on the hair, brushing, washing, and trimming. This has been the cause of much devastation wreaked on expensive dolls that parents might have hoped would be carefully preserved. The child, subjected to many haircuts herself, may reckon that if the doll is as real as she imagines it to be, its hair will soon grow back. When she was little, Doris cut *Rose Vanilla*'s (real) blond hair to shreds, and for nearly a century she has had to hide her shame under a little embroidered cap (picture 9). Eileen G. remembers: "I had my mother's doll when I was little. Her doll would go back to about 1906 or 1908. And it had a long wig with curls, but they made me have a Dutch bob. And I didn't know what I was thinking but I cut my doll's hair. . . . It was just why should she have curls when I didn't? That was it."

Eileen's grandchildren are up to the same game:

Q: Do you like Barbie? Do you have any Barbies?
A: I had one, which I shaved his head—her head. [Laughter]
Q: Why?
A: I don't know! I just felt like it. She's like—keeechh! [whipping hair off]
Q: Did you actually cut it all off with scissors?
A: Yeah—it still has a little hair.
E: We actually got rid of most of our Barbies. I just have about three now.
A: We were cutting their hair before we got rid of them. And I thought it looked really cool with a shaved head.

While some have criticized the hipless, skinny-legged design of Barbie as a fashionable inducement to anorexia, the more plausible explanation emerges if you watch little children at play: Barbie's legs function as a handle (picture 10). This is one reason why the wide-hipped "Happy-to-Be-Me" substitute offered to progressive mothers never caught on. Even a very small child can grasp Barbie's legs in one fist, while the hair (profuse and loose on the basic play versions) is groomed vigorously with the other hand. For the convenience of the

Picture 9: *Rose Vanilla*, **without her bonnet.**
Doris's doll, acquired sometime between 1910 and 1920. Porcelain head
and full, painted composition body, about 15 inches, made in Japan.
Rose Vanilla was named after a favorite dessert. She wears Doris's own
first baby dress. As a child Doris cropped its hair.
Photo by A. F. Robertson.

Picture 10: Rosie, age 3, grooming Barbie.
Photo by Elizabeth Stanger.

budding hairdresser, there are Barbie-type dolls which consist simply of a head, mounted bustlike on a stable plinth. There are even "cut-and-come-again" models which allow the child to pull more hair out through holes in the scalp after each trim.

Attention is drawn to the hair explicitly in 17 percent of the PCD advertisements. Catering for the play-display ambivalence, a few of the more expensive dolls have hair that's brushable. Neatly and permanently coiffed hair is an important selling line, and TV presenters point out that up-market dolls get the individual attention of "real live hairdressers." It is clear that hair can be overdone, especially if it gives the toddler or child doll a precocious, adult appearance. A common criticism was that the hair on some PCDs was "just too much." One little girl described *The Gibson Girl's* emphatically big hair as "flumpy." As for color, all the blond-haired dolls (38 percent of our sample) were of course Caucasian. We classified 34 percent as "brown" or "auburn," 14 percent "black," and 5 percent "red." All of these were clear, positive hairdresser hues. We identified 5 percent as "fair," that almost uncategorizable "mousy" color so common in Caucasian populations, which is rather too drab for the doll reality.

EXTREMITIES: HANDS, LEGS, AND FEET

"From her crimped honey-blonde tresses to her shapely pink toenails, she's absolutely detail-perfect" (*Sunday's Child*). Although a little lower on the schedule of design priorities, the limbs, hands, and feet of the PCDs can be very important in building the illusion of reality. Legs are referred to in 27 percent of the advertisements, mostly to affirm that they are fully modeled in porcelain. Convincing articulation of the limbs to the torso is another big challenge. Historically, "well-designed thighs were an essential feature in a doll, to enable her to sit as naturally as possible."[46] Like real infants, baby dolls usually have curving legs, the soles of their feet pointing inward to assist balance. All-porcelain dolls can feel clunky, but the joins between cloth or beanbag bodies and the porcelain extremities on the "partial" dolls can be disconcerting.

"Everywhere, one trait parents play close attention to is how plump the baby is." Unlike many other mammals, a human infant is designed to survive for many days off its own body fat.[47] No doubt high infant mortality rates in the nineteenth century made pudgy dolls particularly appealing. The hands of play dolls often look like stubby paws. Accurate details seem to matter less than the capacity to pass easily through sleeves, or to grasp with opposed thumbs and fingers. For their part, the PCD advertisements linger lovingly on "chubby little hands" and "delicate curled toes." Hands don't seem to have quite as much sensuous appeal as feet. Detailing the crinkles and crevices adds to the affective allure of a doll—indeed there is a whole barefoot doll collection called "Footsies." *Good as Gold*'s "pudgy baby toes look so real, you expect them to wiggle!" *Hannah*'s have "the natural dimples of a little girl," and *Little Bit of Sunshine* has toes that have "the natural creases of an infant." On *Holly*, "even her miniature toenails have been painted." The advertisement for *Playing Footsie* asks us to admire how it "pulls its bootee off and wiggles those tiny pink toes!" (note the avoidance of gender pronouns for this infant):

> Superbly sculpted in a lifelike pose, the baby actually seems to be caught in action. Just look at that exuberant expression, those chubby legs and the dimpled hand tugging at the bootee! The baby's head and limbs are crafted from fine bisque porcelain to reflect every adorable detail. Its precious features are painted entirely by hand. Notice the radiant complexion and rosy knees. Even the baby's eyebrows are delicately colored to match its wispy blond hair. From head to toe Playing Footsie is a collecting treasure!

Scrupulous attention may be paid to shoes (mentioned in 8% of the advertisements):

> "*Kimberly*' is amazingly realistic, from the top of her glossy dark curls to the tips of her pretty summer shoes."

> " . . . from her bright little face to her polished shoes, [*Roxanne*] looks a picture."

One of the Shirley Temple dolls boasts "lace-trimmed white socks and white lace-up shoes on her little feet." A selling point on the most expensive dolls is that the shoes are made by "a real shoemaker."

CLOTHES AND ACCESSORIES

Clothes and shoes have a sensuous quality that is very important in realizing the dolls. "Peeking from below her dress are pristine white pantaloons and a slip trimmed in delicate white lace. And, her real leather shoes are tied with blue satin ribbons!" (*Virginia*). Clothes are very important for the "play" element in PCDs:

> "Mommy has just finished dressing little 'Stephanie' in her brand new pink romper. Accented with dainty flowers, mauve piping and delicate bow collar, it's just the outfit for such a precious little girl."

> *Lauren* "has been trying so hard to be good! Mommy said she could wear her new pink romper all day long if she promised to be a precious little angel."

> *Danielle* is "all cozy and warm in a custom-designed romper suit of softest flannel and delicate lace, with lovely little rosebuds around the neckline. With a matching bonnet and darling, hand-tied booties."

Describing clothes is plainly important in conveying quality and value, and on this topic the advertisements are in full gush. Sensuality matters a great deal, but so too do the material values. A change of garments, even a few home-made touches, can decimate the value of a "serious" collector doll. Here, the copywriter can make technical connections with the dress-making skills of enthusiasts. *Alicia, the Gibson Flower Girl* wears "pretty peach shoes adorned with lovely baby rosebuds" and is "authentically dressed in sumptuous ivory satin with five full yards of delicate lace and 180 full inches of pretty peach ribbons." "*Tiffany's*' costume has been lavished with loving detail too, from the rosebuds and lace on her bonnet, to the eyelet and ribbon trim of her pale pink dress, with scalloped lace edged petticoat and ribbon tied shoes peeking from beneath." But it's not necessarily all lace and frills: *Buckwheat* may be "crafted of fine, hand-painted bisque porcelain," but "he is dressed just as we remember him . . . baggy sweater, shorts, droopy socks and scruffy shoes that were always too big."

Eighty-one percent of our PCD sample were "accessorized" in some specified way, other than their garments. These objects ranged from rocking horses to toilet paper, from caterpillars to kittens, and from bowers to bassinets. Flowers and fruit made frequent appearances, often in conjunction with the name of the doll: *Apple Dumpling, Sweet Strawberry, Peaches and Cream, Cherry Pie, Blackberry Blossom, Blushing Rose, Shy Violet, Lavender Dreams*. Accessories are very important in adding verisimilitude: the advertisements invite us to marvel at the *real* wooden chair, or 24-carat gold-plated charm, or "silvery" buttons.

AUTHENTIFICATION

The text that accompanies the dolls—the advertising copy, packaging, birth and adoption certificates, the guarantees of satisfaction—works hard to authenticate them and to boost the illusion of reality. A word that crops up frequently in the advertisements is *faux*, French for "false." This is applied to clothes, accessories, trimmings, and even to body parts: "faux fur," "faux pearls," "faux eyelashes." Faux is a classier word than "imitation" or such kitsch phrases as "leather-like," "suade-cloth," or "pearlized." The ambiguous reality of the dolls is often maneuvered into "quotes" or *italics*: *Little Teardrop*'s "tiny mouth seems to quiver as she '*weeps*,' and her hand-set blue eyes are filled with tenderness." The dolls' names and title themes, their miniature accessories, and many other hyperreal touches are rendered this way.

The way we use the word "incredible" these days is loaded with irony. We usually mean that something is "wonderful" or "amazing," rather than literally "unbelievable." Still, the frequent use of the word in the doll advertisements seems to put our credibility to the test:

"This baby is incredibly lifelike" ("Someone to Watch Over Me").

"Such an incredible likeness of Shirley Temple—from her

renowned dimples, to her cute button nose and radiant smile—has never before been available in a collector doll!"

"Elke Hutchens has given *Little Eagle Dancer* a charming, incredibly lifelike face."

"Expertly sculpted; incredibly lifelike" (*Julia*).

Stretching credibility is dangerous. Take it in one direction or another and it becomes either brilliant or stupid, blissful or dreadful. Such effects should never amount to more than simple reality in the eyes of the beholder for whom they are intended. In the case of the PCDs this involves some delicate collusion between producer and consumer.

THE ARTIST AS TECHNICIAN AND MAGICIAN

"Let the grace of Ann Timmerman's artistry take you to a more perfect world" (*Apple Dumpling*). The artist-designer (some prefer the phrase "doll artisan") is the central figure in this collaboration between manufacturer and collector.[48] She is technician and magician, the link between craft and art. It is she who authenticates the doll as an object with both life and material value. She puckers lips and curls eyelashes, and her name is stamped on the back of the finished product along with the registration number and logo. Her reputation translates into cash values. She is almost indispensable to the presentation of the product—only 13 percent of the PCDs in our sample of advertisements have no named artist-designer.

It is possible that a manufacturer could achieve the full hyperreal effects by evolutionary trial and error of the sort imagined by Dunbar (see above), or by employing a skillful cynic who has studied the development of the product. Competition has certainly brought ruthless imitation of one manufacturer by another. But these are clumsy and risky tactics when it is possible to capture and incorporate into the production process the imagination of the collector herself. This is done very directly. There is ample testimony that many of the "doll artists" are, or were, enthusiasts like the collectors themselves.

Manufacturers are well aware that such women can cut through the mysteries to design the little masterpieces that sell so well. The companies advertise in the same media they use for sales (magazines, TV, the Web) for people with a flair for design. They are invited to submit samples for inspection, and if they are successful they are recruited on a freelance basis, part of the "outsourcing" network on which the industry depends. With the development of a personal profile and possibly a name change, they may eventually be contracted to the company as a star designer, like Ann Timmerman and Pamela Phillips of the Georgetown Collection, Elke Hutchens of Danbury, or Diana Effner and Kathy Barry-Hippensteel of Ashton-Drake.

The identity, real or possibly fictitious, of the "doll artist" responsible for each individual creation has become a central feature of the PCD merchandising and packaging of the dolls. She is written up in the magazines and makes celebrity appearances on the TV specials. She is represented to the clientele as a sort of spiritual sister with the special capacity to "bring the dream to life." *My Little Ballerina*, for example, "is issued exclusively from the Ashton-Drake Galleries under Ms Hippensteel's *From Her Heart to Your Home* seal, your assurance of the finest in quality and craftsmanship." Although she is very rarely pictured, the doll artist is represented in the advertisements as a vibrant youngish woman with special gifts and qualifications in art and design. She appears on the TV merchandising shows as an older woman who has made a hobby of modeling and dressing dolls, and has graduated to "serious" craft work. Her children have grown up, and she now has the time and resources to experiment, sculpting and firing her own dolls and selling them on a modest scale.

On the Home Shopping Network's *Gallery of Dolls* sales show, Rose Pinkul tells the host, Tina Berry, how she came to design dolls like *Heidi* ("a closed edition, only 500 pieces worldwide, two payments of $69.50 . . . "):

> I used to be a design draftsman, and I worked with men all day. I supervised the drafting room, and I had to get out with some women, I just really did. And so I went to a doll class—I just happened to be passing a doll shop, and I said wow! I didn't know people did this! So I went in, and I started taking classes. I'm an old

art student from way back, I've always been a painter and I've sold work in galleries and things like that, so I picked it up pretty quickly. And in pretty much no time at all I was sculpting my own dolls. I was a victim of the recession and got laid off, and my husband said, well, you know, you've always wanted to do something with the dolls, now's the time. And he stood behind me, and I started sculpting and really surprised myself, because I never thought I'd be a sculptor. I was always into graphics.[49]

Rose has designed PCDs including *Brittany—All Tuckered Out* for Danbury, but also makes one-off originals that sell for more than a thousand dollars. "My men and ladies are around fifteen hundred. But they wear silk, and human hair wigs, glass eyes . . . "

In the advertisements the artists are "acclaimed" or "celebrated," and a large proportion of them have won industry prizes. The French and German origins of the antique dolls means that any sort of European connection is stressed in the advertisements: *Nicolette* offers "exquisite European artistry at a noteworthy price!" *Danielle*, designed by "renowned European doll artist Gudrun Haak," is "an heirloom selection from Franklin Heirloom Dolls' exclusive European Doll Artists Collection. This outstanding collector doll represents the 'best of the best' from Europe's top artists."

Only 5 percent of dolls with named artists in our sample were designed by persons who are not clearly identifiable as women. The most conspicuous of the male PCD designers is "Titus Tomescu," whose "Cute as a Butt-on" was a best seller and a winner of the industry's Doll of the Year award in 1994. This all-porcelain doll comes from the "Barely Yours Baby Doll Collection," and appears in the advertisements with her buttocks coyly displayed. The artist's first design for Ashton-Drake, it "touched a responsive chord in the public's heart." The company's Web site explains: "As a classically trained artist influenced by the European Great Masters, Tomescu's understanding of human physiology extends beyond his ability to craft lifelike facial features. Collectors also exclaim over the realistic sculpts of his dolls hands and feet. With care and sensitivity, he suggests the play of muscle and tendon beneath porcelain 'skin.'"[50] People of both sexes tend to rate this as one of the "most realistic" dolls in our sample of advertisements. Like other dolls designed by men it is more simply "childlike" than other dolls in the PCD range that incorporate adult female facial characteristics. The men also design explicitly female adult mannequin dolls. There are a few male designers who enjoy a special celebrity status among the enthusiasts for their costly custom-made dolls. Those produced by Phillip Heath are among the most spectacularly realistic, by any standards, we have ever seen.

HYPERREALITY

For Baudrillard, the French philosopher who gave currency to the term, "hyperreality" is the situation when a model of something becomes in some respects more real than the thing it is supposed to depict. In the past, for example, we drew maps by looking at landscapes, but now we make landscapes by drawing maps.[51] In some respects the PCDs have become a means for measuring-up children rather than the other way round, in the way that we depend on maps rather than the landscape itself tell us "how things really are." Feminist scholars have written a great deal about how dolls have served as models of etiquette and lady-like behavior for young girls over the last couple of centuries.[52] Popular phrases like "she's a doll" suggest that we do indeed project doll qualities (perfect looks, perfect passivity) onto women.

The designers play on the ancient magic of dolls—their power as imitations of ourselves and the people around us, or as we would wish ourselves and those around us to be. Simply scaling down a real child and turning it into porcelain would not be enough. The effects must be boosted by deforming the body, especially the facial features, in particular ways. What is excluded (genitals, movements, sounds) is as interesting as what is added—the manipulations of the eyes and mouths, or the inscription of numbers and signatures. Also intriguing is the way the dolls play on a different combination of senses (sight, touch, smell) than are normally at play in our perceptions of real kids. As if to compensate for the difference, manufacturers stress the authenticity of brushwork, clothes, accessories, and biographical details.

The dolls are locked into the bodies and lives of the collectors in ways that the women can *feel* even if they cannot find the words to describe it. It is the rest of us, lacking the passion that gives the dolls their veracity, who are at a loss to understand. For the collectors, "perfect" (occurring in 16 percent of the advertisements) is never too finely distinguished from "real" (21 percent). Of course, it's the skeptical observer rather than the women themselves who think the realism is overdone. The collectors are content with the plain, breathtaking actuality they see, and regard the likeness of doll and child as a bit of magic that allows them to establish a virtually human relationship.

Many doll makers, especially the smaller artisanal ones producing special and expensive dolls, have a very explicit sense of vocation—they are proud and happy in their magic-making. This is not without risks: the magic of any doll is its capacity to foster make-believe, but overstepping the bounds of reality in the creation of a doll (making a fantastically accurate imitation of a child, or *believing* that a chunk of wood or a bundle of rags *is* a child) can be dangerous. The company of dolls can be immensely gratifying or very dreadful, depending on how the thing looks and how you feel about it.

A central theme of this book is that the doll collectors themselves are complicit in this magic, and in the making of the commodity at every level. They know what they want, and they are able and willing to talk about it. But they cannot answer all our questions—why this eye shape rather than some other, why the delicate lip puckering that few children's dolls bother with. To know more about why the PCDs look the way they do we have to dig more deeply into the lives of the collectors than even they themselves may be able to dig. Ironically, this means that we have to part company with them for a while, to use a bit of physiology to detect exactly which features of these dolls are distorted in the pursuit of hyperreality.

We have touched several times on one basic aspect of the unreality of the PCDs that requires an agonizing suspension of belief: unlike the collector herself, the doll defies death. She or he is a small bastion against the ravages of time as they affect us as mere human beings, a consolation for the absence of real children or their loss to the wider world, and for the shadowy immanence of our own mortality. But it is this very inertia, this stillness of the doll, that allows us to inscribe on it any truth, or any lie, we wish.

Chapter Seven

Forever Young

"Her timeless features are alive with curiosity."

In this chapter we return to our title theme: these dolls are lifelike, but in the collector's dreams life is also doll-like: stable, immortal, perfected. The magic of the dolls is in their exquisite resolution of the contradiction that they must look so much alive, while defying the most basic principle of life, that change is inevitable. So much is expected of them: they must convey perfected, timeless images of children who were never born and children who have grown up. But most challenging of all, they hold a magic mirror up to the collector herself, presenting palpable, composite images of childhood enriched by a lifetime of experience and yet secure from the ravages of time.

In this chapter we look more closely at how these complicated expectations are realized in the bodies of the dolls. What are the techniques for constructing the physical features of the dolls so that they can, in the eyes of these particular beholders, say more about human bodies than even a real human body can?

CAN DOLLS GROW?

The question is a matter of anxiety to some children. "Will my dolly ever grow up to be a real lady doll?" asked one child a century ago. In their classic study, Hall and Ellis found that children often imagined that their dolls grew as they did, although some were perplexed by the illusion that as they themselves got bigger the dolls seemed to grow smaller. In the hands of their owners, dolls could live expansive family lives. The dolls of one twelve-year-old got married and had children: "She tucked them up under the clothes and pretended they were born the regular way, when they grew up one was Longfellow and the other Louise Alcott [*sic*]."[1]

For developmental psychologists, the doll is a "transitional object," whose function is to assist its owner in moving from one life stage to another—infancy to childhood, pubescence to adulthood. In practice, there is some ambiguity about this: must the doll part company with the owner, or can it accompany her? Transitions are painful: the effectiveness of the doll's mediating role depends on how thoroughly it has bonded with the child, but this only makes the agony of eventual separation more intense. In guiding this process, adults can appear horribly capricious. It is usually they, not the children, who choose the dolls in the first place, and encourage the child to identify with them. We have, says Bernard Mergen, "a subtle mirroring process in which the adult world imagines the child in the form of the doll while the child is simultaneously encouraged to recognise itself in that form."[2] And then, having encouraged the child to be doll-like (stable, charming, docile), the adults insist that the child "grow up" and put away childish things. "Persius tells us how the young Roman girl, when ripe for marriage, hung up her childhood's dolls as a votive offering to Venus."[3] Little wonder that the shock of separation can then be intense and very confusing. Around 1812, Jane Welsh, an only child who was later to marry the writer Thomas Carlyle, was admonished by her middle-class parents that "a young lady reading Virgil must make an end of doll play." Taking the literary cue, Jane decided that her favorite doll "should die like Dido." She staged an elaborate suicide, in which the doll stabbed herself and set herself ablaze. When the flames dramatically engulfed the funeral pyre, Jane collapsed in a fit of hysterics.[4]

When its transitional task is done, the best a doll may expect of the human growth cycle is to retire to a closet to await the appearance of the next generation of children. As she enters this limbo the bond between herself and her owner may be marked in some special way. When *Rose Vanilla* (see picture 9) was retired, Doris put her own christening gown on her, investing the doll with part of her childhood. This is a variant of the custom in which a woman put the dress of her last baby on a doll, usually her own, sometimes that of her child. The doll would then be displayed as a token of the transition of the woman out of the childbearing stage of her life.

But owners who have invested much of themselves in their dolls may hope to see them accomplishing life's transitions in parallel. The classic teddy bear seems to have had a knack for fudging his age and continuing to live companionably with his owner. The multiple manifestations of Barbie make her more versatile than other dolls in adapting to her owner's changing expectations (hair-on-a-handle, fashion mannequin, cabinet collectible). But if she is to survive, the doll may also have to be given a thorough makeover to meet the redefined expectations of the adult. Or else a new actor, like the PCD, may be brought into play.

"Today's baby dolls are so realistic that they can do everything except grow."[5] But that may be their greatest virtue for the woman who feels abandoned by her children, relegated to the empty nest, and confronted with old age and intimations of mortality. The irony for the doll is that she must be both *lifelike* and *timeless*—an eternally ambiguous "transitional object." Translating this into body language is an intriguing technical challenge in the manufacture of the doll.

MAKING FACES

The facial signals of the PCDs may at first sight seem confusing. Some aspects are babyish, others are very adult, and the "unnatural" mixture disturbing. Various analogies came up: the playful incongruities of Mr. Potato Head and his infinitely variable plastic features; police Identikit or Photo-Fit pictures; or the "age progressions" on the missing-children cards that accompany junk mail.

Malleability of this sort is actually important for the development of real bodies. Our various parts (legs, guts, noses) are genetically programmed to develop together in a particular way, but there are subtle differences in the arrangement of details that give each of us our distinctive—and changing—appearance. Later in childhood, for example, our feet get embarrassingly large, in preparation for the additional body weight that puberty will pile up on top of them. The fact that the basic scheduling of body-part development can be "rearranged" is very interesting for biologists: the potentially variable timing of the growth of one body part in relation to others ("heterochrony") is one of the mechanisms of evolution. A much-discussed aspect of humans, for example, is that three quarters of our cranial growth is delayed until *after* we have been born. Compared with our primate relatives we look premature, but we are predisposed to think of this as "cute."

For us ordinary mortals, appearances of "normal timing" are basic to our understanding of good looks. We are unhappy if we have a very old-looking nose in the middle of our otherwise young-looking face, and we may make big cosmetic efforts to disguise the incongruity. Our understanding of our changing selves lags: we usually feel younger than we evidently are, and we resent that nose, these ears, or this stoop for betraying the more youthful selves we would prefer to be. If we are a bit vain, we work on our bodies continually, seeking to arrest or redirect natural processes of growth, whether by dress, diet, makeup, or surgical interventions. But the best we can do is tinker with the different parts of our bodies before the battery of clocks that control them finally snuff us out altogether.

The doll is immune to the way of all flesh, and on her we can play at will with tricks of heterochrony, reassembling body parts, changing proportions, hiding and revealing, overlaying older features with younger ones. On the doll we can reorganize the human physique, refashioning in porcelain images of ourselves that are freed from the constraints of time and growth. Like a surgical nose job or the application of rouge, the effects will be a "lie," pleasing some and startling others. One effect of these manipulations is to make it difficult to give a doll (or someone heavily made up) a precise "age."

Unlike us, dolls can deviate from normal patterns of growth. They can ignore genetic rules and "grow younger" as well as older. In surveying and measuring the PCDs we noticed both these apparently contradictory tendencies. Some dolls have regressed: although dressed and described as little children, they have the facial proportions of newborn infants. A larger proportion in the PCD range have developed in the opposite direction: they look precociously adult. This older appearance can be difficult to pinpoint because it is usually superimposed on the babylike face: the doll has been simultaneously infantilized and matured—"adultified." Although this very ambiguous appearance can be achieved by tinkering with all parts of the facial mask, the most noticeable tendency is to keep the upper part of the face babylike, while making the lower part, especially the mouth and jaw, look grown-up.

In the following discussion of these two sorts of facial distortion, the infantile and the adultified, we shall compare the PCDs with the faces of some *real* children. We must recognize, of course, that the arrangement of these kids' features is continually developing, and matching their growth with the "ageless" dolls is tricky. Nor should we hold up any of these children as an ideal: there is no such thing as 100 percent normal growth, which is why some children sometimes look prettier, or older, or more doll-like than others. Nevertheless, there are some striking contrasts.

LOOKING CUTE: INFANTILIZATION

"The brink of toddlerhood is a time when a child's proportions seem so perfect—so rounded, cuddly and appealing," says Diana Effner, the designer of *Angel Face, Sugar Plum,* and other successful Ashton-Drake dolls. Our word for this is "cute," which usually means, says biologist Sarah Blaffer Hrdy, "a round head, big eyes, and plump cheeks."[6] In tests, people give higher "cuteness ratings" to faces with more prominent foreheads, lower eye heights, bigger eyes, and smaller features below eye level—the immature faces in our growth diagrams.[7] These infantile characteristics seem to be the foundation on which we build a lifetime's appreciation of good looks. Careful testing indicates that even babies like looking at babies; and young adults prefer little children's faces to older faces.[8] "Mean," an older-sounding quality, is usually the word offered in these experiments as the opposite of "cute," especially in children's ratings.[9]

Why little children should like cute dolls, and why this preference should linger on in the PCDs, is not entirely obvious. If, as is often argued, the business of play is to socialize children, would we not expect to see a lot more adult-looking dolls? Instead we find, around the world, a more obvious tendency for children to have dolls that are younger, "cuter" looking than themselves.[10] The conventional, adult logic here is that the children are practicing to be parents. This is what doll play often looks like, and some people's memories of this are very categoric. When she clapped eyes on the baby doll she had longed for on Christmas morning, one little girl was deeply moved: "I don't remember being able to speak at all. I simply clutched my baby to me in ecstasy. . . . It was very like birth. I was a mother, no doubt about it."[11]

A view that has surfaced relatively recently is that the doll is at least as likely to be substituting for a younger *sibling* as for a daughter or son. Little children are not simply "playing" at being fathers and mothers, they are enacting their very serious responsibilities as auxiliary parents ("alloparents").[12] Human babies can—and need to be able to—attach themselves to anyone who will care for them. If our physical survival and socialization depends so much on the attention of people even just a little older than ourselves, then signaling our cuteness and dependency to *everyone* is a vital adaptation. In the hurly-burly of the subsistence community, the most immediately accessible "alloparents" are likely to be siblings or other children. Anthropologists in the field are very familiar with the sight of tiny children competing to lug even tinier siblings around on their hips or backs. Those who lack little brothers and sisters make do with doll substitutes. "As the child grows he or she may need a charge of some kind," says doll specialist Audrey Vincente Dean, "and it is then that the doll—requiring to be dressed, undressed and tended—comes into its own."[13]

The small child may make little distinction between a new doll and a real baby, which is why the gift of a baby doll may successfully

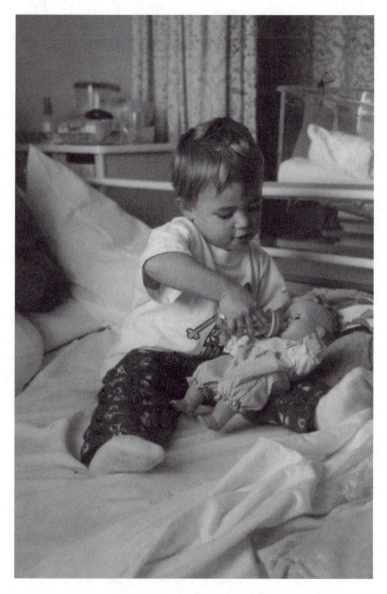

Picture 11: Rosie nursing doll.
Rosie, age 2, was given the doll by her grandmother upon the birth of her brother.
Photo by Elizabeth Stanger.

distract its attention from the arrival of new brother or sister (picture 11). This may partly explain why little boys, unless they are specifically discouraged by social rules, may be as interested in dolls as are girls. They are not "mothering" or "fathering" so much as "brothering." If the experience of alloparenting comes before parenting, it might even make more sense to think of mothering as a development of sisterly practice. It may also explain why "the oldest child often cares less for dolls or is interested in them later than the younger children."[14] The elder child is busy looking after the "real thing," and it's the younger child who has to make do with a surrogate.

This view of doll play doesn't square with the entrenched psychological view of siblings as potentially lethal rivals. Is it our modern, patronizing view of the incompetence of children which leads us to assume that play that is affectionate and careful rather than hostile or abusive is "mothering" rather than "sistering" or "brothering"? Should we not think of the child-child bond, and its extension to doll play, as an aspect of human reproduction separable from the usual adult, sexualized sense of the word? The Freudian assumption that a small child sees in her doll an image of the penis she envies or of her own self in erotic entanglements with her mother seems a good deal less obvious than the simpler notion that she is commonly charged with the care of people younger than herself—and may feel anxious or guilty about being negligent. If so, the signals to which children respond in play dolls (yielding bodies, big searching eyes, extended arms and clinging fingers), may be subtly different from those directed at the breast-feeding mother. Study of doll "play" would surely tell us something important about how humans organize reproduction, but alas "the doll barely exists in psychological theory. . . . Together with the psychology of the female child, [dolls] have been dismissed from the history of psychology."[15] In the meantime we are left with more questions about the "infantilization" of dolls in general, and the PCDs in particular, than we can hope to answer. But at least we are alerted to the probability that the PCDs contain layers of imagery extending back to the experiences both of the care-receiving infant and the care-giving child.

Some PCDs push infantile appeal very close to the fetal form. The downward displacement of *Sarah Jane*'s facial mask and the size of

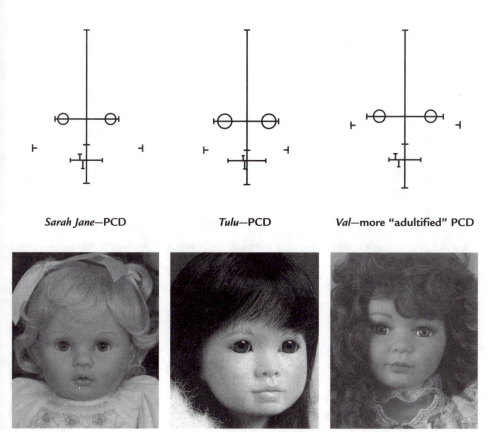

Sarah Jane—PCD   *Tulu*—PCD   *Val*—more "adultified" PCD

Figure 7-a: Infantilization.
Sarah Jane, photo by A. F. Robertson.
Tulu, © Linda Mason.
Val, photo by A. F. Robertson.

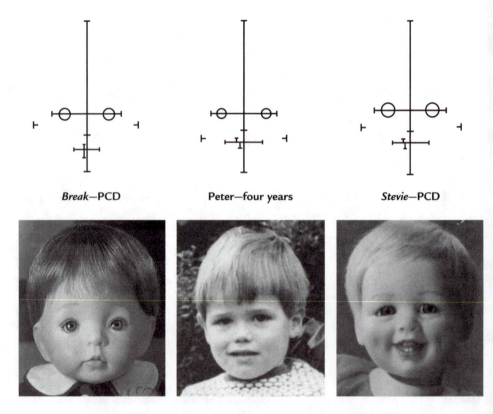

Break—PCD Peter—four years *Stevie*—PCD

Figure 7-b: "Infantilized" and "normal" boys.
Break ("You Deserve a Break Today") ©: Dianna Effner.
Peter age four years—photo by ELizabeth Stanger.
Stevie ("Catch Me if You Can")
© The Ashton-Drake Galleries. Mary Tretter, Artist.

Tulu's eyes are exaggeratedly babylike (see figure 7-a). To the extent that they are distorted at all, the boy dolls are infantilized, not adultified—they do not bear detectable traces of either adult female or adult male features. *Stevie*, often rated "quite normal-looking" has exaggeratedly large eyes compared with the real four-year-old Peter, but looks much less fetal than the "You Deserve a Break Today" doll (see figure 7-b). Early in the project we thought that the boys would be made to look effeminate, but on closer inspection we could see few indications of this. Skewing of physical features toward those of girls would in any case be hard to detect, since in reality children of both sexes have very similar bodily proportions until puberty. Nor was there any tendency toward the frocks and frills in which Victorian mothers dressed up their little boys. Instead, cute boylike behavior was more likely to be stressed (dirtiness, mischief, busyness, and so on), eliciting motherly attention. "Catch me if you can," cries *Stevie*, "a mischievous little boy caught in the act" of unfurling toilet paper.

LOOKING ATTRACTIVE: ADULTIFICATION

Studies of what people find appealing in faces have noted a basic distinction between the "cuteness" of little children and the "attractiveness" of adults.[16] "Attractive" has more sexual undertones than "cute": perhaps we could say that while little children emanate cuteness to solicit caring responses from all parties, attractiveness draws the attentions of adults to one another.[17] From an evolutionary point of view, an implication of this, not always pleasing to women themselves, is that "looking attractive" is basically about pleasing men. Visible nubility (hormonal status, fecundity) has been the key to a "well-designed female," says the evolutionary psychologist Donald Symons. "That adult female sexual attractiveness declines systematically with observable cues of increasing age is a theme that runs through the ethnographic and historical records, folk tales, great literature, less-than-great literature, movies, plays, soap operas, jokes, and everyday experience."[18] Little wonder that older women should prefer to hark back to their reproductive heyday in visualizing "good looks."

Women also find women attractive, but how their ideas differ from those of men is still, we have found, wide open to happy-hour debate. The differences are not simply a matter of cultural conditioning or personal whim; they diverge according to age and growth. Set the experimental task of designing "beautiful" female faces, 40 20-year-olds (20 men, 20 women) produced a composite whose nose-chin proportions were significantly *shorter* ("typical of an 11- or 12-year-old girl") than the composite of their *own* faces. The "beautiful" ideal also had fuller lips in the vertical dimension and smaller mouth. They looked, we might say, pretty cute. What, Symons wonders, is the evolutionary logic of this apparent enthusiasm of fertile males for prepubescent females? And why should their female age-mates concur? The answer seems to be that for all its infantilization, the beautiful composite still "appears to be a sexually mature woman."[19]

Our conclusion is that these 20-year-olds (drawn from that inexhaustible experimental pool of college students) have a characteristic way of assembling an idealized face that includes features younger than their own—some of which may be a holdover of the sibling care signals. Certainly, they are not assembling an attractive face in a way that would appeal to doll collectors some 30 to 60 years their senior. The dainty jaws and "pouty" lips of earlier mating days may matter to some of these women, but others evidently like a more robust jaw. This, Symons notes, is a characteristic women acquire during and after childbearing. The assertion of this motherly feature in the PCDs confirms his intuition that the template for attractiveness is not static or confined to a single life stage, but is "updated throughout life."[20]

CUTE *AND* ATTRACTIVE

How our appreciation of facial attractiveness *grows* is not well understood.[21] It seems that as we grow up our aesthetic preferences do not so much change as accumulate, adding new layers of definition to what we consider appealing. Since people generally rate younger faces as more attractive, middle-aged and elderly people give relatively high attractiveness ratings to more mature (female) faces.[22] This has interesting implications for the PCDs: older people may find certain features attractive that younger people would find displeasing.

While baby dolls designed for little children don't have to do much more than imitate babies, many of the PCDs look beyond the child and add facial features that are distinctly adult. It is as though these dolls, making their late entry into women's lives, look back across a wide range of life experiences, bringing a broader conception of attractiveness to bear on design. The doll is thus less an idealization of a child at a *particular* age than a collage of features that were idealized at different ages. The simplest example of this is the ever-popular bridal doll, which appears not only as an adult effigy but as a child or baby doll wearing a wedding dress: a fusion of two blissful but separate transient episodes in a woman's life. It is the tendency of many of the dolls to include *nubile* features that observers find sublimely disturbing. If a child's face and body are designed to inspire nurturing and protective behavior rather than eliciting a sexual response, more mature come-on signals are disconcerting.

The nubile component was added to the PCDs mainly by keeping the eyes unnaturally large and the cheeks plump, while emphasizing the cheekbones and increasing the proportions of the lips and jaw. *Caroline* (see figure 7-c) is a fair representative of these tendencies. In the words of her designer, Pamela Phillips, she is "both childlike and ladylike." She has a very different facial mask from the more infantilized *Gwendolyn*, although the prominence of *Gwendolyn*'s lips adds adult weight to the lower part of her face. The Lenox Christening Doll is a curious example of the tendency to adultify (picture 12). Her mouth and jaw are much more robust than we would expect of an infant. "Crafted of bisque porcelain and meticulously hand painted, she is portrayed sleeping sweetly, with an expression of pure innocence."

Careful examination of all the doll faces in our sample suggested that a convenient measure of the general tendency to infantilize or adultify was the height of the nasal septum (where the nose meets the upper lip) in proportion to the length of the whole face. An infantilized face with a small jaw and large forehead would tend to draw the septum down the center line of the face; and an adultified face would tend to raise it, making way for the bigger jaw. To check this, we picked out 118 of the girl dolls we classified as "children" in our sample, notionally in the post-toddler to pre-pubescent category, and for

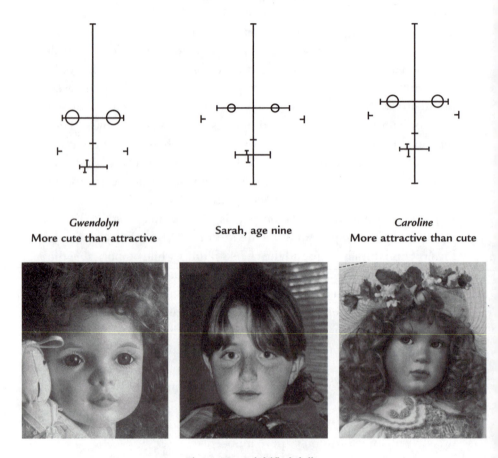

Gwendolyn
More cute than attractive

Sarah, age nine

Caroline
More attractive than cute

Figure 7-c: Adultified dolls.
Gwendolyn © 1992 The Ashton-Drake Galleries. Sandy Freeman, Artist
Sarah, photo by David Lawson.
Caroline © Pamela Phillips, photo by Dave Tuemmler, Stretch Studio.

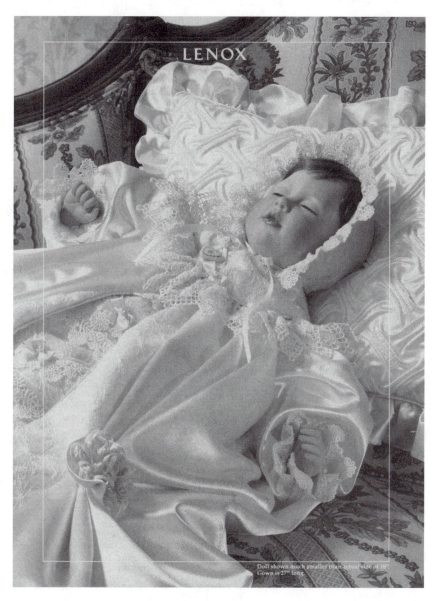

Picture 12: The Lenox Christening Doll.
© Lenox, Incorporated 1992.

which we could take satisfactorily clear measurements. On average, the septum was placed about a third of the way up the chin-to-crown line, but there was a surprisingly wide range of variation in septum height, amounting to a quarter of the length of the face (see figure 7-d). The dolls were distributed quite evenly along this range, with a slight bunching at the higher and lower septum heights—suggestive of the divergent infantilizing and adultifying tendencies.[23] More tellingly, the mean position of the septum—35 percent of the way up the face line from the chin—was considerably higher than one would expect of a real child. Modal images of facial growth suggest a septum height of about 15 percent for toddlers and 26 percent for girls close to puberty.[24] A rapid survey of a dozen (real) girls in the same child category as the dolls produced an average septum height of 25 percent, with a much smaller range of variation—7 percent. Mature adult women have a septum height around 29 percent up the face line.

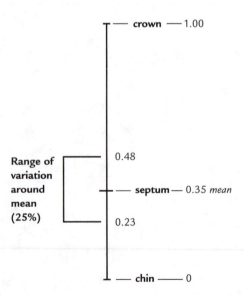

Figure 7-d: Mean and variation in the height of the nasal septum in sample of 118 girl dolls.

We wondered who, specifically, might be the model for the nubile features we detected in the dolls. Assuming that it might be an iconic face from the typical collector's nubile years, we thought the emphasis on cheekbone and jawline suggested Katharine Hepburn. In her studio portraits, the proportions of her lower face are indeed very similar to those of a PCD like *Caroline.* We asked as many women as we could who they regarded as the most conspicuous beauty icon of the 1950s and 1960s, and the answer almost invariably was Marilyn Monroe. Looking at various publicity stills, we could see a strong resemblance to the ambiguous cute/attractive dolls. In many shots, Marilyn's eyes (heavily made up and probably retouched in the photos) look very babylike. Laurence Olivier, with whom she starred in *The Prince and the Showgirl,* is said to have remarked of Marilyn: "Look at her face. She could be five years old."[25] Marilyn herself was painfully aware of the massive public attention paid to her appearance. Among the many rumors (it was even said she had six toes) she is supposed to have had plastic foam implanted very early in her career to correct a receding chin. Cosmetic surgery not long before she died indicated that most of the foam had been absorbed.[26] In her movies and publicity stills she usually drops her jaw, suggesting her concern to emphasize her mouth and chin. Her makeup was less of a secret: her formula for beautiful lips in the 1950s "included three shades of lipstick, plus a gloss of wax and Vaseline."[27] But beyond mere physical appearance there are some affecting similarities between Marilyn and the timeless, lifelike doll. For Gloria Steinem she is "the woman who will not die." In her own unfinished autobiography Marilyn says, "I knew I belonged to the public because I had never belonged to anything or anyone else."[28]

Until we know much more about the forms and functions of bodily appeal later in life, these observations about cuteness and attractiveness can only be speculative. Now that we live so much longer, the physical, social, and emotional processes of aging have become much more interesting, raising such new and intriguing questions as what attracts a child to a grandparent, and vice versa. Nature—so say the biologists who study it—is not much concerned with what happens to the organism when its reproductive days are over. But we, as individual organisms, have a personal interest in our continuing lives that may or may not have much to do with the survival of our species. Theories of evolutionary adaptation and natural selection, preoccupied with the activities of nubile women, could not readily predict the face forms that would please a woman who has already grown up and raised a family, or which of these she would want to see inscribed on a doll. At this stage in her life it seems likely that her preferences are retrospective, more concerned with how she has actually lived than with her mating prospects. A doll that can express her cumulative experiences as a child, a mother, and a grandparent may be particularly gratifying. Superficially, the appearance may be disturbing to others, but to "read" this palimpsest you need a sympathetic understanding of the life that it inscribes.

We are ruled by time. In real life our bodies and our experiences are inexorably arranged in sequence, connected by the imperfect links of memory. As life proceeds we need to stem the flow, to make some durable sense of our own identity: "This is who I am, because this is who I have been." We try to make the things that matter to us tangible. Transposed to the doll, life's experiences are inscribed in three dimensions, not four: the memories are laid one on top of the other, a palimpsest that begins with a child's doll and an antique fashion doll, and piles upon it images of a son, daughter, or grandchild, and serial memories of a self. The result, from the perspective of biological science, is of course an intricate lie.

NARCISSISM AND NOSTALGIA

On reflection, it is understandable that the collectors should have found it hard to pin down for us exactly who they felt a particular doll represented. A much-loved doll could bring together images of somebody else's child, of the collector's child, of her own self, or of all three. This triple identity is hinted at in advertisements: "Stevie is sure to bring a smile of recognition to anyone who has raised a family . . . or was ever a child!" Nostalgia is an ever-present motif. *Roxanne* "looks a picture":

> With butterflies in her tummy and pencil and notebook at the
> ready, Roxanne takes her seat at her brand-new desk. And she pre-

pares herself for the most exciting day of her life. Because now,
she's "almost a grown-up," you see. Immaculately dressed in her
new green-and-white checked uniform, she's made sure her straw
boater is on straight. Her well-brushed hair shines in a perfect
plait, complete with matching green ribbon. And from her bright
little face to her polished shoes, she looks a picture—just the way
you did on your first day at school.

The practical problem so cleverly addressed in PCD design is how to
convey on one small porcelain body an image of childhood refracted
by the experiences of parenthood. Sibling, child, other, self, youth,
maturity. . . . If dolls have to say so many things, is it any wonder you
might need to collect a couple of hundred of them to hear all the
voices?

What does a collector really mean when she says of a doll, "She
reminds me of me"? The most obvious answer is that she sees in the
doll an image of herself at some specific, blissful, earlier stage in her
life. For many collectors, that may be enough. But viewing the dolls as
reflections of the full passage of a woman's life suggests another interest: their design was not simply bent on capturing the qualities of
childhood but also of the collectors' own emergent adult selves. This
makes the adultification of the dolls look less simply erotic. The doll
can compound a series of autobiographical images that superimpose
memories of being a mother on memories of being mothered; and
memories of being an attractive young woman on memories of being
a cute child.

The child is ever present in all of us. How could it be otherwise?
You only get to be an adult by virtue of having been a child—not the
other way round. The difference today is that we have become more
self-conscious about this inherent childishness to the extent that we
have turned it into *another self,* a little person crouching inside us,
rather than an accumulation of life experiences which *actually are* us.
"Inside every woman is an adult and a child" says an advertisement for
Barbie Collectibles. "They should get to know each other better."[29]
"The child in you will dream of bright summer days in the park. . . .
The adult in you will admire her authenticity, craftsmanship and timeless quality."[30] Marilyn Ivy traces connections between the post-1960s

fixation on child abuse, the ADVO cards ("Have you seen me?") for missing children that accompany junk mail, and the adult's quest for the lost "inner child" today. All three are concerned with *finding* and *healing*, and restoring the *functional family*. "To assert that we can reclaim our inner child," says Ivy, "is potentially to deny the fragility of a temporally limited childhood in a desperately narcissistic attempt to subsume child, adult, and parent within oneself."[31]

Many of the PCDs seem bent on this act of healing, of encapsulating a self and a whole life. "Dolls are a passion and a fantasy to me," says Coleen E. of Virginia:

> I came from an abusive home and was moved around quite a bit;
> each time my favorite dolls and toys were left behind in the shuffle.
> I have been able to replace these long-lost dolls. I can play with
> them and look at them, seeing their beauty and feeling that I can
> almost rewrite my childhood to one of beauty and pleasure with
> carefree thoughts as it should have been.[32]

The fusion of self and doll is an old tradition that lives on. In the nineteenth century, little girls were given dolls that supposedly looked like them and with whom they could identify directly in play. Early in the twentieth century doll manufacturers sponsored annual "Children's Days," featuring doll contests and parades in which girls dressed as dolls competed with one another for prizes.[33] A current version of this is the American Girl series, in which the child can dress like the doll and act out the various "historical" personalities described in the accompanying texts. In 1993, the My Twinn Doll Workshop of Englewood, Colorado, struck the mother lode of matching dolls. The firm specializes in dolls

> individually created to resemble one special person . . . your child.
> Starting with the Personal Profile (TM) and recent color photos of
> your child, artisans carefully select the face shape, skin tone, eyes
> and hair color. Then they cut and style the hair, paint the eye-
> brows, fit the eyelashes, and more, to capture your child's look . . .
> right down to the freckles. My Twinn dolls are created to be more
> child-like than doll-like, which makes them more fun to play with.

They are soft, cuddly, and durable; and they become a treasured keepsake for years.[34]

The My Twinn Workshops place much of the responsibility for composing the doll on the purchaser, who must select eyes, skin color, face shape, hairstyle, and so on. from the catalog. Parents tend to be more delighted with the results than are the children, which is good enough for the manufacturer. Sarah sent hers back for remedial treatment, and other girls we spoke to were frankly skeptical (picture 13). Anna does not identify with her American Girl look-alike (see picture 8), a doll produced on the same principles: "the hair's too long, for a start." Other firms have been quick to get onto the bandwagon, producing more exact replicas of the child—for a price. These of course are more likely to be display dolls for parents rather than play dolls for the child. We know of at least one case where a doll was produced to memorialize a child who had died.

The My Twinn repertoire has expanded to include matching clothes for the child and the dolls, and a mass of other accessories like beds and stands. Further spin-offs from the original idea are Cuddly Sisters and Cuddly Brothers dolls for your My Twinn doll (even dolls need dolls); and Lovable Sisters, a pair of dolls, one on the same scale as My Twinn (20 inches) and one smaller (14-inch) Cuddly Sister. The next development was seemingly inevitable. The firm now offers the When She Was a Child doll, which is assembled by referring to photos which the buyer supplies. "Now teens, mothers and grandmothers can also have a My Twinn doll made to resemble them when they were 3–12 years old. . . . Like portraits, these beautiful dolls become personalized home decor pieces."[35] This narcissism offers much scope for psychoanalysis. Of all toys "the doll comes closest to imitating the child's own body."[36] The child becomes the doll becomes the adult: at one stage it acted out the child's grown-up fantasies (playing parent, teacher, doctor, shopkeeper). Resurrected later in life as a PCD it acts out an adult's place in the child's world: the adult becomes the doll becomes the child. This may involve some subliminal auto-eroticism. One of our researchers found evidence of this in the passionate hues (reds, purples, mauves) and the persistent theme of consumption (peaches, cherries, cream, candy, lollipops) that abound in the PCDs.

Picture 13: Sarah with her My Twinn, and My Twinn's own look-alike doll.
Photo by David Lawson.

But "it should be noted that I never found a boy doll with a piece of fruit."

The nostalgia and narcissism have another dimension. "To collect artifacts from the past is to own the past—and sometimes to imagine a better past than the one that actually existed."[37] If the dolls help to place the person in a life, they also help to place that life in history, real or imagined. "Those innocent eyes . . . that soft loveliness. Where have you seen such a girl before? In the Portraits you remember—of children long ago" (*Peaches and Cream*). The dolls are of course ideal-izations: "That's how I wanted to be." Most little girls like to look grown-up now and then, and many of the dolls are depicted dressing up, making up, and looking precocious. Imitating antiques, many of the dolls reach back to the older woman's own childhood, and bear her back to a "sweeter, calmer, gentler" world. "*Alice* recalls the very feeling of a place and time you thought was gone forever." These vari-ants on the PCD theme are described as "Victorian" or (in the United States) "turn-of-the-century" or "1900s" or, more vaguely, "period" dolls. In this category too are "portrait" dolls, some of them "recre-ated from famous paintings." But these nostalgic dolls could never be mistaken for a nineteenth-century Bru or a Jumeau with their bulbous cheeks, tiny mouths, and bug eyes. "I think the features on the more modern dolls have softened and seem to reflect some long-lost mem-ories and/or innocence for us collectors. . . . For me they become part of my family and home. And, of course, they know they are loved."[38]

Dolls are "transitional" in the further sense that they help us to find our place in society, as children and then as grown-ups. We take our places in history as particular sorts of persons (rich, French, black, female), and the dolls take their place in history as particular styles (Kewpie, Bébé Bru, Kachina). Our understanding of how we were or how we are, at particular times and in particular places, may in some small way be measured by the sorts of doll we treasured. Already, the collector doll of the late twentieth century is becoming a curiously distinctive marker of a particular sort of person and histori-cal period. But, to complete the circle, if a particular type of doll, famous in one period of history, fails to "grow" and change, she dies— she becomes junk or, at best, museum stock. The marvel of Barbie (two are sold every second) is that she has developed, moving cautiously along the fine line of teen/preteen trendiness, pleasing those who love her "timeless" qualities while adapting to the next generation of enthusiasts.[39] "I was a Barbie girl," a young mother told us, a little ruefully. "So is my daughter."

DEATH AND RESURRECTION

The PCD advertisements are rich in the vocabulary of timelessness: forever, endless, always, cherish year after year, for years to come. But the agony of imminent mortality always seems to lurk behind those assurances of permanence. The memento mori is the death of the doll in its owner's adolescence, often at the hand of the owner herself: witness the guilty allusions to abuse and abandonment, and the purposeful efforts to make reparations through doll collecting later in life. The often vexatious role of the doll in life's transitions may make it ambiguously an object of hate as well as love. In his poem *Hope*, written in 1782, William Cowper declared:

> Men deal with life, as children with their play,
> Who first misuse, then cast their toys away.

Hall and Ellis's inquiries turned up numerous cases of doll abuse by children, echoed in the guilty admissions of careless treatment by the women with whom we spoke.[40] Dolls have been spanked, whipped, stabbed, hanged, and dismembered; and more routinely scolded, or deprived of sleep, food, and company. Designing dolls that can withstand the punishment is a challenge for manufacturers. Perhaps the most advanced abusable doll is "My Blim Blam Baby," designed in Canada and made by Zapf in England, whose vinyl body "can sustain any amount of manipulation."[41] Is it a little ironic that dolls, on the receiving end of so much violence, should be used so widely in the diagnosis and treatment of the abuse of small children?[42]

In the nineteenth century, death was a central feature of children's doll play. Children fantasized endlessly about languishing illnesses, funerals, burials, and resurrections.

We had a regular graveyard at the end of the garden where we
buried pets and dolls. When dolly had lain there a few days we dug
her up and played she was a new baby and dressed her in long
clothes.

When my brother set the dog on my doll, it was so badly torn that I
put it in a box and had a funeral. We cried real tears, but at night
it pained me so that I went alone and dug her up, kissed, hugged
her and said I was sorry.[43]

When her much-repaired doll finally broke, one little girl had a little
funeral for her in the backyard with a cold cream jar for a headstone.
"And it broke my heart," she later recalled.[44] Mourning clothes were
routinely included in the wardrobes of more elaborate French dolls
in the mid- to late-nineteenth century. In the United States, middle-
class girls were encouraged to imitate the fashionable funeral rituals,
and "fathers constructed doll-sized coffins for their daughters' dolls
instead of what we consider the more usual dollhouses."[45]

We should remember that in those days death was a frequent and
intimate domestic fact of life, and that one of the advances of the
twentieth century was to make it much less so. People normally died
at home, and their bodies were laid out there. The heavy toll of infant
mortality made small corpses—and the anguish, guilt, and fear they
inspired—all too familiar. For centuries, dead infants had been
fetishized as cherubs, and it seems very probable that the putti that
swarm over Baroque religious architecture influenced doll design—
or possibly vice versa. In Freudian analysis, "The angel is the idealized,
pure form of Eros prior to organic involvement and differentiation
into sexes—the archetypal image of primary narcissism. The doll, on
the other hand, embodies the victory of death and destruction over
the life of the organism—the archetypal image of primary
masochism."[46] If this is so, it makes the angel-dolls in the PCD range
(a dozen in our sample of advertisements) doubly and dreadfully
interesting (picture 14).

Part of this morbid ritualization was the assertion that the dolls
had *souls*. "Doll funerals probably appealed to girls in part because
the domestification of heaven (along with the beautification of ceme-

Picture 14: *Noelle*, the Christmas Angel.
Georgetown Collection, c. 1996.
Photo by A. F. Robertson.

teries where families found rest and recreation) made the afterlife sound fun. For others, the staging of doll funerals was an expression of aggressive feelings and hostile fantasies"—dramas of resistance, according to Formanek-Brunell.[47] We could find no evidence of doll collectors today having funerals for their dolls, but something very evocative of burial and resurrection is apparent in the rituals of wrapping and unwrapping, opening and closing boxes, which are so much a part of PCD play (picture 15). The link to the antique tradition of the "trunk doll"—one that "lives" in a display box, along with her wardrobe and accessories—is sustained in recent PCDs like "My Little Ballerina."

If nineteenth-century children were much affected by the immanence of death at home, the doll collectors today are more affected by the immanence of death in their own lives. Unlike the earlier period when this was a routine, even fashionable topic of conversation, death in our times has been described as a kind of obscenity. It was not easy to pursue this topic with our informants; indeed denial of mortality seemed to be central to the passion for dolls.

Twenty percent of the doll advertisements use the word "forever," but in two distinct sorts of context. The first suggests that the doll, your relationship with it, and the special gifts it brings will be immortal:

"Reach for the sunlight, and bring warmth into your heart forever." (*Amber*)

"You are assured of *Shannon*'s heirloom quality—in a signed, hand-numbered, limited edition that you will treasure forever."

"A Victorian Beauty of unparalleled splendor. An heirloom to cherish forever." (*Rose*)

"Order now . . . To enjoy the magic forever." (*Winter Romance*)

A best friend to last forever! (*Mary Elizabeth*)

The second context suggests an altogether darker meaning:

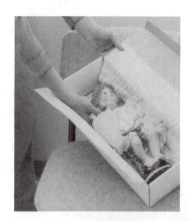

Picture 15: Unwrapping and wrapping
Noelle, **the Christmas Angel.**
Photos by A. F. Robertson.

"Issued in an edition ending forever in 1994, after which molds for
this doll will be broken and no more porcelain will ever be made."
(*A Friend in Need*)

"Hurry . . . *Boo Bear and Me* is issued in an edition ending forever
in 1991, after which molds for this doll will be broken and no
more porcelain will ever be cast."

". . . limited forever to 100 firing days." (*Clarissa*)

"A hand-numbered Limited Edition which will close forever after
just 45 firing days." (*Heather*)

Here, the collision between the sacred object and the commodity is
devastating. Little wonder that quite early in the 1990s the advertisements steered away from dreadful words like "broken." The advertisement for *Cute as a Button* explains more palliatively that she is
"issued in an edition ending forever in 1995, after which no more
porcelain will be cast." Today, even the hellish evocation of "firing" is
used very sparingly.

These double promises of immortality and mortality express the
age-old ambiguity of the doll as a live/dead object. The passion of life
and the dreadful intimations of death that are embodied in dolls are
densely evident within and beyond the Western traditions. The theme
runs through paintings, literature, drama, the movies. Maybe men,
already very much on the edge as far as dolls are concerned, are more
sensitive to their dangerous ambiguities. For observer Dan Fleming,
dolls like *Fiene*, "a little girl of curly-haired, pouting, dark-eyed
provocativeness is unforgettable in a slightly disturbing way: except
for enthusiasts immune to the thought, it is somewhat unnerving to
find such a 'realistic' child frozen for our gaze."[48] The most famous
discussion of this is an essay by the German poet Rainer Maria Rilke
on the macabre wax dolls created by the artist Lotte Pritzel early in
the twentieth century. He could be reacting to the PCD genre today:

To determine the realm in which these dolls have their existence,
we have to conclude from their appearance that there are no chil-

dren in their lives, that the precondition for their origin would be
that the world of childhood is past. In them the doll has finally
outgrown the understanding, the involvement, the joy and sorrow
of the child; it is independent, grown up, prematurely old; it has
entered into the unrealities of its own life.[49]

Rilke dreaded dolls, and in his later writing raged against them and
toys in general, mainly because they would not express the "real live"
feelings he expected of them:

At a time where everybody made an effort to give us quick and
soothing answers the doll was the first who made us suffer this
immense silence. And finally, the doll lies before us without disguise: as that gruesome alien body for which we have wasted our
purest warmth; as that superficially painted drowned corpse, lifted
and carried by the floods of our tenderness until it dried out and
we forgot it somewhere in the bushes.[50]

If we are happy and well adjusted as children, we may return to
the doll with nostalgic affection. If we are Rilke, we return to it in fearful, vengeful, masochistic mood.[51] In Freudian terms, the doll can be
a source of *uncanny* experience, which we carry through our lives.[52]
This may be the dark wellspring of creepy stories and horror movies:
The doll *really* comes to life, this time with truly malicious intent. One
of the most memorable contemporary evocations of this is the movie
Child's Play, in which "Chucky," the reincarnation of a murderer,
comes back to torment a small boy (see appendix E). Such stretches
of the imagination give us a clue why many people find the hyperreality of the PCDs disturbing, even ghastly. If it is *too* lifelike, or if it con-
fuses distinct phases of a normal person's development, or if the doll
were *really* to cross the line from passivity to life as many children have
dreamed, the chances are it would end up on the side of evil rather
than good.

Our researchers kept encountering people with a dread of one
sort of doll or another—mannequins, clowns, antiques. Lili G., 52, is
so terrified of the statue in front of Bob's Big Boy restaurants that she
can't drive past, far less eat there. A lot of people couldn't bear the

ventriloquist Edgar Bergen's dummy, Charlie McCarthy. Once again, it's the eyes that do much of the signaling. The PCD manufacturers labor mightily to make them warm, touching, expressive, but if they are too large, or too blue, or if the pupils are a little too big or too small, they cross the danger line. Big, limpid eyes can have a disconcerting emptiness, reminiscent of the studied blankness of beggar children in Asia, or pictures of African kids dying of starvation, or of a corpse. Eyes watch, eyes fascinate, and the sense that they are staring at you and into you can be very alienating. For small children one of the virtues of mechanical eyes is that they can be closed and the doll put innocently to sleep.

Marilyn, in her twenties, has lots of dolls from her childhood from which she finds it very difficult to be parted. She says she has never formed a personal relationship with them, but they sit on shelves around her bedroom, watching and waiting. Marilyn explains:

> I make the nightly ritual of turning my dolls around towards the
> wall. If I merely close my eyes, I feel as if they are looking at me,
> and I would never be able to sleep with a feeling that my dolls are
> watching and waiting until I'm asleep. I feel that if they cannot see
> me, they do not know when I am asleep . . . They have no power if
> they do not see me when I am most vulnerable. If you do not let
> them see you in a vulnerable state, they cannot attack.

Somewhere close to the heart of the matter is the tragedy that we grow out of our dolls: in a sense they die long before we do. To the adult women collectors, the PCDs are a gesture of resistance, an affirmation that this need not happen, and that in old age we can still embrace the childish magic. Gathering around you not just one or two but hundreds of dolls is a vivid gesture of resurrection. Collectors often talk of exultation, rejuvenation, revitalization. "With my dolls," Annie K. told us, "I feel so much more alive."

In the guise of angels, some of today's PCDs come quite close to the icons of "serious" religion. We might even say the same of the numerous Princess Diana and Jackie Kennedy figurines, which have certain cult qualities. Whether in religion or in play, we make dolls, and we may hope that they in turn may make us. A recurrent theme in the advertisements for PCDs is the promise of change and redemption:

> Sunshine and joy are her golden gifts—making all your wishes come true! . . . She's Adriana, the Harvest Angel, and bringing nature's glory to the waiting world is all she's ever wanted to do. Every whisper of her wings showers the earth with her love—and the golden promises of nature are fulfilled! Let an angel's love make your wishes come true. . . . Send for Adriana today!

"I wish . . . Oh, I wish . . . " exclaims *Lavender Dreams*. And then, "Lost in a daydream, she turns into a beautiful princess from long, long ago. . . . Lavender Dreams is issued as a hand-numbered, limited Artist's Edition. Make your own wish and keep her forever. Send for your Lavender Dreams today!"

Chapter Eight

Innocence and Fear

"The precious innocence of a little boy sound asleep, warmly captured in fine porcelain."

I have been fascinated with dolls since I was 10 years old. . . . In early adulthood I sort of lost touch with my hobby. But I still loved dolls and bought some occasionally, but my focus (time-wise and financially) was taking care of my family. A little over a year ago I discovered ebay, because a family member auctions glassware there. I checked out the Dolls category, and all my enthusiasm came back. I bought some dolls that I owned as a child but lost, and then I expanded my interests. I realized that I didn't know alot about dolls, so I bought books, joined a doll club, and took every opportunity to learn about dolls. I live in North Carolina and have a daughter beginning college this year. (She has NO interest in dolls.) My other passion is lilies of the valley. I collect anything with lilies of the valley—china, hankies, etc.[1]

In this book I have used the small matter of doll collecting to draw attention to larger questions of how people's personal lives are actively intertwined with history and culture. I have explored the intimate connections between the physical forms of the PCDs, their diffusion as a commodity through time and space, and the lives of the women who collect these dolls—sometimes in large numbers. The lineage of the PCDs extends back through some of the more elaborate children's dolls of the twentieth century to the fashion dolls of the nineteenth century that are now prized as antiques. The lives of today's collectors are threaded through a large part of this history. Many of them were born in hard times, raised their families in the years of postwar recovery, and are now aging in relative isolation and loneliness. Others have deferred or forgone child rearing in their pursuit of other opportunities. Their needs and the demands they place on manufacturers and markets are structured by their experiences, and it is hardly surprising that they should want things that do not interest other people—notably their own offspring.

Having focused in this book on what it is about these dolls that enthralls and delights some people, I must finally return to what repels and disconcerts others. Such an emphatic difference of attitude reminds us that we are seldom in complete agreement about the meaning of the things that surround us—that "culture" does not always imply consensus. Meaning does not have an independent, stable existence, floating "out there" in social space. It is variable and mutable because it is body-bound and life-bound. Culture lives in the intergenerational transactions of life itself: people take it and make it very selectively as they grow, inevitably believing that what matters to them today is what matters most.

Since supposedly we were all children once, it is astonishing how thoroughly, with the imperative of "growing up," we suppress our earlier understandings. What is it about adulthood that disrupts our sentimental attachment to our dolls? Why are they so variously the stuff of dreams and of nightmares? Is the guilty pleasure of doll collecting later in life a delayed rebellion against earlier parental hegemony? Or is the disjunction something inherent in the dolls themselves, the tragedy that while we grow, they can't?

All dolls, in varying degrees, distort, merge, confuse "real" bodily appearances, and all of them are, potentially, dangerous. In her study *Purity and Danger*, the anthropologist Mary Douglas draws attention to how we use our bodies as very basic frameworks for thinking about and symbolizing all sorts of social and moral qualities. For example, we use our right and left hands to make important contrasts (dextrous and sinister, this or that political party) and we use "head" and "foot" to signify political or economic distinctions (head of state, foot the bill). What bothers us is when something doesn't fit the normal body scheme, or is not in its proper place. Saliva in my mouth is warm, friendly, and lubricating; if I spit into a glass and let it cool, it seems very unappetizing, even to me. By metaphoric extension, boots on the dinner table, or a priest in a brothel, is matter out of place—"dirty." But what really troubles us is when we can't clearly categorize something, when we can't tell for sure if it's in or out of place: it's neither left nor right, good nor bad, food nor shit. Ambiguity, says Douglas, is *dangerous*. To deal with it we need special rules and procedures (rituals, medicines, laws). The trouble is, the natural processes of growing confront us continually with hazardous changes: the dangerous condition of adolescence is neither childhood nor adulthood, and around the world we humans have quite elaborate coming-of-age ceremonies to get us safely across the threshold.[2]

Dolls can be dangerous. I have already noted many of their ambiguities: they seem poised on the threshold between life and death, the real and unreal, persons and things; and thresholds, according to Mary Douglas, can be the most dangerous place in the house (neither inside nor outside). Dolls that take some features that properly belong in one stage of bodily growth (the nubile mouth and jaw) and add it to what is otherwise a baby face may be more than usually dangerous.

The biologist Eibl-Eibesfeldt remarks that "in commercial art the childish attributes of women are frequently exaggerated as well as the sexual attributes."[3] If infantilizing is a familiar way of enhancing adult feminine appeal, why should features of adult attractiveness not be used to enhance the appeal of little children? The very thought rouses indignation: "Only in a nation of promiscuous puritans could it be a good career move to equip a six-year-old with bedroom eyes," laments journalist Richard Goldstein.[4] The sense of outrage is not new. Shirley Temple—still the most favored "live" model for the current collector dolls—was the ideal child of the Depression years. In

1936 Graham Greene, then editing the magazine *Night and Day*, pointed out her sexual coquettishness. In the resulting storm of protest, he was sued for libel, and the magazine was forced to close.[5]

Today, says Marina Warner, the precocious eroticization of children has become especially fearsome—"little angels, little monsters."[6] It subverts our efforts to keep childhood in its proper place: "Never before have children been so saturated with all the power of projected monstrousness to excite repulsion—and even terror."[7] Loading a doll with these different meanings can be magically gratifying for the collectors. But for others whose lives are not in sympathy with this collage, the effect is of physical abnormality, freakishness.

In the cynical, knowing world of the new millennium, the mixture of *cute* and *attractive* is explosive, but whatever erotic effects there may be, they are repressed by the doll collectors themselves. We found it virtually impossible to discuss with these women the possibility that they might be sexually aroused by the dolls; tentative inquiries made clear that such questions were ridiculous or offensive. *Innocent* is a key word in selling the dolls. It occurs in 12 percent of the advertisements, apparently seeking to reassure but also betraying some moral anxiety on the manufacturers' part (see appendix C). "Victorian Lullaby" is advertised as "a timeless portrait of innocence"; but was childhood in Victorian times really so "innocent"? And are children today as "innocent" as we would wish? It is "an entirely modern view of childhood," says cultural theorist Neil Postman, that it should be "sheltered from adult secrets, particularly sexual secrets." This gives "innocence" an awkward twist: "*without a well-developed idea of shame, childhood cannot exist.*" The problem today, Postman complains, is that modern media give children ready access to adult secrets, stripping them of innocence and of childhood itself.[8]

A favorite example of the decay of innocence and the confusion of infancy and nubility are the baby shows and pageants so popular in Middle America. These have "blurred the boundary between child and adult" and deepened our confusion about the meaning of innocence.[9] They became the object of international media attention through the unresolved murder in 1996 of child beauty pageant star JonBenet Ramsey. It is not hard to understand why people looking at the PCDs for the first time should remark on their resemblance to JonBenet—the child's facial proportions and elaborate makeup match quite a few of our "adultified" PCDs. "The JonBenet Ramsey case revealed not only how regressive notions of femininity and beauty are redeployed in this conservative era to fashion the fragile identities of young girls but also how easily adults will project their own fantasies onto children."[10] Part of the public censure resulting from the case was that in being made to look more adult, JonBenet seemed to be inviting abuse—an extension of the old innuendo that women who contrive to look more feminine are "asking for it." Suspicions in this case have been loaded with assumptions about "bad parenting."

It is strange that although we now claim much professional understanding of the rights, needs, and capacities of the child, we are as much at a loss as we ever have been about the "Eros of childhood" and, even more troublesome, the "Eros of parenthood." The angst seems to have turned against child raising itself, witness the rash of fin de siècle book titles like *Who's Fit to Be a Parent?* Uneasiness about the PCDs reflects the moral crisis about childhood, in which *all* kinds of physical interest in children, even the "maternal," is suspect. Noelle Oxenhandler protests: "Not touching children can also be a crime."[11] The idea that "sibling appeal" is an important part of a child's (and a doll's) physical appearance may mitigate some of our fears about the attractions of small children, and help us to understand how and why the Eros of child care and the Eros of conjugality differ.

In recent history our attitudes to these matters has been far from stable. In some ways the PCDs are heirs to the Victorian bourgeois tradition that produced mawkish, naively erotic images of children. The twentieth century saw middle-class intellectuals vacillating between extremely repressive and very liberal attitudes on child rearing. The work of Freud and his disciples has served both purposes. A repressive attitude at the turn of the century (mechanical restraints for sucking and masturbation) was followed by more lenient attitudes in the 1930s and 1940s. The writings of Spock, Kinsey, Mead, and others fostered a tolerance of infantile sexuality. For all the rigors of the Depression, it was a relatively benign time to be raised: ordinary kids were less likely to be tortured with guilt and could still enjoy the company of their peers in the streets and parks with little fear of wicked prowlers. If the 1960s are remembered for naked flower children and freely available pornography, it was also the decade in which child abuse was officially "discovered" by the medical profession in the United States, preparing the way for the sexual molestation paranoia of the '80s and '90s and a harsh backlash against earlier "permissiveness."[12] The sexual libertines of the 1960s were now overwrought parents, scrutinizing the most intimate details of their children's lives, and subjecting them to mountains of profoundly ambiguous professional and literary wisdom. "We know what you're thinking—we've been there."

According to psychologist James Kincaid, the problem is that while we insist on the innocence of childhood, we have found that innocence itself erotic and have become hopelessly confused by it.[13] We turn our own guilt on the child, "and in despair, in an attempt to protect, we demand even greater disclosure of the child to the adult." We strip away the child's privacy, leaving it "little with which to protect itself from the invasions of the adult."[14]

The dolls would seem to allow a fantasy of total possession, power, and knowledge—a perfect guilt-free innocence. And yet the power of the dolls also lies in the secrets that are implanted subliminally by both their owners and their manufacturers. In the eyes of some beholders, the wantonness of some of the dolls is very striking (the dilated pupils, the pouty mouth, the plump limbs). But for the collectors, if there is any obscenity it is in the cheapest and crudest dolls or, more likely, in the prurient eyes of these other beholders.

In writing up this project I was goaded by three memorable comments from senior anthropologists. The first was a woman, the other two were men. They were respectively a cultural, a biological, and an economic anthropologist, and all were in their fifties. Having listened patiently to an illustrated talk on the dolls, the woman's comment was succinct: "Nauseating." The biological anthropologist was struck by the fact that "everything about these dolls is a lie." And looking over an early draft of our report, the economic anthropologist doubted the general interest of our topic. There have been hugely successful books on other commodities, "sugar and cod come to mind—but these are heroes of economic history with universal consequences," he said. A reader whose great virtue is his unremitting candor, he declared that he "could never bring himself to care about what seems to be a relatively arbitrary feature of western U.S. culture in the late twentieth century."

Why some serious and thoughtful people should find these dolls disgusting, mendacious, or boring, while others are sufficiently beguiled to buy them in large numbers, is a passionate difference of opinion on which I would wish to bring to bear our analytical framework of growth. I value these scholarly comments, but I recognize that they are also the opinions of real human beings, historically situated in Europe and North America at the turn of the twenty-first century, with lifetimes of particular experiences, and well equipped with the visceral feelings that underlie such judgments. Collegial protocol disallows a detailed description of who they are and how they have lived, but it will already be clear that none of them is in the market for porcelain collector dolls.

How much does something have to matter—and to whom—before it can be counted as "culture" and thus as a truthful and respectable object of academic attention? In classic ethnography, religious beliefs, myths, taboos, and the orderly structures of kinship were all thought of as constituting the hard core of culture. The anthropological task was to tease out the important, general, and durable from the trivial, local, and ephemeral. Classically, this meant seeking out the authoritative old men who, unlike the diffident children and women, had a well-rehearsed tale to tell. To ethnographers interested in trivia (decoration, children's games, dress, cooking) the challenge was to show how even such details slotted into the cultural master plan. What has always been unclear is the logic that justifies these greater and lesser degrees of ethnographic relevance. *Why* should dolls be of lesser account in the cultural catalog than, for example, religious icons? The reason, it seems, is not simply a bias of anthropology—it's a bias of adulthood itself.

As we grow up, things drop into and out of our lives. One meaning elides with another, linked by our cumulative experiences of life.

We put away childish things, only to rediscover them later, through our own children, and perhaps again in the second childhood of old age. Such changes and mutations are not irrelevant to culture, they are the living processes that sustain it and imbue it with emotional meaning.

"Culture," as anthropologists and others have sought to define it, is at best a very partial truth: fragmentary images of something that is presumed to be an inclusive dynamic whole but that can be described only in static parts and from particular points of view. It is the abstraction of a few ideas and actions from the immense busyness of real life, which we immobilize and pin like a butterfly on the academic display board. "Culture" is *life like*, but in much the same limited way that the collector dolls are life like. Both struggle to represent living things, in written texts or on porcelain, but these images are basically *timeless*. We can write and rewrite the grand outlines of culture, but as a compound of millions of lived lives stretched out through history its whole truth is beyond our intellectual grasp. One of the well-known frustrations of ethnography is that however comprehensive we try to make it, our audience is very narrow, and books are destined to be unreadable and unrecognizable by nearly all the people they beg to portray. Similarly, the record of past lives inscribed on the small body of the doll caters to a very narrow range of perceptions. It will always be a partial record, profoundly meaningful to some and perplexing or repugnant or simply meaningless from other life-bound points of view.

Today, contemporary cultural studies have worked hard to help us come to terms intellectually and morally with social difference. A better intellectual grasp of race, class, gender, religion, or nationality has improved our tolerance of these social categories. It is now unlikely that we would describe any of these manifestations of "otherness" as nauseating, mendacious, or boring, but there are evidently other axes of social difference that we have not yet learned to treat in the same tolerant terms. What we loosely describe as "generation" is embedded in the experience of every one of us, and yet has persistently eluded our best analytical efforts. However, recent changes in the demographic history of our societies make the need to understand these relations of human growth a matter of increasing political, economic, and social urgency. The cultural phenomenon of the generation gap widens inexorably with each passing decade. Today the old and the young live apart as they never did before, but they still communicate through intensely "feelingful" objects like dolls. For reasons that run deeper than culture or history, little children may come to terms much more readily than their parents with why Grandma should do something so weird as fill her home with lifelike dolls.

It is a biohistorical fact of some importance that there are a lot more grandmas around now than ever before. Greater longevity has increased the risks of isolation in old age, but it has also expanded the scope for relationships across the life span and through history. In our study, these life experiences were shared, sometimes very poignantly, in conversations between grandmothers and granddaughters. Our challenge has been to translate some of these sentiments back into words. While we may find it difficult to make objective, scholarly sense of the PCD phenomenon, the contradictions are resolved for the women themselves at the level of *feelings*. They do not care to dwell on the psychology, economics, sociology, or semantics of their passion for dolls. That is our scholarly business, and if the collectors (and the manufacturers) are not very sympathetic to us, it's because our analyses impinge on their enthusiasm in rather dry, surly, critical, and sometimes guilt-inducing ways.

Modern intellectual styles tend to split things rather than see them as continuous wholes: dolls are for children, not adults; for girls rather than boys; they are *either* for play *or* display; they are things, not persons. In the disciplinary mosaic of modern scholarship, the doll makes its fragmentary appearance in pediatrics or gerontology, museology, or developmental psychology. It appears definitively intact in the arms of a child; and once again, changed by the passage of a life, in the arms of an elderly woman.

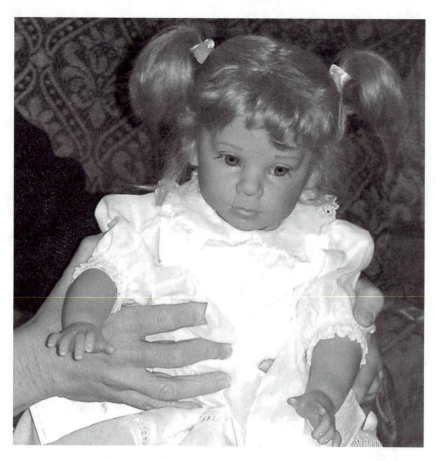

Picture 16: *Mary Jane.*
Photo by A. F. Robertson.

"Precious"

some quotations from the sample of PCD advertisements

Precious and all porcelain, she's *Cute as a Button.*

Accented with dainty flowers, mauve piping and delicate bow collar, it's just the outfit for such a precious little girl. (*Stephanie*)

"Angel Face" is a precious and gentle girl dressed like a little angel for her preschool pageant.

Little "Sugar Plum" has a big sister in ballet class and tries to be just like her. But without taking a single step, this sweet baby girl is as precious a ballerina as you could ever wish for!

Make this precious little girl with her sweet-but-sad expression your very own. Submit your reservation for "Kayla" today.

The precious innocence of a little boy sound asleep, warmly captured in fine porcelain. (*Ryan*)

Kimberly's precious features are expertly painted by hand.

She's Sunshine, Lollipops, and precious as she can be!

Sweet and precious and adorable in all porcelain, she's "Clean as a Whistle," a baby doll you'll love to "shower" with love and affection.

Award winning doll artist Gudrun Haak brings to life a precious heirloom baby doll. An exclusive offering in the prestigious European Doll Artists Collection!

Dolls as precious as little girls' dreams. (*Erin*)

Joshua's head, arms and legs are superbly crafted of fine bisque porcelain, and his precious facial features are lovingly painted by hand.

It's a precious scene from the gentle, sunlit world of a child's imagination. (*Brittany*—Tea for Teddy)

Her precious features brought to life in fine porcelain, painted by hand. (*Baby Bliss*)

As pink and precious as the flower she's named for! (*Sweet Carnation*)

His precious facial features are skillfully painted by hand in soft, natural colors. (*Karl*)

Precious in porcelain, with a poseable beanbag body. (*Baby Mickey*)

Appendix B-1

Doll Words
Analyses of the doll advertisements

GENDER AND FREQUENTLY USED WORDS IN THE COLLECTOR DOLL ADVERTISEMENTS

The words are arranged in order of the frequency with which they occur in the sample of 267 advertisements. Extensions of all the listed words are included: * marks stems which are not complete words. For example, LOVE* includes lovely, loveliness, and so on; LOV* includes all of these, plus lovable, loving, lovingly, and so on.

Words which occur in more than 10% of the ads in one list but not the other are <u>underlined.</u>

QUALITY WORDS
(Occurring in more than 20% of advertisements):

Girls	Boys
LOV*	LOV*
BEAUTIFUL	TIME
LOVE	JOY
TIME	REMARKABL*
SWEET	LOVE
ACTIV*	SWEET
HEART	ACTIV*
ADOR*	ADOR*
DELIGHT	DELIGHT
FOREVER	HEART

(Occurring in 10–20% of advertisements:)

PRECIOUS	FOREVER
ADORABLE	FAVO(u)RITE
CHARM	PROUD
JOY	CAPTIVAT*
EXQUISITE	MISCHIE*
INNOCEN*	FUTURE
GENTLE	HAPPY
BEAUTY	CUTE
ENCHANT	ENCHANT
ANGEL	IRRESISTIBLE
IRRESISTIBLE	
SPARKL*	
REMARKABL*	
INSPIR*	

RELATION WORDS
(Occurring in more than 10% of the advertisements:)

Girls	Boys
HOME	HOME
FRIEND	FRIEND
	DADDY
	MOMMY
	PERSONALITY

ACTION WORDS
(occurring in more than 20% of advertisements:)

Girls	Boys
CAN	CAN
COME	COME
BRING	PLAY
	LOOK
	SLEEP
	MAKE
	FUN

(occurring in 10–20% of advertisements:)

LOOK	BRING
PLAY	WONDER
MAKE	EXPRESSI*
WONDER	CUDDL*
LOVING	LOVING
SMILE/ing	SMILE/ing
NEED	NEED
EXPRESSI*	DREAM
WISH	
EXPRESSION	

BODY WORDS
(Occurring in more than 10% of the advertisements:)

Girls	Boys
LITTLE	LITTLE
EYES	BOY
DRESS	EYES
GIRL	DRESS
CHILD	LEGS
LEGS	FACE
FACE	CHILD
BABY	BABY

TOUCH WORDS
(Occurring in more than 10% of the advertisements:)

Girls	**Boys**
<u>DELICATE</u>	SOFT
SOFT	WARM
WARM	

REALITY WORDS
(Occurring in more than 10% of the advertisements:)

Girls	**Boys**
ACTUAL	ACTUAL
LIFE	LIFE
REAL	REAL
LIFELIKE	LIFELIKE

COMMODITY WORDS
(Occurring in more than 20% of the advertisements:)

Girls	**Boys**
COLLECT	COLLECT
FINE	GUARANTEE
GUARANTEE	FINE
COMPLETE	COMPLETE
EXCLUSIVE	VALUE
VALUE	SATISFACTION
HEIRLOOM	<u>AFFORD</u>
SATISFACTION	EXCLUSIVE
QUALITY	QUALITY
<u>CONVENIENT</u>	PREMIER
PREMIER	HEIRLOOM

TECHNICAL WORDS
(Occurring in more than 20% of the advertisements:)

Girls	Boys
HAND	HAND
ARTIST	ARTIST
CRAFT	CRAFT
EDITION	FIRST
FIRST	BISQUE
BISQUE	EDITION
AUTHENTIC	AUTHENTIC
SCULP*	<u>HANDCRAFT</u>
	SCULP*
	<u>CAPTURE</u>

Appendix B-2

Words which are more likely to be used in advertisements for girl dolls than boy dolls: (i) quality words, (ii) action words

For example: in (i) below, "beautiful" occurs in 32% of the advertisements for girl dolls and just 7% of the advertisements for boy dolls—that is, it occurs in 25% more of the advertisements for girl dolls than boy dolls. "Mischief" occurs in 16% of the boy advertisements and just 1% of the girl advertisements—a difference of 15% in favor of boys. "Enchant" is as likely to occur in advertisements for girl dolls as boy dolls—roughly 11% in both sets of advertisements.

(i) Quality Words: Difference between < Girl Words and Boy Words >

(ii) Action Words: Difference between
< Girl Words and Boy Words >

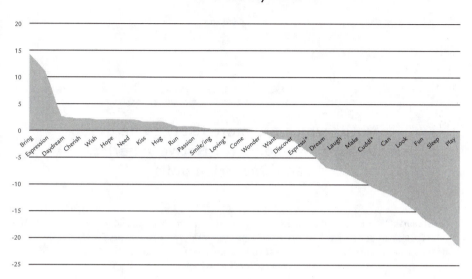

Appendix B-3

Words which are more likely to be used in advertisements for Native-American and Caucasian dolls

For example: "Artist" is used in 93% of the advertisements for Native American dolls, and 66% of the Caucasian dolls—that is, it occurs in 27% more of the advertisements for Native American dolls. "Little" occurs in 62% of all the advertisements for Caucasian dolls, 26% more than in the advertisements for Native American dolls.

**Words Occurring in 10% or More of the Advertisements: Differences between
< Native American Dolls and Caucasian Dolls >**

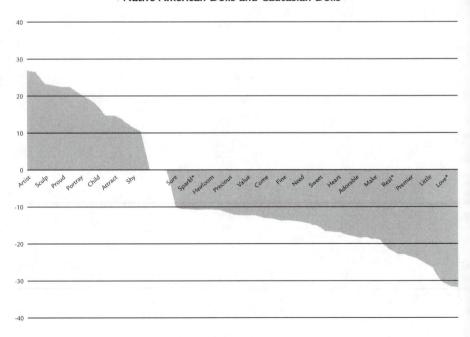

240

Appendix B-4

Native American/Caucasian/African American contrasts in frequently used words in the collector doll advertisements

The words occur in more than 10% of the adverts in each category, and are arranged in order of the frequency with which they occur. Extensions of *all* the listed words are included; * marks stems which are not complete words. For example, LOVE* includes lovely, loveliness, and so on; LOV* includes all of these, *plus* lovable, loving, lovingly, and so on.

ACTION WORDS

Native American	Caucasian	African American
COME	COME	COME
LOOK	CAN	CAN
BRING	BRING	LOOK
DREAM	PLAY	WANT
WONDER	LOOK	BRING
LOVING*	MAKE	MAKE
SMILE/ing	WONDER	WONDER
SLEEP*	LOVING*	SMILE/ing
	NEED	DISCOVER
	SMILE/ing	
	EXPRESSI*	
	SLEEP	
	WISH	
	DREAM	

QUALITY WORDS

Native American	Caucasian	African American
BEAUTIFUL	LOV*	LOV*
TIME*	TIME*	LOVE*
PROUD	LOVE*	ACTIV*
ATTRACT	SWEET	HEART
TALE	BEAUTIFUL	FOREVER
LOV*	ACTIV*	FAVO(u)RITE
SWEET	ADOR*	TIME*
ACTIV*	HEART	DELIGHT
FOREVER	DELIGHT	JOY
CHARM	FOREVER	INNOCEN*
REMARKABL*	PRECIOUS	BEAUTIFUL
BEAUTY	ADORABLE	IRRESISTIBLE
INSPIR*	JOY	GENTLE
CAPTIVAT*	CHARM	HAPPY
SHY	REMARKABL*	SWEET
	ENCHANT	PRECIOUS
	EXQUISITE	CHARM
	INNOCEN*	BEAUTY
	IRRESISTIBLE	ANGEL
	SPARKL*	PROUD
	GENTLE	DARLING

Doll Technicalities
"Full Socketed Head"

Tina Berry is presenting a sequence of collector dolls in classic Home Shopping Network mode: lingering closeups on the product, continuous suasive, quasi-technical patter, while sales and other details are posted permanently on a window on the left of the screen. There is a clublike atmosphere, but the mood is urgent: phones ring, sales meters click away each item, a clock counts the seconds to the closure of the sale. The indomitably cheerful Tina, more motherly than glamorous, projects herself as a serious collector in her own right. She wears sensible, dark clothes, perhaps not to out-glamorize the dolls. Her hands, continually working the dolls over, are clearly important, seriously manicured, with long, chisel-shaped, heavily enameled nails. Tina urges persistently "Don't let this one slip through your fingers!" The program is punctuated by chats with dial-up shoppers, who much appreciate Tina's bright personality:

> *Sandy, from North Carolina:* I watch every doll show you do. You give them so much life. It's almost like you invest a personality in each doll.

> *Tina:* Oh you're so sweet. What did you pick up tonight?

Sandy: I got Heather, and while I was on hold I saw the number for another one that I'm going to check back with the operator, to see if they still have it. It's really funny—I'm single, and a lot of times somebody will ask me to go out, and I say, "No, no, no, my doll show is tonight.". . . It's amazing—I have cats, and they know not to bother my dolls. . . . I just sit here, and even if it's one I know I'm not going to get, I enjoy listening to you—you describe them *beautifully*.

Tina: It does take having a passion, and I can tell you, as a collec-tor, we have here my extra, extra special favorites, and here tonight we have been able to offer you just a random sampling of some of the finest dolls from all over the world. . . .

Here, Tina is selling *Tamsin* by artist Christine Orange (Court of Dolls, price $198.75) on the HSN program *Gallery of Dolls:* "Look at how believable this little girl is. And you're going to find of course she has her legs gently crossed, you'll also notice that her little arms are down by the sides supporting, if you will, the overall body. I want to share with all of you out there just the extensive amount of porcelain that goes into this one, because there's quite a bit." Tina at this point pulls the larger-than-average, 36-inch doll out of the chair where Tina herself usually sits, and wrestles her around so that she can unbutton the back of the dress and expose the neck and shoulder areas, which bear stamps and signatures, and where some important mechanics of the doll are normally hidden. The doll is unsmiling, impassive, her head clunking on Tina's shoulder. Those crossable legs flop about as Tina works.

Here you can see the artist's signature mark, and also the limited edition piece at the back of the neck, the beautiful pearlized but-tons that hold this beautiful dress together, and there's the breast plate, OK? Quite an extensive breast plate as well. Notice some-thing else that's the mark of quality: wherever the porcelain is joined to porcelain you'll see a little bit of felt in here and that keeps it, of course, from grinding, because porcelain is a form of glass and you want to of course have that separation. . . . OK? Full

socketed head, huge upper body done in porcelain, there's a *lot* of
porcelain that goes into this doll. . . .

Take a look at these faces—they so much look like real children.
And because of the size, the structure and the size of them, you're
going to find that you may place these in any room of your home,
people will actually come in, look at them, and think they're talking to real children.

The doll's name is Tamsin, and she is an exceptional masterpiece
. . . even down to the little satin shoes.

[Home Shopping Network, *Gallery of Dolls* (host Tina Berry), February
17, 1999, 10–12 P.M. Pacific time.]

"Innocence"

some quotations from the sample of PCD advertisements

Cherry Pie is as sweet as her name . . . so gentle and innocent, she's like a picture from a perfect world.

"Gwendolyn"—a masterpiece of elegance and innocence!

"Special Delivery"—A PORTRAIT OF INNOCENCE

"Chelsea" is everything collectors love in a Connie Walser-Derek original—innocence, charm and captivating personality.

Donna RuBert has captured all of the heartwarming innocence and wonder of childhood in this astonishingly lifelike doll. (*Sara*)

"Beneath the Mistletoe," by artist Titus Tomescu, is a fine-porcelain collector doll that will fill your home with childhood innocence.

"Lauren's" big blue eyes are fringed with long, sweeping eyelashes and her sweet, innocent face is brightened by an endearing smile and rosy-pink cheeks.

Look at the way Grace's face lights up . . . with those chubby cheeks
. . . those innocent dimples.

A heartwarming new porcelain collector doll capturing a special
moment of childhood innocence. (*Brittany*)

To complement her innocent sweetness, *Kimberly*'s dress is hand-tailored of rosebud-patterned fabric with a pink ribbon sash.

"Hope" is the first issue in a collection called *Gardens of Innocence.*

This face, rounded cheeks, and handpainted, pursed lips convey a
timeless portrait of innocence. (*Victorian Lullaby*)

"Amber" will surely delight your heart, and add a very special touch of
childlike innocence wherever she is delivered. Order now.

"Snowbird's" head . . . the look of innocent wonder in her beautiful
brown eyes.

Hand-set eyes in innocent blue. (*Jack and Jill*)

Amber Afternoon draws you into her golden world of innocence.

You can see she's full of hope and innocence, and right now just a little bit shy. Tansie is also everything you could wish for in a collector's
doll.

Those innocent eyes . . . that soft loveliness. Where have you seen
such a girl before? In the Portraits you remember—of children long
ago. (*Peaches and Cream*)

An adorable porcelain collector doll capturing the innocent playful-
ness of a little boy. (*Bobby*)

The minute you see Brian's winsome face and the wishful expression in his big blue eyes, you'll recognize Elke Hutchens' magical ability to evoke the innocence and sweetness of young children.

Her delicate beauty and tender innocence are as sweet as the blossoms she carries. (*Shy Violet*)

An adorable first edition collector doll capturing a little boy's innocent charm. (*Christopher*)

Jessica captures the tender innocence of a child.

An adorable porcelain collector doll capturing a baby's playful innocence. (*Playing Footsie*)

She's tiny. Angelic. Blushed with innocence. It's love at first sight with adorable Baby Bliss.

Look into her soft brown eyes, and see all the love and innocence that makes babies irresistible! She's "Sweet Carnation."

Chucky's Back!

In movies, the bad-doll genre flourished with early animation techniques. In *The Devil Doll* (MGM, 1936), an adaptation of Arthur Merritt's novel *Burn, Witch, Burn!*, an old woman sends her dolls on stealing and killing missions. But she is in fact a he, a convict on the run, played by Lionel Barrymore in drag, and the dolls are actually little people (Grace Ford and Arthur Hohl) trained to wreak vengeance on his behalf. "Creepy," concludes a recent *New Yorker* review (April 5, 1999). "Some bits are fairly certain to return in nightmares."

Much the same could be said of *Child's Play* (MGM-United Artists, 1988) the best-known modern version of this genre. The plot is rudimentary: single mom (Catherine Hicks) raising small son on wretched shop job buys "Chucky" doll from peddler who stole it from a toy store burned down by thunderbolt as Strangler, gasping vengeance against detective who has just shot him, migrates into convenient doll.

Chucky, alias the Strangler, is very much a child's doll, but with features hyped along the scary axis: big blue eyes, small pupils, nasty little mouth with sharp teeth. He is from a doll series called Good Guys ("He wants YOU to be his Best Friend," say the boxes stacked up in the toy store). He is intended as a sibling surrogate for six-year-old

Andy (Alex Vincent) who, with his big blue eyes, dainty chin, and dolichocephalic head looks somewhat hyperreal himself. The movie plugs away at the theme that dolls can get real despite adult skepticism. Chucky makes his point by ejecting Andy's skeptical aunt/babysitter messily from the apartment window, early in the movie. Later, the detective's sidekick is bouncing Chucky's head around like a football to show the principals that the doll is just a doll—at which point Chucky's scorched and dismembered torso tears into him. Only when he is shot through his newly forming heart (spatter-spatter) by the detective (Chris Sarandon) does Chucky quiet down—biding his time for resurrection in *Bride of Chucky*. The movie closes with the Chucky-afflicted principals heading out of the apartment, stabbed and chewed, wondering how they will break the news of doll hyperactivity to the rest of the world.

Key to Face
Diagrams

These diagrams focus on the facial mask, the arrangement of primary features (eyes, nose, mouth) to which we pay most attention in looking at faces. In the diagrams, the length of the head from crown to chin (A-B) is held constant to show proportional differences and changes in the mask. The breadth of the face (D-E) is recorded by noting the greatest width of the cheeks: this is much closer to the level of the mouth in the case of infants, and usually at the height of the cheek bones, just below the eyes, for adults. Key coordinates are the eye line (G-H), centered on each pupil and extended to the corners of each eye; the point (N) on the crown-chin line at which the upper lip meets the nasal septum; and the point (M) at which the line of the mouth, from its corner creases, meets the crown-chin line. The diagrams also note two other important facial signals: the width of the irises (L), and the thickness of the upper (R-S) and lower (R-T) lips.

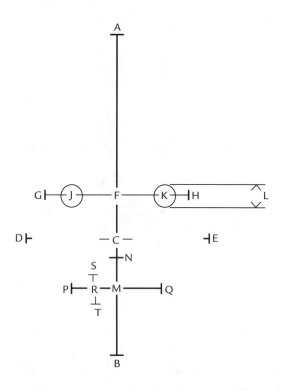

Appendix F: Key to Face Diagrams

A-B	Crown-chin (MAIN index line). Base of chin (first if double!) to scalp at highest point of crown estimated where not fully visible. Height of open mouth is deducted from MAIN line.
D-C-E	Cheek width: face at widest point below eye line.
B-F	Chin to eye line running through center of pupils.
G-H	Eye width: between *corner* of each eye, centered on MAIN line.
J-F-K	Distance between pupils, centered on MAIN line.
L	Iris diameter.
B-N	Nasal septum height: chin to septum at lip crease.
B-M	Mouth height: chin to mouth line below center of upper lip.
P-Q	Mouth width, corner to corner.
R-S	Upper lip at point of maximum width along mouth line.
R-T	Lower lip at point of maximum width along mouth line.

Notes

PREFACE

1. See especially Robertson 1991, 1996, 2001.

CHAPTER 1

The epigraphs opening this and subsequent chapters are all drawn from our sample of doll advertisements.

1. *Stevie* is illustrated in figure 7-b. In this book we shall use the convention that the names of dolls will be in italics, real people in normal type.
2. Novelist Anne Rice, http://www.dollreader.com/vampire_0898.html (February 15, 2001).
3. *Star Free Press* (Ventura, California), March 6, 1994.
4. Hall and Ellis 1896: 171.
5. Lorna Scott Fox's review of Rand's *Barbie's Queer Accessories* (1995), in the *London Review of Books* (July 20, 1995: 13). "But the premise of mickey-mouse academics is often fruitful: that the least cultural droppings are microcosms of a wider political dynamic, to be prodded and tested in a reflexology of the social body."
6. When Caroline died in 1824, age nine, she was about 20 inches tall—about the same size as the larger PCDs in our sample.
7. Simms 1996: 663–64.
8. C. Carter 1993: 16–17.
9. "In Memory of the Late Mr. and Mrs. Comfort." Fashion photo essay by Richard Avedon, *New Yorker*, November 6, 1995.

10. Rossi 1985, Woodward 1995.

11. Bengtson, Rosenthal, and Burton 1990: 270.

12. Wise 1990: 5.

13. Hall and Ellis 1896: 165, 172–73.

14. Hall and Ellis 1896: 167–68.

15. See, for example, Wilson 2002, Pearce 1995: 211.

16. Dean 1997: 108–11.

17. Hall and Ellis 1896: 161.

18. Kenneth Loyal Smith, http://www.virtualdolls.com/kensmith.htm (November 6, 2000).

19. Hall and Ellis 1896: 159.

20. Piot 1999: 84–86.

21. LaFleur 1992: 8–9.

22. L. Martin 1994: 20.

23. I have described this biohistorical perspective in much greater detail elsewhere: see Robertson 1991, 1994, 1996, 2001.

24. Toren 1993: 474. Toren rejects conventional views of the child as an asocial and ahistorical receptacle for adult meanings: "The child is taken to be biologically an a-social individual who becomes social/cultural by virtue of actions performed upon it by others. Thus the child is made the locus of a split between 'individual' and 'society,' between 'biology' and 'culture,' and processual relations with others are reified as 'structures' that are outside and beyond the particular persons who are cognitively constituting them as such" (469).

25. "The child's toys and the old man's reasons are the fruits of two seasons," said William Blake two centuries ago (quoted in Mergen 1984: 149). And "beads and prayer books are the toys of age," said Alexander Pope a century before that.

26. See especially Aries 1962, Atran 1990, Elder, Modell, and Parker 1993, Cox 1996, James, Jenks, and Prout 1998, Walkerdine 1997.

27. Cox 1996: 207.

28. Students of culture, says Sahlins, need take little interest in biology, beyond recognizing that it places "a set of natural limits on human functioning" and "puts at the disposition of culture a set of means for the construction of a symbolic order" (Sahlins 1976: 66).

29. Birke 1999: 138, 157.

30. Birke 1999: 2.

31. Birke 1999: 172.

32. Birke 1999: 157.

33. McDonough and Braungart 2002.

34. Hard-nosed journalists have encountered the same problems. *Forbes* magazine's Phyllis Berman (1992) found that Theodore Stanley, the boss of Danbury (one of the main PCD producers), "is an extremely private person who doesn't even meet with the big-name artists like Roger Tory Peterson who design collectibles for his company. . . . Stanley has taken care to avoid publicity for MBI products,

but why take a chance on telling some journalist what he makes and how much he makes?" (Berman 1992)

35. See, for example, Rand 1995; and Fleming 1996: 207.

CHAPTER 2

1. Fleming 1996: 87.
2. Fleming 1996: 109.
3. Barbie is classified as a "fashion doll" by the advertising trade (Mansfield 1983).
4. Dean 1997: 118–19.
5. Dean 1997: 130, 131.
6. Dean 1997: 104–107.
7. Fleming 1996: 87.
8. Hall and Ellis 1896: 134.
9. Dean 1997: 178.
10. Postman 1994: 67.
11. Hall and Ellis 1896.
12. Formanek-Brunell 1998: 371.
13. Formanek-Brunell 1993: 186.
14. Dean 1997: 189.
15. Postman 1994: 123.
16. Mansfield 1983.
17. Taylor 1999.
18. Appadurai 1986: 41.
19. Ehrenreich and Ehrenreich 1979: 325.
20. Appadurai 1986: 41.
21. Appadurai 1986.
22. Loro 1995a.
23. Loro 1995a.
24. The remaining 26 advertisements in our final selection included dolls manufactured by several smaller producers, including Gorham and Paradise Galleries. The list is a selection, based on what appeared during the 1990s in the print media. It is far from comprehensive—for example, Harper's Bazaar established its own range of porcelain dolls in the mid-1990s (Underwood 1996).
25. Loro 1995.
26. Berman 1992: 54–5.
27. Berman 1992.
28. Ashton-Drake: http://www.collectiblestoday.com (October 15, 2000).
29. Loro 1995a.
30. *Moody's Company Data Report, 1998*, Moody's Investors Service.
31. Dean 1997: 132.
32. Loro 1995b.
33. Shiffrin 1995.
34. Byrnes 1995: 44.
35. *Moody's Company Data Report, 1998*, Moody's Investors Service.

36. U.S. Department of Commerce 1983, 1993, 1997.

37. *"Hand"* came out top of our list of key words, occurring in some form in 84 percent of the sample of 267 PCD advertisements.

38. Dean 1997: 74, Ogando 2000: 64.

39. Harvey 1990: 300.

40. Berman 1992.

41. *Moody's Company Data Report, 1998*, Moody's Investors Service.

42. "America Past and Pleasant," *Economist*, no. 337 (December 16, 1995), p. 62.

43. We have no artist names for the five Lenox dolls in our sample, but all of them were offered for sale in 1991–92.

44. Ashton-Drake Galleries: http://www.collectiblestoday.com (October 15, 2000).

45. Home Shopping Network, *Collectors Day* (hosts Tina Berry and Tim Luke) April 13, 2001, 4–5 a.m. Pacific time.

46. QVC-TV, *Dolls by Pauline–7th Anniversary Show*. November 4, 2001, 10–11 P.M. Pacific time.

47. Of the 95 clearly named doll artists in our advertisement sample, 12 were male, including 3 working in male-female couples. The remaining 86 artists were female (judging by their names), and between them they designed 95 percent of the dolls that bore an artist's name.

48. *Sunday Post Magazine* (UK), April 6, 1997.

49. M. Carter 1994.

50. Home Shopping Network, *Gallery of Dolls* (host Tina Berry), February 17, 1999, 10–12 P.M. Pacific time.

51. Seiter 1993: 14

52. Loro 1995b.

53. Hodges and Loro 1995: 4.

54. Loro 1995a.

55. Loro 1995a.

56. Schiffrin 1995; *Moody's Company Data Report, 1998*, Moody's Investors Service.

57. Hodges and Loro 1995.

58. Loro 1995b.

59. Schnorbus 1987.

60. Loro 1995b.

61. http://www.mylittlepeople.com (May 2, 2001).

62. Loro 1992.

63. *Star Free Press* (Ventura, California) March 6, 1994.

64. Dowling 1997.

65. http://www.DollHaus.com; http://www.dollmarket.com (April 2, 2001).

66. Fenn 1985.

67. Ashton-Drake Galleries: http://www.collectiblestoday.com (November 15, 2000).

68. Dean 1997: 158.

69. Home Shopping Network, *Gallery of Dolls* (host Tina Berry), February 17, 1999, 10–12 P.M. Pacific time.

70. Quoted in Loro 1995b: 33.

CHAPTER 3

1. http://www.collectdolls.guide (chat room) (November 1, 2000).
2. Dale Graham, publisher of *Antiques and Collecting Hobbies*, reported in Ehrenfeld 1993.
3. Harrison 1996: 15.
4. Pearce 1995: 274.
5. Murphy 2000: 176.
6. See, for example, Pearce 1995.
7. Pearce 1995: 412.
8. Fulkerson 1995: 17–18.
9. Contributor CWEATHER to Doll People chat room at http://www.collectdolls. guide (November 1, 2000).
10. Pearce 1995: 272–75.
11. *New York Times*, May 15, 2002.
12. Ehrenfeld 1993: 94.
13. Harrison 1996: 19.
14. Harrison 1996: 17.
15. Ehrenfeld 1993: 98.
16. One collector professes to be a member of 30 car clubs and 15 train clubs (Ehrenfeld 1993: 97).
17. Murphy 2000.
18. Harrison 1996: 17.
19. Pearce 1995: 190.
20. Murphy 2000.
21. Ehrenfeld 1993: 95.
22. Murphy 2000, Wilson 2002.
23. Ehrenfeld 1993: 94.
24. "Above all, play is not trivial," says Bernard Mergen sternly. Mergen quotes Johann Huizinga's definition of play as "a free activity standing quite consciously outside 'ordinary' life as being 'not serious,' but at the same time absorbing the player intensely and utterly" (Mergen 1984: 149).
25. Stephens 1995: 345.
26. Ogando 2000.
27. Washburn 1997: 127.
28. Baudelaire 1994 [1853]: 24.
29. Seiter 1993: 131.
30. "Displaying Your Doll Collection," http://www.dollreader.com/display.html (February 15, 2001). And see Dean 1997: 214.
31. Loro 1992.
32. "Displaying Your Doll Collection," http://www.dollreader.com/display.html (February 15, 2001).
33. Seiter 1998: 303; and see Cowan 1986.
34. *Los Angeles Times Magazine,* June 9, 2002.
35. *Home and Life*, October 1997.

36. The classic account of this is William J. Goode's *World Revolution and Family Patterns* (1970).

37. Survey in 1994 by Unity Marketing, reported by Jennifer Fulkerson (1995: 17–18).

38. Home Shopping Network, *Collectors Day* (hosts Tina Berry and Tim Luke), April 13, 2001, 4–5 A.M. Pacific time.

39. *Sunday Post* (UK), August 10, 1997.

40. Pearce 1995: 253.

41. Pearce 1995: 253.

42. http://www.dollreader.com/vampire_0898.html (February 15, 2001).

43. Pearce 1995: 237.

44. Contributor DEBBIESDOLLI to Doll People chat room at http://www.collect-dolls.guide (November 1, 2000).

45. *Home and Life*, October 1997: 58.

46. The following paragraphs draw on my book *Greed: Gut Feelings, Growth, and History* (Robertson 2001: 111–39).

47. Lord 1994: 282.

48. Ehrenreich 1989.

49. Counts and Counts 1985: 138.

50. Kant 1978 [1796]: 182.

51. See especially Meillassoux 1981.

52. Coser 1974: 98.

53. See, for example, Demos 1970, Garrett 1977, Noddings 1989.

54. Harrison 1996: 17.

55. *Los Angeles Times*, March 16, 1985. "Greed—for lack of a better word—is good," says Gordon Gekko, anti-hero of the movie *Wall Street*. "Greed is right. Greed works. Greed clarifies, cuts through, it captures the essence of the evolutionary spirit. Greed in all of its forms: Greed for life, for money, for love, knowledge, has marked the upward surge of mankind, and greed—you mark my words—will not only save Teldar Paper, but that other malfunctioning corporation called the USA." *(Applause).*

56. Ehrenfeld 1993: 97.

57. Ehrenfeld 1993: 96.

58. Letter from Sherrie H. of Wheaton, Maryland, in *Dolls—The Collector's Magazine*, August 22, 1996 (responding to the editor's question "What is a doll?").

59. "Heirloom" occurs in 23 percent of our sample of advertisements (*Polly*—"Heirloom quality at only $78") and is a generic label for several manufacturers ("Franklin Heirloom Dolls").

60. Pearce 1995: 251.

61. See, for example, Goody 1976.

62. Pearce 1995: 211.

63. Pearce 1995: 248.

64. Pearce 1995: 176, 235, 272.

65. Ehrenfeld 1993: 96.

66. *Times* (London), March 7, 1998.
67. Roha 1992.
68. Harrison 1996.
69. Home Shopping Network, *Collectors Day* (hosts Tina Berry and Tim Luke) April 13, 2001, 4–5 A.M. Pacific time.
70. Woman caller on Home Shopping Network, *Collectors Day* (hosts Tina Berry and Tim Luke) April 13, 2001, 4–5 A.M. Pacific time.
71. Berman 1992.
72. Fulkerson 1995: 17.
73. Fulkerson 1995: 17–18.
74. Fulkerson 1995: 17–18. "The average doll collector is willing to spend more than $600 annually and may have 200 to 400 dolls," according to one firm's product planning director" (Mansfield 1983).
75. Seiter 1993: 202.
76. My grandmother was a slave to the Indian Tree pattern of crockery, my mother a devotee of the Regency pattern. Each of these was collected diligently over many years. My wife and I fell heir to the Indian Tree.
77. Berman 1992.
78. *Woman's Realm* (UK), April 1998.
79. QVC-TV, *Dolls by Pauline—7th Anniversary Show.* November 4, 2001, 10–11 P.M. Pacific time.
80. Ehrenfeld 1993: 98.

CHAPTER 4

1. Seiter 1993: 74, 129.
2. Scheper-Hughes and Stein 1998: 186–87. The authors report that at Christmas 1985 a new line in doll orphans appeared—the Rice Paddy Baby, which came with "a British passport and voice that coos 'I want to immigrate. Will you sponsor me?'"
3. The name Lenci is an acronym for *ludus est nobis constanta industria*—"To us, play is a constant industry." The Lenci factory in Turin employed over 1,000, specializing in child dolls with "striking eyes" and notably colorful clothes (Dean 1997: 172–73).
4. See, for example, Berry 1994: 38–42.
5. I have discussed this at length in Robertson 2001.
6. Berry 1986: 82.
7. Bâ 1981: 28–29.
8. See especially Anderson 1985, Hess 1985, Wells 1971, and U.S. Census Bureau: *Statistical Abstract of the United States,* 1999.
9. Hall and Ellis 1896: 139.
10. See especially Elder 1999 [1974], *Children of the Great Depression.* The Oakland study was supplemented by a slightly later Berkeley study, augmenting later-life data, reported in Clausen 1993, *American Lives: Looking Back at the Children of the Great Depression.*

11. In their forties, a third of the women in the sample "engaged in crafts and hobbies—painting, knitting, gardening, and a wide variety of types of collecting" at
least once a week. More than half of men and women had such pursuits when
they were in their seventies (Clausen 1993: 438, 479).
12. Elder 1999: 57, 272–75.
13. Elder 1999: 18.
14. Elder 1999: 51.
15. Elder 1999: 5.
16. Elder 1999: 28.
17. Kline 1993.
18. Elder 1999: 80–82.
19. Elder 1999: 278.
20. Elder 1999: 215.
21. Elder 1999: 112.
22. Elder 1999: 293.
23. Elder 1999: 117.
24. Elder 1999: 226.
25. Elder 1999: 238.
26. Elder 1999: 5.
27. Elder 1999: 212.
28. Elder 1999: 206.
29. Clausen 1993: 433–34.
30. Lopata 1971: 363.
31. Elder 1999: 297.
32. Clausen 1993: 504–505.
33. Clausen 1993: 503.
34. Clausen 1993: 505.
35. *Star Free Press* (Ventura, California), March 6, 1994.
36. Fee 1995.
37. Wise 1990: 5.
38. Hewlett 2002: 257.
39. See especially Robertson 1991, Roberts 1993, U.S. Census Bureau: *Statistical
Abstract of the United States,* 1999.
40. Hewlett 2002.
41. Hewlett 2002: 91–92.
42. Hewlett 2002: 253.
43. Hewlett 2002: 27.
44. Hewlett 2002: 254.
45. Hewlett 2002: 194, 189.
46. Ehrenfeld 1993.
47. Hewlett 2002: 99–100.
48. Hewlett 2002: 102.
49. According to Melanie Klein, "Beneath the little girl's ever-recurring desire for
dolls there lies a need for consolation and reassurance. The possession of her

dolls is a proof that she has not been robbed of her children by her mother, that she has not had her body destroyed by her and that she is able to have children" (Klein 1975: 56–57).

50. http://www.dollsales.com/dolls/Doll%20Factory/original%20newborn. htm (October 6, 2000).

51. Flo, who has been collecting Barbie dolls for some 11 years, "underwent a mastectomy, which required extensive corrective and reconstructive surgery. Flo now has a complete collection of the outfits manufactured by Mattel for Barbie, and it is difficult not to relate her satisfaction at this completeness, associated as it is with the very full feminine form of the dolls, with her own difficulties following the removal of her breasts. Flo's Barbies are the acceptable face of vamping, desirable but well within the accepted constraints of Middle America" (Pearce 1995: 211). It may be more than a coincidence that Barbie's designer, Ruth Handler, was herself a breast cancer survivor, and a pioneer of post-mastectomy implants.

52. Formanek-Brunell 1993: 157–59.

53. Formanek-Brunel 1993: 85–88.

54. Darlin 1995.

55. www correspondent RMS4–collectdolls.guide chat room (November 13, 2000).

CHAPTER 5

1. Hall and Ellis 1896: 159. After more than a century there is still no parallel for Stanley Hall and Caswell Ellis's remarkable *Study of Dolls*. A pioneer psychologist, sociologist, and educator, Hall started the *Pedagogical Seminary* as a forum in the psychology of teaching, to which schoolteachers around the United States and in the United Kingdom contributed. Hall and his colleagues typically issued a list of queries or test stimuli, which were then administered voluntarily by interested teachers. The results were collected, computed, and analyzed by Hall. In this way, hundreds, sometimes thousands of "cases" could be drawn into the study framework. Topics in Vol. 4 of the *Pedagogical Seminary* include children's capacity to remember details of a story; analysis of their drawings; "suggestibility"; "youthful degeneracy"; teasing and bullying; and notes on "peculiar and exceptional children."

2. Hall and Ellis 1896: 135.

3. Baudelaire 1994 [1853]: 24.

4. Hall and Ellis 1896: 132–34, 159.

5. Hall and Ellis 1896: 134.

6. Webster's *New World Dictionary*.

7. Mead 1967 [1932].

8. Pearce 1995: 251.

9. "Mattel introduced Magic Nursery Babies in 1990 (the 'magic' being that the doll had to be brought home and a special packet immersed in water before discerning the doll's sex)" (Seiter 1993: 203).

10. Baudelaire 1994 [1853]: 16.

11. See, for example, Woodward 1995.

12. QVC-TV, *Dolls by Pauline–7th Anniversary Show*, November 4, 2001, 10–11 P.M. Pacific time.

13. Internet chat room: http://www.suite101.com/print_article.cfm/1973/42795.

14. http://www.collectiblestoday.com (November 15, 2000).

15. See Clausen 1993: 431, 451.

16. QVC-TV, *Dolls by Pauline—7th Anniversary Show*. November 4, 2001, 10–11 P.M. Pacific time.

17. This is very evocative of the Barbie experience: "Just as the Native American Barbie does not copy the uniform of a specific tribe but reflects an outsider's interpretation of Native American identity, the upper-class Barbies reproduce not real upper-class clothing, but an outsider's fantasy of it." They are "a proletarian daydream of how a rich person would dress" (Lord 1994: 186).

18. Formanek-Brunell 1998: 373.

19. Seiter 1993: 88.

20. Bordo 1993: 265.

21. U.S. Census Bureau: *Statistical Abstract of the United States*, 1999.

22. Hall and Ellis 1896: 147–48.

23. Home Shopping Network, *Gallery of Dolls* (host Tina Berry), February 17, 1999, 10–12 P.M. Pacific time.

24. *Los Angeles Times*, October 29, 2001.

25. Home Shopping Network, *Collectors Day* (hosts Tina Berry and Tim Luke), April 2001, 4–5 A.M. Pacific time.

26. Formanek-Brunell 1998: 372.

27. Neal 1992.

28. "America Past and Pleasant," *Economist*, no. 337 (December 16, 1995), p. 62.

29. Home Shopping Network, *Collectors Day* (hosts Tina Berry and Tim Luke) April 13, 2001, 4–5 A.M. Pacific time.

30. Correspondent HELENEKAREN, chat room—http://www.collectdolls.guide (November 1, 2000).

31. These were all offered as a sequence of trial subscriptions by http://www.magazine-of-the-month.com.

32. QVC-TV, *Dolls by Pauline—7th Anniversary Show*, November 4, 2001, 10–11 P.M. Pacific time.

33. http://www.marianllc.com (November 20, 2002).

34. http://www.collectiblestoday.com (October 28, 2000).

35. http://www.collectiblestoday.com (October 28, 2000).

36. QVC-TV, *Dolls by Pauline—7th Anniversary Show*, November 4, 2001, 10–11 P.M. Pacific time.

37. Formanek-Brunel 1993: 2.

38. Formanek-Brunel 1993: 1.

39. See especially Rand 1995: *Barbie's Queer Accessories*.

40. *Los Angeles Times*, April 28, 2002. Any of these original Barbies now fetch up to $10,000 in auction.

41. *Los Angeles Times*, February 8, 2002.

42. *New York Times*, June 15, 2002.

43. See Chin 1999, Rand 1995.

CHAPTER 6

1. Hall and Ellis 1896: 160.

2. Alley 1988: 58.

3. See Wood 2002.

4. Harris 2000: 11.

5. Hall and Ellis 1896: 140–42.

6. Dean 1997: 200.

7. Rilke 1994 [1913].

8. I have a hand-puppet raccoon who is a master at deceiving humans, but not dogs (although I must admit to a moment's anxiety while testing this hypothesis on a neighbor's pit bull terrier).

9. Alley 1988: 55.

10. Berry and Zebrowitz-McArthur 1988: 81.

11. See McCabe 1988: 92.

12. Alley and Hildebrant 1988: 136–38.

13. Berry and Zebrowitz-McArthur 1988: 83–84.

14. Mark, Shaw, and Pittenger 1988: 19.

15. Alley 1988: 51.

16. See for example Alley and Hildebrant 1988: 110.

17. Lorenz 1950, *Ganzheit und Teil in der Tierischen und Menschlichen Gemeinschaft*, cited in Gould 1980: 100–101.

18. Bogin 1988: 98.

19. Gould 1980: 100.

20. Hinde and Barden 1985.

21. Hinde and Barden 1985; Dunbar 1998: 96.

22. Hrdy 1999: 472.

23. Alley 1988: 53–54.

24. Harris 2000: 5–6.

25. Formanek-Brunel 1993: 5, 117–34.

26. Moyers and Carlson 1988: 276.

27. Alley and Hildebrant 1988: 134.

28. Dean 1997: 28.

29. Dean 1997: 95.

30. Berry and Zebrowitz-McArthur 1988: 67.

31. Berry and Zebrowitz-McArthur 1988: 64.

32. Chin 1999: 315.

33. Dean 1997: 124.

34. Alley and Hildebrant 1988: 109.

35. Landau 1989: 97.

36. According to Sarah Blaffer Hrdy, "Human infants have been selected to be activists and salesmen, agents negotiating their own survival" (1999: 484).
37. Landau 1989: 132.
38. Landau 1989: 86.
39. Early in the twentieth century the German firm of Kammer and Reinhardt produced "character dolls" with open wet mouth, smallish eyes, and big ears (Dean 1997: 122–23).
40. Dean 1997: 31.
41. Dean 1997: 137.
42. Alley 1988: 60.
43. Alley 1988: 51.
44. Dean 1997: 30.
45. Dean 1997: 32–33, 74.
46. Dean 1997: 24.
47. Hrdy 1999: 474, 476–83.
48. See, for example, http://www.thedollmarket.com/artist.html (March 23, 2001).
49. Home Shopping Network, *Gallery of Dolls* (host Tina Berry), February 17, 1999, 10–12 P.M. Pacific time.
50. http://www.collectiblestoday.com (October 27, 2000).
51. Baudrillard 1998. In this context, Shakespeare's amusingly arrogant "Summer's Day" sonnet (XVIII) comes to mind as an early claim to hyperrealism. He tells his lover that by turning her into a poem he will make her immortal,
    . . . When in eternal lines to time thou grow'st.
    So long as men can breathe, or eyes can see,
    So long lives this, and this gives life to thee.
52. See especially Formanek-Brunell 1993.

CHAPTER 7

1. Hall and Ellis 1896: 14, 135, 150.
2. Mergen 1984: 150, and see Fleming 1996: 86–87.
3. "Veneri donatae a virgine puppae" (Hall and Ellis 1896: 157).
4. Hall and Ellis 1896: 157.
5. Dean 1997: 198.
6. Hrdy 1999: 474.
7. Alley 1988: 53.
8. Alley 1988: 52.
9. Berry and Zebrowitz-McArthur 1988: 71.
10. Hall and Ellis 1896: 136.
11. Formanek-Brunel 1993: 184.
12. Hrdy 1999: 493–510.
13. Dean 1997: 8–9.
14. Hall and Ellis 1896: 135.
15. Simms 1996: 664.
16. Alley & Hildebrant 1988: 133.

17. Alley 1988: 60–61.
18. Symons 1995: 88.
19. Symons 1995: 98.
20. Symons 1995: 107.
21. Alley 1988: 58–59.
22. Alley and Hildebrant 1988: 104.
23. Although the differences were not large, the septum height of two thirds of the African American dolls was below average, whereas three quarters of the Native American dolls were above average.
24. See Landau 1989: 34.
25. Wagenknecht 1969.
26. BBC-TV program *Hollywood Knives* broadcast May 2, 2001.
27. Landau 1989: 222.
28. Steinem and Barris 1986: 9.
29. http://www.barbie.com (February 12, 2002).
30. Advertisement for *Promenade in the Park Barbie. Homes and Gardens*, November 1998.
31. Ivy 1995: 98.
32. Letter from Coleen E. of Virginia, in *Dolls—The Collector's Magazine*, August 22, 1996.
33. Formanek-Brunell 1993: 178.
34. My Twinn catalog, August 1998.
35. My Twinn catalog, August 1998.
36. Simms 1996: 672.
37. Lord 1994: 283.
38. Letter from Kelly L. of Truckee, California, in *Dolls—The Collector's Magazine*, August 22, 1996.
39. *Los Angeles Times*, December 20, 1996.
40. Hall and Ellis 1896: 148–49.
41. Dean 1997: 200.
42. See Simms 1996: 664.
43. Reported in Hall and Ellis 1896: 139. Thirty children in Hall and Ellis's survey reported digging up their buried dolls "to see if they had gone to Heaven, or simply to get them back."
44. Formanek-Brunell 1993: 163.
45. Formanek-Brunell 1998: 370.
46. Simms 1996: 676.
47. Formanek-Brunell 1998: 374–75.
48. Fleming 1996: 88.
49. Rilke 1994 [1913]: 26–27.
50. Rilke, "Dolls" in *Werke*, Vol 3, pp. 357–58, 535–36, translated here by Simms (1996: 670).
51. Eva-Maria Simms subjects Rilke to some stern Freudian psychoanalysis, focusing on his macabre story about Frau Blaha's maid, who gives birth to a child which

she strangles, wraps in a blue apron, and keeps as a doll in her trunk. When he was little, Rilke's mother dressed him as a girl and for a while called him Sophie. Simms says "I think that a large part of the rage, hatred, and aggression against the doll is a memory of the lost union with the mother, for which the doll is merely a poor substitute." The child has to *work hard* to imbue the object with "life," and "part of the terror the doll inspires in Rilke comes from her life-lessness and her indifference and unresponsiveness to the child's emotions." "The toy would not absorb the narcissistic urges as would a mother—hence its transitional function in the child's discovery of self-consciousness, and the doll's eventual 'death.'" How, we may wonder, could loving parents inflict such a "thickly forgetful, hate-inspiring body" on their child? (Simms 1996: 663, 670–71.)

52. *Uncanny*: "weird: unearthly: savouring of the supernatural: ungentle: formidable" (*Chambers Dictionary*). "An uncanny experience" says Freud, "occurs when either infantile complexes which have been repressed are once more revived by some impression, or when primitive beliefs which have been surmounted seem once more to be confirmed" (quoted by Simms 1996: 674).

CHAPTER 8

1. Contributor CWEATHER to Doll People chat room at http://www.collectdolls.guide (November 1, 2000).
2. Douglas 1966.
3. Eibl-Eibesfeldt 1971: 21.
4. Goldstein 1997: 48.
5. Walkerdine 1998: 259.
6. Warner 1994: 43–62.
7. Warner 1994: 56.
8. Postman 1994: 9.
9. Giroux 1998: 270.
10. Giroux 1998: 270.
11. Oxenhandler 1996. "Between the two extremes of the molested child and the withered child, we make our way" (Oxenhandler 2001: 302).
12. See Hacking 1999: 125–62.
13. Kincaid 1998.
14. Cox 1996: 206.

Bibliography

Abbott, Andrew. 2001. *Chaos of disciplines.* Chicago: Chicago University Press.

Alley, Thomas R. 1988. The effects of growth and aging on facial aesthetics. In *Social and applied aspects of perceiving faces*, ed. Thomas R. Alley. Hillsdale, NJ: Lawrence Erlbaum, pp. 51–62.

Alley, Thomas R., and Katherine A. Hildebrant. 1988, Determinants and consequences of facial aesthetics. In *Social and applied aspects of perceiving faces*, ed. Thomas R. Alley. Hillsdale, NJ: Lawrence Erlbaum, pp. 101–140.

America past and pleasant. 1995. *Economist* 337, no. 7945: 62.

Anderson, Michael. 1985. The emergence of the modern life cycle in Britain. *Social History* 10, no. 1: 69–87.

Appadurai, Arjun (ed.). 1986. *The social life of things: Commodities in cultural perspective.* Cambridge: Cambridge University Press.

Aries, Philippe. 1962. *Centuries of childhood: A history of family life.* New York: Alfred Knopf.

Atran, Scott. 1990. *Cognitive foundations of natural history: Towards an anthropology of science.* Cambridge: Cambridge University Press.

Bâ, Mariama. 1981. *So long a letter.* African Writers Series, London: Heinemann.

Bateson, Gregory. 1972. A theory of play and fantasy. In *Steps to an ecology of mind: Collected essays in anthropology, psychiatry, evolution, and epistemology.* San Francisco: Chandler.

Baudelaire, Charles. 1994 [1853]. The philosophy of toys. In *Essays on dolls*, ed. Idris Parry and Paul Keegan. Harmondsworth: Penguin, pp. 13–25.

Baudrillard, Jean. 1988 [1986]. *America*, London: Verso.

———. 1998. *The consumer society: Myths and structures.* London: Sage.

Behrents, Rolf G. 1990. Adult facial growth. In *Facial growth*, ed. Donald H. Enlow. 3rd ed. Philadelphia: W. B. Saunders, pp. 423–443.

Beisel, David R. 1984. Thoughts on the Cabbage Patch Kids. *Journal of Psychohistory* 12, no. 1: 133–142.

Berman, Phyllis. 1992. Getting even. *Forbes*, vol. 150, no. 5, pp. 54–55.

Bengtson, Vern, Carolyn Rosenthal, and Linda Burton. 1990. Families and aging: Diversity and heterogeneity. In *Handbook of aging and the social sciences*, ed. Robert H. Binstock and Linda K. George. New York: Academic Press, pp. 263–287.

Berry, Chistopher J. 1986. *Human nature*. London: Macmillan.

—— 1994. *The idea of luxury: A ocnceptual and historical investigation*. Cambridge: Cambridge University Press.

Berry, Diane S., and Leslie Zebrowitz-McArthur. 1988. The impact of age-related craniofacial changes on social perception. In *Social and applied aspects of perceiving faces*, ed. Thomas R. Alley. Hillsdale, NJ: Lawrence Erlbaum Associates, pp. 63–87.

Birke, Lynda. 1999. *Feminism and the biological body*. Edinburgh: Edinburgh University Press.

Björk, A., and V. Skieller. 1976. Postnatal growth and development of the maxillary complex. In *Factors affecting the growth of the midface*, ed. James A. McNamara. Craniofacial Growth Series Monograph 6, Center for Human Growth and Development. University of Michigan, Ann Arbor, pp. 61–99.

Blacking, John. 1977. Towards an anthropology of the body. In *The anthropology of the body*, ed. John Blacking. London: Academic Press, pp. 1–28.

Bogin, Barry. 1988. *Patterns of human growth*. Cambridge: Cambridge University Press.

——. 1998. Evolutionary and biological aspects of childhood. In *Biosocial perspectives on children*, ed. Catherine Panter-Brick. Cambridge: Cambridge University Press, pp. 11–44.

Bordo, Susan. 1993. *Unbearable weight: Feminism, western culture, and the body*. Berkeley and Los Angeles: University of California Press.

Burdi, Alphonse R. 1976. Biological forces which shape the human midface before birth. In *Factors affecting the growth of the midface*, ed. James A. McNamara. Craniofacial Growth Series Monograph 6, Center for Human Growth and Development. University of Michigan, Ann Arbor, pp. 9–42.

Burman, Erica. 1994. *Deconstructing developmental psychology*. London: Routledge.

Byrnes, Nanette. 1995. Are those Marie Osmond dolls really worth $12 million? *Business Week*, no. 3440, p. 44.

Camaren, Marjorie Marian. 1968. Dolls as causal agents effecting socialization behavior. Master's thesis, University of California, Los Angeles, Education Deparment.

Carneiro da Cunha, Manuela. 1995. Children, politics and culture: The case of the Brazilian Indians. In *Children and the politics of culture*, ed. Sharon Stephens. Princeton, NJ: Princeton University Press, pp. 282–291.

Carriker, Kitti. 1998. *Created in our image: The miniature body of the doll as subject and object*. Bethlehem, PA: Lehigh University Press.

Carter, Curtis L. 1993. Eye of the doll: Art and personal identity. In *Dolls in contempo-*

rary art: A metaphor for identity, ed. Curtis L. Carter. Patrick and Beatrice Haggerty
  Museum of Art, Milwaukee, Wisconsin, pp. 7–32.

Carter, Meg. 1994. Kitsch pickings, *Marketing Week* 17, no. 2: 34–35.

Caspi, Avshalom, and Glen H. Elder Jr. 1988. Childhood precursors of the life
  course: Early personality and life disorganization. In *Child development in life-span
  perspective*, ed. Mavis E. Hetherington, Richard M. Lerner, and Marion Perlmutter.
  Hillsdale, NJ: Lawrence Erlbaum Associates, pp. 115–142.

Cederquist, Robert. 1990. General body growth and development. In *Facial growth*,
  ed. Donald H. Enlow. 3rd ed. Philadelphia: W. B. Saunders, pp. 396–422.

Chan, J. C. M., D. Sculli, and S. K. Wong. 1988. Costs of production in the Shenzhen
  special economic zone of China. *Engineering Costs and Production Economics* 14, no.
  3: 199–209.

Chin, Elizabeth. 1999. Ethnically correct dolls: Toying with the race industry.
  American Anthropologist 101, no. 2: 305–321.

Clark, Alison J. 1997. Tupperware: Product as social relation. In *American material culture: The shape of the field*, ed. Ann S. Martin and J. Ritchie Garrison. Knoxville:
  University of Tennessee Press, pp. 224–250.

Clausen, John A. 1993. *American lives: Looking back at the children of the Great Depression.*
  New York: The Free Press.

Coser, Lewis A. 1974. *Greedy institutions: Patterns of undivided commitment.* New York:
  The Free Press.

Counts, Dorothy Ayers, and David R. Counts (eds.). 1985. *Aging and its transforma-
  tions: Moving toward death in Pacific societies.* Lanham, MD: University Press of
  America.

Cowan, Ruth Schwartz. 1986. *More work for Mother.* New York: Basic Books.

Cox, Roger. 1996. *Shaping childhood: Themes of uncertainty in the history of adult-child
  relationships.* London: Routledge.

Cross, Gary. 1997. *Kids' stuff: Toys and the changing world of American childhood.*
  Cambridge, MA: Harvard University Press.

Darlin, Damon. 1995. Dolls from hell. *Forbes*, vol. 156, no. 12, pp. 186–187

Dean, Audrey Vincente. 1997. *Dolls.* Glasgow: HarperCollins.

Demos, John. 1970. Underlying themes in the witchcraft of seventeenth-century New
  England. *American Historical Review* 75, no. 2: 1311–1326.

Douglas, Mary. 1966. *Purity and danger: An analysis of concepts of pollution and taboo.*
  London: Routledge and Kegan Paul.

Dowling, Melissa. 1997. Mailer dolls up dolls. *Catalog Age*, vol. 14, no. 9, p. 22.

Dullemeijer, P. 1971. Comparative ontogeny and cranio-facial growth. In *Cranio-facial
  growth in man*, ed. Robert E. Moyers and Wilton M. Krogman. Oxford: Pergamon,
  pp. 45–75.

Dunbar, Robin. 1998. Behavioural adaptation. In *Human adaptation*, ed., Geoffrey
  Harrison and Howard Morphy, Oxford: Berg, pp. 73–98.

Ehrenfeld, Temma. 1993. Why executives collect. *Fortune*, vol. 127, no. 1, pp. 94–98.

Ehrenreich, Barbara. 1989. *Fear of falling: The inner life of the middle class.* New York:
  Harper Collins.

Ehrenreich, B, and J. Ehrenreich. 1979. The professional-managerial class. In *Between labor and capital*, ed. Pat Walder. Boston: South End Press, pp. 5–45.

Eibl-Eibesfeldt, Irenäus. 1971 [1970]. *Love and hate: On the natural history of basic behavior patterns*. London: Methuen.

Elder, Glen H. 1999 [1974]. *Children of the Great Depression: Social change in life experience*. Boulder, CO: Westview.

Elder, Glen H., Jeffrey K. Liker, and Bernard J. Jawarski. 1984. Hardship in lives: Depression influences from the 1930s to old age in postwar America. In *Life-span developmental psychology: Historical and generational effects*, ed. Kathleen A. McCluskey and Hayne W. Reese. New York: Academic Press, pp. 161–201.

Elder, Glen H., John Modell, and Ross D. Parker (eds.). 1993. *Children in time and place: Developmental and historical insights*. Cambridge: Cambridge University Press.

Elsner, John, and Roger Cardinal (eds.). 1994. *The cultures of collecting*. London: Reaktion Books.

Enlow, Donald H. (ed.). 1990a. *Facial Growth*. 3rd ed. Philadelphia: W. B. Saunders.

———. 1990b. The structural basis for ethnic variation in facial form. In *Facial growth*, ed. Donald H. Enlow. 3rd ed. Philadelphia: W. B. Saunders, pp. 222–228.

Ennew, Judith. 1986. *The sexual exploitation of children*. Cambridge: Polity Press.

Erikson, Erik H. 1977. *Toys and reasons*. New York: Norton.

———. 1980. *Identity and the life cycle: Selected papers. Psychological Issues* 1, no. 9.

Fee, Rich. 1995. Nine children and hundreds of dolls. *Successful Farming* 93, no. 9: 66–69.

Fenn, Donna. 1985. Private Lives: Profiles from the Inc. 500—#39: Shader's China Doll. *Inc. Inc.* 7, no. 12: 91.

Fleming, Dan. 1996. *Powerplay: Toys as popular culture*. Manchester: Manchester University Press.

Formanek-Brunell, Miriam. 1993. *Made to play house: Dolls and the commercialization of American girlhood, 1830–1930*. New Haven: Yale University Press.

———. 1998 [1993]. The politics of dollhood in nineteenth-century America. In *The children's culture reader*, ed. Henry Jenkins. New York: New York University Press, pp. 363–381.

Fowles, Jib. 1996. *Advertising and popular culture*. Thousand Oaks, CA: Sage.

Frank, Robert H. 1988. *Passions with reason: The strategic role of the emotions*. New York: Norton.

Friedland, Roger, and A. F. Robertson (eds.). 1990. *Beyond the marketplace: Rethinking economy and society*. New York: Aldine de Gruyter.

Fulkerson, Jennifer. 1995. Don't play with these Barbie dolls. *American Demographics* 17, no. 5: 17–18.

Garrett, C. 1977. Women and witches: Patterns of analysis. *Signs* 3, no. 2: 461–470.

Giroux, Henry A. 1998. Stealing innocence: The politics of child beauty pageants. In *The children's culture reader*, ed. Henry Jenkins. New York: New York University Press, pp. 265–282.

Goldstein, Richard. 1997. The girl in the fun bubble: The mystery of JonBenet. *Village Voice*, June 10.

Goode, William J. 1970 [1963]. *World revolution and family patterns.* 2nd ed. Glencoe, NY: Free Press.

Goody, Jack. 1976. Inheritance, property and women: Some comparative considerations. In *Family and inheritance: Rural society in Western Europe, 1200–1800,* ed. J. Goody, J. Thirsk, and E. P. Thompson. Cambridge: Cambridge University Press, pp. 10–36.

Gould, Stephen Jay. 1980. *The panda's thumb: More reflections on natural history.* New York: Norton.

Gupta, Akhil. 2002. Reliving childhood: The temporality of childhood and narratives of reincarnation. *Ethnos* 67, no. 1: 33–56.

Hacking, Ian. 1999. *The social construction of what?* Cambridge, MA: Harvard University Press.

Hall, G. Stanley, and A. Caswell Ellis. 1896. A study of dolls. *Pedagogical Seminary* 4, no. 2: 129–175.

Harris, Daniel. 2000. *Cute, quaint, hungry and romantic: The aesthetics of consumerism.* New York: Basic Books.

Harrison, Barbara Grizzuti. 1996. Collecting the stuff of life. *Harper's,* vol. 292, no. 1752, pp. 15–20.

Harvey, David. 1990. *The condition of postmodernity: An enquiry into the origins of cultural change.* Oxford: Blackwell.

Hess, Beth B. 1985. Aging policies and old women: The hidden agenda. In *Gender and the life course,* ed. Alice S. Rossi. New York: Aldine, pp. 319–331.

Hewlett, Sylvia Ann. 2002. *Baby hunger: The new battle for motherhood.* London: Atlantic Books.

Hinde, R.A., and Barden, L. 1985. The evolution of the teddy bear. *Animal Behavior* 33: 1371–1373.

Hodges, Jane, and Laura Loro. 1995. Collectibles cut budgets. *Advertising Age* 66, no. 46: 4.

Hrdy, Sarah Blaffer. 1999. *Mother nature: Maternal instincts and how they shape the human species.* New York: Ballantine.

Hwang, C. Philip, Michael E. Lamb, and Irving E. Sigel (eds.). 1996. *Images of childhood.* Hillsdale, NJ: Lawrence Erlbaum.

Ivy, Marilyn. 1995. Have you seen me? Recovering the inner child in late twentieth-century America. In *Children and the politics of culture,* ed. Sharon Stephens. Princeton, NJ: Princeton University Press, pp. 79–104.

James, Allison. 1998a. Confections, concoctions, and conceptions. In *The children's culture reader,* ed. Henry Jenkins. New York: New York University Press, pp. 394–405.

———. 1998b. From the child's point of view: Issues in the social construction of childhood. In *Biosocial perspectives on children,* ed. Catherine Panter-Brick. Cambridge University Press, Cambridge, pp. 45–65.

James, Allison, Chris Jenks, and Alan Prout. 1998. *Theorizing childhood.* New York: Teachers College Press.

Jenkisn, Henry (ed.). 1998. *The children's culture reader.* New York: New York University Press.

Johnson, Mary. 1984. Women and the material Universe: A bibliographic essay. In *American material culture: The shape of things around us*, ed. Edith Mayo. Bowling Green, OH: Bowling Green State University Popular Press, pp. 218–255.

Johnston, Lysle E. 1976. The functional matrix hypothesis: Reflections in a jaundiced eye. In *Factors affecting the growth of the midface*, ed. James A. McNamara. Craniofacial Growth Series Monograph 6, Center for Human Growth and Development, University of Michigan, Ann Arbor, pp. 131–168.

Kant, Immanuel. 1978 [1796]. *Anthropology from a pragmatic point of view (Anthropologie in pragmatischer Hinsicht)*. Translated by V. L. Dowdell. Carbondale: Southern Illinois University Press.

Kessler, Susanne J. 2002. Defining and producing genitals. In *Gender: A sociological reader*, ed. Stevi Jackson and Sue Scott. London: Routledge, pp. 447–456.

Kincaid, James R. 1998. Producing erotic children. In *The children's culture reader*, ed. Henry Jenkins. New York: New York University Press, pp. 241–253.

Klein, Melanie. 1975. *The psycho-analysis of children*. London: Hogarth.

Kline, Stephen. 1993. *Out of the garden: Toys and children's culture in the age of TV marketing*. London: Verso.

Kuhn, Annette. 1998. A credit to her mother. In *The children's culture reader*, ed. Henry Jenkins. New York: New York University Press, pp. 283–296.

LaFleur, William R. 1992. *Liquid life: Abortion and Buddhism in Japan*. Princeton, NJ: Princeton University Press.

Lancaster, Jane B. 1989. Women in biosocial perspective. In *Gender and anthropology: Critical reviews for research and teaching*, ed. S. Morgen. American Anthropological Association, Washington D. C., pp. 95–115.

Landau, Terry. 1989. *About faces: The evolution of the human face*. New York: Anchor Books.

Lasch, Christopher. 1977. *Haven in a heartless world: The family besieged*. New York: Basic Books.

Lopata, H. Z. (ed.). *Widows*. Durham, N.C.: Duke University Press.

Lord, M. G. 1994. *Forever Barbie*. New York: William Morrow.

Loro, Laura. 1992. Magazines make for impressive collections. *Advertising Age* 63, no. 43: S6.

———. 1995a. Infighting nasty for collectibles. *Advertising Age* 66, no. 39: 30.

———. 1995b. Nostalgia for sale at Franklin Mint. *Advertising Age* 66, no. 20: 33.

Mansfield, Matthew F. 1983. Dolls aren't merely child's play. *Advertising Age* 54, no. 26: M4–5, M28.

Mark, Leonard S., Robert E. Shaw, and John B. Pittenger. 1988. Natural constraints, scales of analysis, and information for the perception of growing faces. In *Social and applied aspects of perceiving faces*, ed. Thomas R. Alley. Hillsdale, NJ: Lawrence Erlbaum, pp. 11–49.

Martin, Emily. 2002. The egg and the sperm. In *Gender: A sociological reader*, ed. Stevi Jackson and Sue Scott. London: Routledge, pp. 384–391.

Martin, Laura C. 1994. *Precious Moments last forever*. New York: Abbeville.

McCabe, Viki. 1988. Facial proportions, perceived age, and caregiving. In *Social and applied aspects of perceiving faces,* ed. Thomas R. Alley. Hillsdale NJ: Lawrence Erlbaum, pp. 89–95.

McDonough, William, and Michael Braungart. 2002. *Cradle to cradle: Remaking the way we make things.* New York: North Point Press.

Mead, Margaret. 1967 [1932]. An investigation of the thought of primitive children, with special reference to animism. In *Personalities and cultures: Readings in psychological anthropology,* ed. Robert Hunt. New York: Natural History Press, pp. 213–237.

Meillassoux, Claude. 1981. *Maidens, meal and money: Capitalism and the domestic community.* Cambridge: Cambridge University Press.

Mergen, Bernard. 1984. Toys and American culture objects as hypotheses. In *American material culture: The shape of things around us,* ed. Edith Mayo. Bowling Green, OH: Bowling Green State University Popular Press, pp. 149–157.

Merrow, William W., and B. Holly Broadbent. 1990. Cephalometrics. In *Facial growth,* ed. Donald H. Enlow. 3rd ed. Philadelphia: W. B. Saunders, pp. 346–395.

Mitchell, Juliet. 2000. *Mad men and Medusas: Reclaiming hysteria and the effects of sibling relations on the human condition.* Harmondsworth: Penguin.

Moss, Melvin. 1971. Ontogenetic aspects of cranio-facial growth. In *Cranio-facial growth in man,* ed. Robert E. Moyers and Wilton M. Krogman. Oxford: Pergamon, pp. 109–124.

Mooyers, Robert E., and David S. Carlson. 1988. Maturation of the orofacial neuromusculature. In *Facial growth,* ed. Donald H. Enlow. 3rd ed. Philadelphia: W. B. Saunders. pp. 267–280.

Murphy, Victoria. 2000. They've Gotta Have It. *Forbes,* 158, no. 12: 176.

Neal, Mollie. 1992. Cataloger gets pleasant results. *Direct Marketing* 55, no. 1: 33–37.

Nettleton, Sarah, and Jonathan Watson (eds.). 1998. *The body in everyday life.* London: Routledge.

Noddings, Nel. 1989. *Women and evil.* Berkeley: University of California Press.

Ogando, Joseph. 2000. Engineering Barbie. *Design News* 55, no. 24: 64.

Orlean, Susan. 1997. Beautiful girls. *New Yorker,* August 4, pp. 29–36.

Oxenhandler, Noelle. 1996. The Eros of parenthood: Not touching children can also be a crime. *New Yorker,* February 19, 1996, pp. 47–49.

———. 2001. *The eros of parenthood: Explorations in light and dark.* New York: St. Martin's Press.

Panter-Brick, Catherine. 1998a. Biological anthropology and child health: Context, process and outcome. In *Biosocial perspectives on children,* ed. Catherine Panter-Brick. Cambridge: Cambridge University Press, pp. 66–101.

——— (ed.). 1998. *Biosocial perspectives on children,* Cambridge University Press, Cambridge.

Parke, Ross D. 1988. Families in life-span perspective: A multilevel developmental approach. In *Child development in life-span perspective,* ed. Mavis E. Hetherington, Richard M. Lerner, and Marion Perlmutter. Hillsdale, NJ: Lawrence Erlbaum, pp. 159–190.

Pearce, Susan. 1995. *On collecting: An investigation into collecting in the European tradition.* London: Routledge.

Piot, Charles. 1999. *Remotely global: Village modernity in West Africa.* Chicago: University of Chicago Press.

Postman, Neil. 1994 [1982]. *The disappearance of childhood.* Revised ed. New York: Vintage.

Rand, Erica. 1995. *Barbie's queer accessories.* Durham NC: Duke University Press.

Richards, Martin. 1998. The meeting of nature and nurture and the development of children: Some conclusions. In *Biosocial perspectives on children,* ed. Catherine Panter-Brick. Cambridge: Cambridge University Press, pp. 131–146.

Rilke, Rainer Maria. 1994 [1913]. Dolls: On the wax dolls of Lotte Pritzel. In *Essays on dolls,* ed. Idris Parry and Paul Keegan. Harmondsworth: Penguin, pp. 26–39.

Roberts, Sam. 1993. *Who we are: A portrait of America based on the latest U.S. census.* New York: Random House.

Robertson, A. F. 1991. *Beyond the family: The social organization of human reproduction.* Cambridge: Polity; Berkeley, University of California Press.

———. 1994. Evolving, aging, and making culture. *Ethnos* 59, nos. 1–2: 1–13.

———. 1996. The development of meaning: Ontogeny and culture. *Journal of the Royal Anthropological Institute (N. S.)* 2, no. 4: 591–610.

———. 2001. *Greed: Gut feelings, growth, and history.* Cambridge: Polity.

Roha, Ronaleen R. 1992. A passion for collecting. *Kiplinger's Personal Finance,* 46, no. 7: 70–74.

Rose, Jacqueline. 1984. *The case of Peter Pan.* London: Macmillan.

Rossi, Alice S. (ed.). 1985. *Gender and the life course.* New York: Aldine.

Ruth, Jan-Erik, and Anni Vilkko. 1996. Emotions in the construction of autobiography. In *Handbook of emotion, adult development, and aging,* ed. Carol Magai and Susan H. McFadden. San Diego: Academic Press, pp. 167–181.

Sahlins, Marshall. 1976. *The use and abuse of biology: An anthropological critique of sociobiology.* Ann Arbor: University of Michigan Press.

Scheper-Hughes, Nancy, and Howard F. Stein. 1998. Child abuse and the unconscious in American popular culture. In *The children's culture reader,* ed. Henry Jenkins. New York: New York University Press, pp. 178–195.

Schiffrin, Matthew. 1995. "Okay, big mouth." *Forbes,* 156, no. 8: 47–48.

Schnorbus, Paula. 1987. Sold! (The Home Shopping Network). *Marketing and Media Decisions* 22: 53–56.

Seiter, Ellen. 1993. *Sold separately: Children and parents in consumer culture.* New Brunswick, NJ: Rutgers University Press.

———. 1998. Children's desires/mothers' dilemmas: The social contexts of consumption. In *The children's culture reader,* ed. Henry Jenkins. New York: New York University Press, pp. 297–317.

Shilling, Chris. 1993. *The body and social theory.* London: Sage.

Simms, Eva-Maria. 1996. Uncanny dolls: Images of death in Rilke and Freud. *New Literary History* 27: 663–677.

Steinem, Gloria, and George Barris. 1986. *Marilyn.* New York: Henry Holt.

Stephens, Sharon (ed.). 1995. *Children and the politics of culture.* Princeton, NJ: Princeton University Press.

Strathern, Andrew. 1996. *Body thoughts*. Ann Arbor: University of Michigan Press.

Sullivan, Louis R. 1928. *Essentials of anthropometry: Handbook for explorers and museum collectors*. New York: American Museum of Natural History.

Symons, Donald. 1995. Beauty is in the adaptations of the beholder: The evolutionary psychology of human female sexual attractiveness. In *Sexual nature sexual culture*, ed. Paul R. Abramson and Steven D. Pinkerton. Chicago: University of Chicago Press.

Taylor, Alex. 1999. It worked for Toyota. Can it work for toys? *Fortune*, vol. 4, no. 2, p. 36.

Thompson, D'Arcy Wentworth. 1942 [1917]. *Growth and form*. Rev. ed. Cambridge: Cambridge University Press.

Thorne, Barrie. 2002. Do girls and boys have different cultures? In *Gender: A sociological reader*, ed. Stevi Jackson and Sue Scott. London: Routledge, pp. 291–302.

Toren, Christina. 1993. Making history: The significance of childhood cognition for a comparative anthropology of mind. *Man* (NS) 28, no. 3: 461–478.

Turner, Terence. 1994. Bodies and anti-bodies: Flesh and fetish in contemporary social theory. In *Embodiment and experience: The existential ground of culture and self*, ed. Thomas J. Csordas. Cambridge: Cambridge University Press, pp. 27–47.

Underwood, Elaine. 1996. Licensing 96: Hearst's hustling act. *Brandweek* 37, no. 26: 22–24.

U.S. Deparment of Commerce and U.S. Bureau of the Census. 1983. *Manufactures—Industry Series: Industry 3942*, dolls and stuffed toys. Washington, DC: U.S. Government Printing Office.

———. 1993. *Manufactures—Industry Series: Industry 3942*, dolls and stuffed toys. Washington, DC: U.S. Government Printing Office.

———. 1997. *Manufactures—Industry Series: Industry 3942*, dolls and stuffed toys. Washington, DC: U.S. Government Printing Office.

Victor, Adam. 1999. *The Marilyn encyclopedia*. New York: Overlook Press.

Wagenknecht, Edward. 1969. *Marilyn Monroe: A composite view*. Philadelphia: Chilton.

Walkerdine, Valerie. 1997. *Daddy's girl: Young girls and popular culture*. Cambridge MA: Harvard University Press.

———. 1998. Popular culture and the eroticization of little girls. In *The children's culture reader*, ed. Henry Jenkins. New York: New York University Press, pp. 254–264.

Warner, Marina. 1994. *Six myths of our time: Little angels, little monsters, beautiful beasts, and more*. New York: Vintage Books.

Washburn, Dorothy K. 1997. Getting ready: Doll play and real life in American culture, 1900–1980. In *American material culture: The shape of the field*, ed. Ann S. Martin and J. Ritchie Garrison. Knoxville: University of Tennessee Press, pp. 105–134.

Wells, Robert V. 1971. Demographic change and the life cycle of American families. *Journal of Interdisciplinary History* 2 no. 2: 273–282.

Wilson, Mark. 2002. Well hello, dolly. *Sunday Star Times (Auckland)*, January 6, p. D5.

Wise, David A. 1990. Overview. In *Issues in the economics of aging*, ed. David A. Wise. Chicago: University of Chicago Press, pp. 1–11

Wolfenstein, Martha. 1998 [1955]. Fun morality: An analysis of recent American child-training literature. In *The children's culture reader*, ed. Henry Jenkins. New York: New York University Press, pp. 199–208.

Wood, Gaby. 1998, *The smallest of all persons mentioned in the record of littleness*. London: Profile.

———. 2002. *Living dolls*. London: Faber.

Woodward, Kathleen. 1995. Tribute to the older woman: Psychoanalysis, feminism, and ageism. In *Images of aging: Cultural representations of later life Routledge*, ed. Mike Featherstone and Andrew Wernick. London: Routledge, pp. 79–96.

Zelizer, Viviana A. 1985. *Pricing the priceless child: The changing social value of children*. New York: Basic Books.

Index

abortion, 97, 109, 110, 147
abuse:
    of children, 208, 212, 225
    of dolls, 5, 79, 119, 212
accessories, 24, 52, 71, 153, 182
acrylic, 169
Action Man, 27, 70
adolescence, 77, 78, 104–5, 132–33,
    148, 167, 190, 199
adoption, 97, 110, 122
adultification, 25, 193, **199–206**,
    223, 225
advertisements:
    of porcelain collector dolls,
        18–19, 29, *30*, 54, 58, 129, 153
    vocabulary of, 19, 40, 58, 92, 97,
        99, 123, 129–33, 150, 155, 181,
        182–83, 187, 220, 224–25,
        231–42, 246–48
advertising, 24, 28, 33–35, 36,
    46–48, 95–96

African American dolls, 52, 53,
    135–37
ages:
    of dolls, 132
    of doll collectors, 88–89
akuaba, 8
Alexander, Madame, (Beatrice
    Alexander Behrman), 28, 69,
    149
alloparenting, 194–96, 200, 225
American Girl dolls, 43, 50, 141,
    153, *154*, 208, 209
angels, 213, *214*, 219, 220
anthropology, xvii, xviii, 10, 15, 17,
    85, 136, 226–29
antique dolls, 6, 17, **21–24**, 27, 64,
    83, 84, 89, 103, 145, 160. *See
    also* neo-antiques
artists, 29, 40, 44–46, 53, 58, 108,
    145–47, 148–49, 166, 183–86,
    256

Ashton Drake Galleries, 36, 38, 44,
    47, 50, 52, 53, 54, 55, 57, 71,
    89, 121, 122, 145, 146, 153,
    184, 185, 193
attractiveness, 160, 168, **199–206**,
    224
authenticity, 54, 182–83, 186

baby boom, 109
baby shows, 224–25
Barbie, 6, 19, 23, 27, 45, 67, 69, 70,
    76, 85, 89, 114, 133, 136, 141,
    143, **147–48**, 153, 176–79, 191,
    207, 211, 261, 262
Barry-Hippensteel, Kathy, 146, 184
Baudelaire, Charles, 70, 119, 123
beanbag bodies, 29, 155
bébé dolls, 6, 24, 25, 29, 100, 211
Bello, Yolanda, 44, 54, 90, 145–46
bereavement, 86, 102, 113, 120, 138
Beverage, Frank Stanley, 37–38
biology, xv, 10–12, 14–17, 162, 193,
    254
Bjonness-Jacobsen, Pauline, 45, 91,
    146–47
black dolls. *See* African American
    dolls
bodies, xv, 14–16, 91, 98–100,
    152–59, 186, 206
body fat, 180
body symbolism, 16, 222–24
boudoir dolls, 25
boy dolls, 129–33, 199, 211
boys and dolls, 5, 6, 70, 79, 119,
    142, 196, 218
Bradford Exchange, 36, 38, 47
bride dolls, 22, 132, 201
Bru, Casimir, 6, 24, 25, 134, 211

Butcher, Samuel. *See* Precious
    Moments dolls
Bye-Lo Baby, 114

Cabbage Patch Kids, 27, 97, 153,
    168, 170, 173
Caroline (porcelain collector doll),
    30, 129, 159, 169, 201, 205
celluloid, 26
certification of dolls, 54–55, *56*, 91,
    122, 123
character dolls, 23, 27, 137, 162,
    172
Chase, Martha, 114
cheeks, 172–73, 201, 205
cherubs, 8, 213
child pageants, 224–25
childhood: 13, 17, 77, 79, 102,
    104–6, 225–26
    invention of, 25, 105, 207–8,
    224, 225
Child's Play (movie) 218, 249–50
childlessness. *See* empty womb;
    empty nest
children's dolls. *See* play
China, 23, 43
Chucky (doll), 218, 249–50
class, social, 35, 62, 80, 89, 228
clothes, 103, 112, 153, 160, 167,
    181, 199, 209
clubs, 62, 64, 102, 144
collecting, xviii, 17, 27, 59, 61–93
    art, 86
    history of, 62, 67
    Aserious,@ 53, 61, 64, 68–69, 84,
    88, 89, 103, 144–45
collections, size of, 72, 76, 77,
    84–85, 143

Acoming out@ as a doll collector, 4, 143, 149

commodity, 18, 19, 29, **31–35**, 93, 118, 150, 153, 222, 227

composition dolls, 26, 155

connoisseurship, 63

contraception, 109

corporate collectibles, 55–58

Crachami, Caroline, 4, 253

crockery, 23, 28, 89, 90

crucifix, 8

culture, 8, 10, 11–17, 59, 67, 76, 98, 221, 222, 227–29

cute, 166, 168, 172, 192, **193–99**, 200–6, 224

Danbury Mint, 36, 43, 47, 50, 90, 125, 184, 185

death, 10, 76, 80, 83, 86, 87, 150, 158, 187, 190, 211, **212–20**

decor. *See* display

definitions of dolls, 4, 5, 12, 118–19, 120

Depression (1930s). *See* Great Depression

designers. *See* artists

desire, 99–100

dimples, 172

disgust, 2, 7, 149, 166, 222, 227, 228

display, 25, **67–75**, 120, 139, 155, 179, 209, 257

divorce, 83, 101, 109

Doll of the Year (DOTY) awards, 55, 145, 185

dolls' dolls, 127–28, 209, *210*

domestic space, 72, 77, 108

Don Juan, 81

dwarfism, 4

Early Moments doll, 158

ears, 175

editions:
    limited, 55
    numbered, 55

Effanbee dolls, 28

Effner, Dianna, xix, 121, 184, 193

emotions, *See* feelings

empty nest, xiii, 17, 72, 84, 93, **100–9**, 133

empty womb, xiii, 93, 98, 100, 108, **109–13**, 158

eroticism, 5, 9, 66, 99, 149, 196, 207, 209, **224–26**

ethnicity, 52–53, 77, 134, 179, 228, 240–42

ethnography, 227–28; *See also* anthropology

evolution, 11, 160, 162–66, 183, 192, 206

eyes, 159, 168–71, 201, 219

faces, 136, 158, **159–75**, 191–93, 251–52
    development of, 161–63, 200
    expressions, 159–60, 168–69, 191–94, 219, 251–52

fairs, 50, 103, 145, 149

families, 76, 80–83, 100, 101, 104–6, 109, 124–28, 132–33

fashion dolls, 22–24, 31, 34, 39

fathering, 126–27, 196

fear of dolls, 7, 128, 142, 213, 218–19, 222

feces, 157–58

feelings, xiv–v, xviii, 2, **9–12**, 19, 35, 58, 66–67, 87–88, 91–93, **95–100**, 101, 111, 149, 181, 186–87, 206, 208, 227–29

feet, 158, 160, 180–81, 192
female property, 85, 89
feminism, 13, 15–16, 147–49, 196
fertility, 109, 110
fetishism, 6, 7, 117, 119, 120
fetus, 162, 166, 196–98, 199
firing of porcelain dolls, 23, 55, 217
fostering, 101
France, 23, 24, 50, 51, 58, 160, 185,
    213
Franklin Heirloom Dolls, 36, 37,
    43, 47, 48, 49, 50, 57, 185
funerals, 212–13, 215

gender of dolls, 35, 69, 122,
    128–33, 141–42, 167–68, 228,
    238–39
genitals, 157–58, 186
Georgetown Collection, 29, 36, 38,
    43, 50, 53, 90–91, 121, 129,
    169, 184
Germany, 22, 23, 26, 43, 103, 160,
    185
gifts, dolls as, 22, 33, 138–40
girl dolls, 129–33
grandparents, 11, 70, 78, 102, 103,
    107, 108–9, 111, 124–26, 127,
    141–42, 209, 29
Great Depression (1930s), 17, 25,
    27, **102–7**, 141, 225–26
great-grandparents, 11, 85
greed, 66, 79–87, 98, 110, 258
grief. *See* bereavement
growth, xv-v, **10–17**, 35, 67, 75–78,
    79–87, 100, 107, 118–21,
    160–63, 186–87, 190–93, 200–1,
    206, 207, 222, 223, 227–28
guarantees, 54, 150

guilt, 2, 7, 79, 97, 142, 149, 212,
    213, 229
gum tragacanth, 26
gutta percha, 26, 155

hair, 175–79
Hamilton Collection, 36, 48, 50,
    123, 150
handcraft, 38–40
Handler, Ruth. *See* Barbie
hands of dolls, 160, 180
heads of dolls, 23, 160–63
Heath, Phillip, 186
heirlooms, 33, 55, 66, 83, **84–86**,
    140
heterochrony, 192
hina (Japan), 6
history, xv, 11, 12, 13–14, 16, 17, 76,
    87, 93, 98–99, 102, 211,
    221–22, 225, 227–9
Home Shopping Network (HSN),
    TV shopping channel, 48–49,
    57, 87, 139–40, 43, 184, 243–45
Hutchens, Elke, 184
hyperreality, xiii-xiv, **151–87**, 218,
    264. *See also* realism

identity of doll collectors, 137–38
idols, 7
immortality, xv, 18, 86, 87, 97, 189,
    191, 205, **212–20**, 224
individualism, 10, 62–63, 82, 83, 86
Indonesia, 43
infant dolls, 52, 112, 122, 132, 156,
    158, 160–66, 171
infant mortality, 113, 114
infanticide, 97
infantilization, 130–31, 132,
    164–66, **193–99**, 223

innocence, 147, 221, 224, 246–48
instructional uses of dolls, 113–15,
    140–42, 147, 186
Internet, 19, 44, 72, 78, 115, 143,
    184
investment values, 1–2, 54–55, 71,
    92
in-vitro fertilization (IVF), 110, 111
isolation of older people, 102, 107,
    108–9, 110, 229

Japan, 6, 8–9
jizò (*mizuko-jizò*) 8–9
Jumeau, Pierre François, 6, 24, 25,
    134, 211

kachina, 8, 211
Kellie, Angela, 77, 85
Kestner, Johann Daniel, 23
Kewpie dolls, 9, 26, 27, 166, 211
kitsch, 63, 182
Knickerbocker, L. L. *See*
    Georgetown Collection
Konig di Scavini, Elena. *See* Lenci,
    Madame

Latino dolls, 137
legs of dolls, 179
Lenci, Madame, (Elena Konig di
    Scavini), 45, 97, 259
Lenox Collections, 36, 37, 47, 50,
    59, 71, 201
life expectancy, 11, 83, 205, 229
lifelike, *See* realism; hyperreality
line extension. *See* series of dolls
lips, 173
loneliness, 69, 83, 84, 97, 102, 107,
    108, 229

longevity. *See* life expectancy
look-alike dolls, *154*, 208–11, *210*
Lorenz, Konrad, 162–65
lust, 66, 81, 86, 99

MacArthur, J. Roderick. *See*
    Bradford Exchange
magazines, 34, 47, 48, 55, 62, 143,
    184
magic, 44, 183, 187
maintenance of dolls, 71–75
mannequin, 4, 22–23, 186, 191, 218
manufacture of dolls, 38–46,
    243–45
manufacturers of dolls, 19, **35–38**,
    88, 118, 121, 136–37, 148, 184
marketing, **46–50**, 88, 90–92,
    96–98, 124
marriage, 106, 109
Marx, Karl, 32
Mason, Linda, xix, 197
mass production, 39, 40, 46
Mattel. *See* Barbie
McCarthy, Charlie (ventriloquist's
    doll), 219
McClure, Cindy, 145
meanings, 9–17, 117–18, 222,
    227–28
mechanical dolls, 6, 156–57, 158,
    169–71
memory, 13, 107–8, 206–12
men and dolls, xvi-xvii, 6, 72,
    82–83, 114, 126–27, 149, 213,
    217
    as collectors, 66–67, 75, 81, 82,
    144
    as designers, 6, 185–86
Messenger Doll, 139–40
Mexico, 32, 43

Mickey Mouse, 165
millennium, 87
mind-body split, 16, 98–100
miscarriage. *See* infant mortality
mizuko-jizò (Japan), 8–9
modernity, 63, 82
Monroe, Marilyn, 205
mortality. *See* death
mothering, 11–12, 85, 105, 112,
    123–24, 125–27, 128, 130–31,
    133–34, 137–38, 140, 194, 207
mouths, 172–75, 200, 201, 205
museums, 64, 77, 85, 86, 111, 211
My Twinn dolls, 208–9, *210*

names of dolls, 121–23, 138
narcissism. *See* self-image
nasal septum, 201–4, 252–53, 265
Native American dolls, 53, 134–35
needs, 95–97, 98–100
neo-antiques, **28–29**, 40, 53, 64, 68,
    84, 86, 211
noses, 175, 201
nostalgia, xv, 84, 134, 206–12

Oakland, California, 103–7, 128
old age, 5, 17
O'Neill, Rose, 166–67; *See also*
    Kewpie dolls
Osmond, Marie, 38, 145
outsourcing of production, 32–33,
    43–44, 184

packaging, 32, 46, 53, 69, 122, 215,
    216
papier mâché, 26
passion. *See* feelings
pedophilia, 6, 158, 223–26

personality of dolls, 33, **117–150**,
    129–32, 151, 167
Phillips, Pamela, xix, *30*, 129, 184
physiology, xv, 187
Pinkul, Rose, 184
play, 13, 17, 24–27, 29, 34, 55,
    67–75, 76, 104–5, 139, 153,
    155, 157, 179, 181, 194, 196,
    209, 257
Pleasant Company. *See* American
    Girl dolls
politics, 147–50
polymer resins (synthetic clays), 46
porcelain, 23, 26, 28, 29, 32, 39, 46,
    53, 55, 70, 155, 156, 207
posability of dolls, 133, 155–57
poupées de luxe, 24
poverty, 104
Precious Moments dolls, 9, 38, 62,
    92, 166
pricing of dolls, xiii, 47–48, 50–53,
    58–59, 121, 135
primitive, 7
Pritzel, Lotte, 217–18
prostitution, 4
psychology, 4–5, 66–67, 68, 79, 80,
    91, 104, 113, 119, 124, 168,
    190, 196, 199–200, 218, 226,
    229
puberty. *See* adolescence
puppets, 4, 5, 120, 263
Putnam, Grace Storey, 114
putti (cherubs) 8, 213

Quality Value Convenience (QVC)
    TV shopping channel, 37, 91,
    143, 145, 146
queering, 149

rag dolls, 22
Raggedy Ann, 26
Ramsey, JonBenet, 2, 224–25
realism, xiii-xiv, 2, 23, 24, 29, 44,
    53, 71, 93, 114, 118–21, 132,
    186, 189, 217–18. *See also*
    hyperreality
relations between doll collectors,
    137–38, 142–47
relations between dolls, 133–37
religion, 8, 9, 219–20
reproduction. *See* growth
resurrection, 212–13, 219–20
retirement, 78, 83
Rilke, Rainer Maria, 159, 217–18,
    265–66
role models, dolls as, 22, 138, 208
role-playing of dolls, 122–28,
    129–32, 156
Rowland, Pleasant, 141; *See also*
    American Girl dolls
Royal House of Dolls, 28

sales of dolls, **46–50**, 88, 90–92,
    96–98, 124
Sanitary Dolls, 114
Sasha dolls, 27, 151, 153
science, 15, 16, 166
self-image, xv, 70, 128, 186, 189,
    192, **206–12**
senility, 2, 68, 69, 81, 84, 120
septum, 201–4, 252–53, 265
serial numbers, 54–55
series of dolls, 89–91, 153
shame, 2, 7, 9, 12, 79, 119, 120,
    142, 147, 224
Shirley Temple, 27, 54, 181, 223–24
shoes, 180–81

shops, 49–50, 145
sibling relationships, 127, 194, *195*,
    200, 225
Simon & Halbig, 37, 151, 169
size of dolls, 152, 160, 190
smells, 158–59
social status, 65–67, 80, 86, 105, 211
*Société Française de Fabrication des
    Bébés et Jouets* (SFBJ), 24
spending on dolls, 89, 259
stamp collecting, 61, 64–65, 75, 83,
    90
Stanhome Inc., 37–38, 48
Stieff, Margaret, 45
stillbirth. *See* infant mortality
student researchers, xvii-xix, 18–19,
    103, 129, 132, 133, 136, 137,
    138, 149
stuffed toy animals, 36, 76, 165, 191
Symons, Donald, xix, 199–200

teddy bear, 165, 191
teeth, 173–75
Thailand, 32, 43
therapeutic uses of dolls, 97,
    113–15, 208
thimbles, 91
Timmerman, Ann, 183, 184
toes, 180
Tomescu, Titus, 57, 185
touch, 155–56, 181
transitional object, doll as, 190–91,
    211, 212, 223
TV sales of dolls, 28, 37, 44, 46, 47,
    48–49, 57, 143–44, 149, 184,
    243–45

uncanny experiences, 218, 266
United Federation of Doll Clubs
    (UFDC), 64, 145
United States of America, 25–26,
    41–42, 43, 47, 50, 148
urine, 157–58

value of dolls. *See* investment value;
    pricing
vinyl (polyvinylchloride), 26–27, 29,
    55, 155

Walterhausen Puppenmanufaktur,
    23, 37, 136
Wambach, Laura Lee, 45
wants, 98–100
wax dolls, 26, 175, 217
West Africa, 8, 100–1
widows, 102, 106
witches, 8, 80, 81
World War II, 102
World Wide Web (WWW). *See*
    Internet